T0414309

Ecclesiastes and the Riddle of Authorship

In Ecclesiastes, the authorial voice of Qohelet presents an identity that has challenged readers for centuries. This book offers a reception history of the different ways readers have constructed Qohelet as an author. Previous reception histories of Ecclesiastes group readings into "premodern" and "critical," or separate Jewish from Christian readings. In deliberate contrast, this analysis arranges readings thematically according to the interpretive potential inherent in the text, a method of biblical reception history articulated by Brennan Breed. Doing so erases the artificial distinctions between so-called scholarly and confessional readings and highlights the fact that many modern academic readings of the authorship of Ecclesiastes travel in well-worn interpretive paths that long predate the rise of critical scholarship. Thus this book offers a reminder that, while critical biblical scholarship is an essential part of the interpretive task, academic readings are themselves indebted to the Bible's reception history and a part of it.

Thomas M. Bolin is Professor of Theology and Religious Studies at St. Norbert College in De Pere, Wisconsin. He is the author of *Freedom Beyond Forgiveness: The Book of Jonah Re-Examined*, and *Ezra-Nehemiah*.

BibleWorld

Series Editors: Philip R. Davies and James G. Crossley
University of Sheffield

BibleWorld shares the fruits of modern (and postmodern) biblical scholarship not only among practitioners and students, but also with anyone interested in what academic study of the Bible means in the twenty-first century. It explores our ever-increasing knowledge and understanding of the social world that produced the biblical texts, but also analyses aspects of the Bible's role in this history of our civilization and the many perspectives – not just religious and theological, but also cultural, political and aesthetic – which drive modern biblical scholarship.

Ecclesiastes and the Riddle of Authorship

Thomas M. Bolin

NEW YORK AND LONDON

First published 2017
by Routledge
711 Third Avenue, New York, NY 10017

and by Routledge
2 Park Square, Milton Park, Abingdon, Oxon OX14 4RN

Routledge is an imprint of the Taylor & Francis Group, an informa business

British Library Cataloguing-in-Publication Data
A catalogue record for this book is available from the British Library

Library of Congress Cataloging-in-Publication Data
Names: Bolin, Thomas M., author.
Title: Ecclesiastes and the riddle of authorship / Thomas M. Bolin.
Description: First [edition]. | New York : Routledge, 2017. | Series: BibleWord | Includes bibliographical references and index.
Identifiers: LCCN 2016036760 | ISBN 9781845530730 (hardback : alk. paper) | ISBN 9781315647302 (ebook)
Subjects: LCSH: Bible. Ecclesiastes—Criticism, interpretation, etc. | Bible. Ecclesiastes—Authorship.
Classification: LCC BS1475.52 .B65 2017 | DDC 223/.8066—dc23
LC record available at https://lccn.loc.gov/2016036760

ISBN: 978-1-845-53073-0 (hbk)
ISBN: 978-1-315-64730-2 (ebk)

Typeset in Times New Roman
by Apex CoVantage, LLC

In memoriam—

Edward L. Shirley

Christmas 1953–Assumption 2012

Contents

Preface and Acknowledgments

"I should like to have produced a good book. This has not come about, but the time is past in which I could improve it." So Wittgenstein ends his preface to *Philosophical Investigations* and I begin the preface to a book that has been long in the making and is not even remotely as good as Wittgenstein's *Philosophical Investigations*. The full story of this book's circuitous journey to print merits a brief telling. A decade ago I gave a paper at the Catholic Biblical Association Annual Meeting on how using Foucault's author function helped to describe how readers had imagined the author of Ecclesiastes. At the time, the paper was meant to be but one chapter in a book on Ecclesiastes that would deal with standard historical-critical questions. Other writing projects intervened and put that book on hold. When I came back to it, that chapter had grown into the entire project, placed in conversation with the rapidly growing sub-discipline of reception history. Like an old friend, Qohelet has been with me this entire time. But also, like a host with houseguests who have overstayed their welcome, I am happy to bid him farewell. I have found it hard to write a book about a biblical book that repeatedly says your hard work is pointless. But while I may have grown tired with this particular project, I have not grown tired of the fascinating ways readers have remade the biblical text over the centuries. I hope readers of this book come away from it aware of the importance biblical reception history as an academic enterprise in its own right and its needed role in the overdue self-examination of critical biblical scholarship.

In addition to its being my own contribution to the reception history of Ecclesiastes, I want this book to allow others to engage in that process. To that end, I have included in the body of the text quotations in both the original and in translation of all the readings I discuss. Where not otherwise noted, translations are my own. Those more competent in the various languages will doubtless find mistakes. In keeping with current practice, I use "Ecclesiastes" to refer to the biblical book, reserving "Qohelet" for the author and first-person voice in that book. Bibliographic style adheres to the *SBL Handbook of Style* (2d ed.); where it diverges, the fault is mine. Much academic writing is notoriously bad, as many of my publications over the past twenty years will attest. But there are world-class scholars who are also tremendous writers. They are ideals for the rest of us to admire and emulate. Diarmaid MacCulloch comes immediately to mind. Before writing this book, I read a number of books on effective writing. Among the lessons I learned, two stand out. First, strive for shorter sentences. Second, trust readers more and rely less on all of the helping words academics love: "moreover," "however," "on the one hand," and the like. I have tried to follow both of these directives in this book.

Parts of this book have been presented at various academic conferences off and on over the past decade or began with work I have published elsewhere (duly noted in the text). There are also many things I talk about in this book that I have thought about in print for years. The obligation to direct readers to those publications has left me feeling awkward engaging in so much self-citation.

I am grateful to the many colleagues who have given me correction, advice, and support, often via Twitter and Facebook. Among them, I want to especially thank Sonja Anderson, Mette Bundvad, Timothy Michael Law, Laurie MacDiarmid, Eva Mroczek, Ellen Muehlberger, Ed Silver, Mark Sneed, Matthew Suriano, Ron Troxel, Jacqueline Vayntrub, and Stephen Young. Jeremy Hutton graciously invited me to talk about Qohelet and the Greeks to the Department of Classical and Ancient Near Eastern Studies at UW-Madison, where the faculty and graduate students were ideal conversation partners. Brennan Breed kindly read over my discussion of his work in the introduction. I have tried to do justice to his important book, and any shortcomings in its use are mine alone. It is my happy obligation to mention the impact on my book of Eva Mroczek's volume, *The Literary Imagination in Jewish Antiquity*, which was published as I was nearing the end of my writing. Mroczek's incisive analysis of how modern scholars misconstrue ancient notions about authorship and literary output made clear to me where my thinking on this issue was thin. In the past 21 years literally hundreds of students have been in courses where we have read Ecclesiastes together, and I have learned much each time. The St. Norbert College Office of Faculty Development awarded me several summer research grants that funded writing or relevant conference travel. Special thanks go to Connie Hackl Muelemans, director of Inter-Library Loan at St. Norbert, who never tired of tracking down whatever resource I needed, despite its obscurity. Elizabeth Thomasson and the other editorial staff at Routledge were patient with my progress and forgiving of my delays. Philip Davies was, as ever, an incisive reader. Much of this book was written under the power of both the food and coffee at Luna Café and Roastery in De Pere, Wisconsin, and I am grateful to Mark Patel, Heather Conard, and all the staff. My wife, Megan Wood Bolin, and our two daughters, Elizabeth and Margaret, deserve my thanks along with my apologies.

I dedicate this book to my teacher, mentor, and friend, Edward L. Shirley, who was the reader of my first paper on Ecclesiastes and whose untimely, sudden death brought me face to face with Qohelet's inscrutable deity.

De Pere, Wisconsin, June 2016

Abbreviations

AB	Anchor Bible
ACCS	Ancient Christian Commentary on Scripture
ACW	Ancient Christian Writers
AEL	*Ancient Egyptian Literature*. Miriam Lichteim. 3 vols. Berkeley: University of California Press, 1971–1980
AIL	Ancient Israel and Its Literature
AJSL	*American Journal of Semitic Languages and Literatures*
AnBib	Analecta Biblica
ANES	*Ancient Near Eastern Studies*
ArBib	The Aramaic Bible
ASTI	Annual of the Swedish Theological Institute
BCOTWP	Baker Commentary on the Old Testament Wisdom and Psalms
BHQ	*Biblia Hebraica Quinta*
BibInt	*Biblical Interpretation*
BRev	*Bible Review*
BZAW	Beihefte zur Zeitschrift für die alttestamentliche Wissenschaft
CBQ	*Catholic Biblical Quarterly*
CC	Continental Commentaries
CurBR	*Currents in Biblical Research*
CWS	Classics of Western Spirituality
DCH	*Dictionary of Classical Hebrew*. Edited by David J.A. Clines. 9 vols. Sheffield: Sheffield Phoenix Press, 1993–2014.
DK	Diels, Hermann and Walther Kranz. *Die Fragmente der Vorsokratiker.* Zurich: Weidmann, 1985.
EvQ	*Evangelical Quarterly*
HAR	*Hebrew Annual Review*
HCOT	Historical Commentary on the Old Testament
HS	*Hebrew Studies*
HThKAT	Herders Theologischer Kommentar zum Alten Testament
HUCA	*Hebrew Union College Annual*
ICC	International Critical Commentary
Int	*Interpretation*
IRT	Issues in Religion and Theology

ISBL	Indiana Studies in Biblical Literature
JBL	*Journal of Biblical Literature*
JHebS	*Journal of Hebrew Scriptures*
JJS	*Journal of Jewish Studies*
JQR	*Jewish Quarterly Review*
JSJ	*Journal for the Study of Judaism*
JSOT	*Journal for the Study of the Old Testament*
JSOTSup	Journal for the Study of the Old Testament Supplement Series
JST	*Journal of Theological Studies*
KAI	*Kanaanäische und aramäische Inschriften.* Herbert Donner and Wolfgang Röllig. 2nd ed. Wiesbaden: Harrassowitz, 1966–1969
LAI	Library of Ancient Israel
LHBOTS	The Library of Hebrew Bible/Old Testament Studies
LSJ	Liddell, Henry George, Robert Scott, Henry Stuart Jones. *A Greek-English Lexicon.* 9th ed. with revised supplement. Oxford: Clarendon, 1996
LXX	Septuagint
NCB	New Century Bible
NEchtB	Neue Echter Bibel
NETS	*A New English Translation of the Septuagint.* Edited by Albert Pietersma and Benjamin G. Wright. New York: Oxford University Press, 2007
NICOT	New International Commentary on the Old Testament
NJPS	*Tanakh: The Holy Scriptures: The New JPS Translation according to the Traditional Hebrew Text*
NRSV	New Revised Standard Version
OBO	Orbis Biblica et Orientalis
OLA	Orientalia Lovaniensa Analecta
OSHT	Oxford Studies in Historical Theology
OTL	Old Testament Library
PG	Patrologia Graeca [= Patrologiae Cursus Completus: Series Graeca]. Edited by Jacques-Paul Migne. 162 vols. Paris, 1857–1886
PL	Patrologia Latina [= Patrologiae Cursus Completus: Series Latina]. Edited by Jacques-Paul Migne. 217 vols. Paris, 1844–1864
SBLDS	Society of Biblical Literature Dissertation Series
SC	Sources chrétiennes
SHANE	Studies in the History of the Ancient Near East
SJT	*Scottish Journal of Theology*
TynBul	*Tyndale Bulletin*
VT	*Vetus Testamentum*
VTSup	Supplements to Vetus Testamentum
WBC	Word Biblical Commentary
WUNT	Wissenschaftliche Untersuchungen zum Neuen Testament
ZAW	*Zeitschrift für die alttestamentliche Wissenschaft*

Introduction

Another Book about Ecclesiastes

My first encounter with the book of Ecclesiastes was thirty years ago as an undergraduate in an "Old Testament Survey" course. In addition to working our way through whatever edition of Bernhard Anderson's *Introduction to the Old Testament* was current at the time, we were given a research paper assignment on a text of our choosing. For reasons that time has faded, I chose Ecclesiastes, and armed with the standard English language works then available, I wrote a serviceable paper that received a correspondingly serviceable grade. My only other memory of the entire affair is that I skipped a very large college party to stay up all night writing the paper, a choice that Qohelet might very well have scorned. But Ecclesiastes has remained with me through my graduate education and subsequent teaching career and in the recitations of Eccl 3:1–8 I have heard at funerals.

These are not reasons to write another book on Ecclesiastes. More to the point, while many readers of the Bible would say that it contains an infinite range of meanings, some biblical texts have garnered so much attention as to make further study in them seem an exercise in redundancy. This may be true for Ecclesiastes; the past twenty years have seen a significant amount of published scholarship on the book with no letup in sight.[1] Given the detailed, sustained attention Ecclesiastes has enjoyed from lots of very smart people, it is only fair that I address two questions at the outset of my contribution to the pile: Why another book on Ecclesiastes? What will it add to the conversation?

The very nature of modern biblical studies contains at its heart a paradox. On the one hand, the discipline arose from Renaissance and Enlightenment principles of textual study that aimed at achieving objectivity in interpretation.[2] Many of its early pioneers sought to free the Bible from the doctrinal uses to which it had been subjected by European Christianity and to a lesser extent, Judaism. Baruch Spinoza's reason for engaging in historical investigation of the Bible was precisely to undermine its use by theologians. But as Ronald Hendel notes, Spinoza's project was "domesticated to the interests of the church" so that "in the moderate guild of biblical scholars, theological concerns were never far from the surface."[3] By the mid-20th century biblical scholars regularly spoke of "assured results" in the field with the confidence of scientists describing progress in physics or medicine. These results were almost entirely based on historical claims and reconstructions; but by the 1970s, the quest for interpretive objectivity in the humanities, biblical studies included, was revealed for the illusion that it was: the projection of white, male, Western interpreters and their readings onto texts and their cultural contexts.[4] Acting on this, a small but growing number of biblical scholars began to challenge the "assured" historical claims of the field by demonstrating that many of them were thinly disguised theological beliefs that often distorted or overlooked problematic evidence in the historical record. By the 1990s, a full-blown scholarly battle was underway between "maximalists" and "minimalists," with bitter polemic on both sides.[5] I was a graduate student at the time, and a research assistant for two of the main "minimalist" scholars. My front-row seat to this acrimonious period in biblical scholarship made clear to me what is at stake in the seemingly esoteric textual and artifactual minutiae that biblical scholars often discuss. This debate is far from over. In 2017, on the Washington Mall alongside monuments to American history and politics, the $400 million Museum of the Bible will open, funded by conservative Christians who want to see the Bible play a larger role in American public life, and who draw upon biblical scholarship to help legitimize this aim.[6]

The upshot of the last thirty years is that many biblical scholars have realized that what has long been called "exegesis" (i.e., a "bringing out" of meanings from the text) is in fact a much more complex process of interaction between reader and text whose interpretive results are created rather than discovered. This does not necessarily affirm the theological claim that the scriptures are inexhaustible, but it does realize that the scholarly study of biblical texts demands much more than the discovery of "original" meanings or intentions. Indeed it has also been shown that, given the circumstances surrounding the composition and preservation of biblical texts, alongside the illusory nature of an "original meaning" in biblical studies there is also no concrete "original text."[7] In its place are manuscripts that reflect particular iterations of a text in limited temporal and geographical contexts, versions whose limited contexts might reflect other particular textual iterations, and scholarly reconstructions that hypothesize about what earlier particular iterations might have looked like.[8]

In over twenty years of classroom experience, I am consistently surprised when I teach Ecclesiastes to undergraduates at my small, Catholic institution in the American Upper Midwest. Almost all of my students are white and culturally Christian, although the majority do not practice a religion. Their knowledge of the Bible is based on a very limited exposure to the text early in their lives and can be reduced to a handful of clichés about doing good, having faith, and avoiding divine punishment. I often ask students to go through Ecclesiastes and select the book's most "unbiblical" statement. This activity makes an impression on them. They are easy targets for the biting observations of Ecclesiastes, and the book's contents, sitting there in the Bible, catches them off guard. It shocks them. That is part of the reason why I have them read it: to rattle their rather uncritical and thin understandings of the Bible and to point out to them that they, like the majority of American Christians, assume to know what the Bible says without ever really having taken a look inside one. They most often select as the most "unbiblical" statement in Ecclesiastes Qohelet's denial of life after death in 3:18–21. Anyone who studies the Hebrew Bible will notice the irony, given that the majority of biblical texts agree with Ecclesiastes in this regard. This should remind biblical scholars that what readers see in biblical texts is very much conditioned by their own interpretive presuppositions. This is also true for biblical scholars themselves. I ask students to do this exercise in part to introduce them to the concept of the canon within the canon so that they realize that parts of the canon are absolutized because of their theological claims while texts with differing viewpoints are overlooked. This both clarifies and problematizes the view that sees Ecclesiastes as an outsider, or a radical, or a countercultural voice attacking the standard religious beliefs of his day. This is a stance that has been taken by other readers, including a majority of modern biblical scholars. But it is a stance: a place outside of the text where my students and other readers might situate ourselves. I show the students how their "default" reading of Ecclesiastes sees Qohelet as a biblical outsider, which in turn highlights how their reading of the text is partial and selective. Their newfound awareness of this fact opens them to the fact that multiple interpretive viewpoints are there for the having. It also allows me to show them characteristics of other interpretive stances, all of which are partial and selective. We choose where to stand in order to see some things better than others. Our standing places determine not only what we are able to see; they also render some things invisible. We are therefore obligated to be aware of and responsible for these choices.

I do not subscribe to the position that Ecclesiastes is an "outsider" book in the Hebrew Bible, although this has been the common scholarly viewpoint. In fact, I find this claim intellectually weak, and at times morally repugnant. Ecclesiastes only looks like an outsider when seen from a constructed "center" of the Hebrew Bible—one usually dependent upon Christian theological claims. Scholars have accordingly marginalized Ecclesiastes to the Bible's periphery as "the odd book in," or as one of the Bible's "strange" books.[9] Take for example this claim from a recent major work on the Hebrew Bible

> It is striking how little Qohelet is intertextually related to other parts of the Bible . . . [it] shows a remarkable lack of explicit awareness of Hebrew biblical texts.[10]

In sharp contrast to this, a recent study of Ecclesiastes argues that the book is "a palimpsest of all Israel's history."[11] Here are two books published within a five-year span, one of which claims that Ecclesiastes has very little intertextual connections or even awareness with the remainder of the biblical canon, while the other argues that Ecclesiastes engages with almost all of it. The marginalization of Ecclesiastes is not the only scholarly position under question. Some scholars now argue that the entire subdivision of biblical "wisdom literature" is itself a chimera, a taxonomical tool mistakenly reified by biblical scholars whose interpretation is driven by a mainly Christian theological reading of the Hebrew Bible.[12]

To return to the limited nature of interpretive stances, the statement that every text can be interpreted in more than one way is a truth to which anyone who has ever struggled with tax forms or assembly instructions can attest. The interpretive richness of literary texts is precisely what makes them a pleasure to read. Not only can different readers find different ways to make sense of a text, but the same reader can discover and wrestle with multiple interpretations that will lead her back to the text to re-read and reinterpret. All this goes to show the rather prosaic fact that readings are constructed, shaped by the viewpoint of the reader. Here you might say to yourself, "Well, there's no other way to read, is there?" And you would be right. But the fact that there is no other way to read makes it necessary for us to think deeply about how we read.

My experience with teaching, reading, and writing about Ecclesiastes for the majority of my life has shown me that this particular biblical book offers rich rewards for anyone who wishes to think about how readers construe texts based upon their varied interpretive standpoints, acting in a back-and-forth relationship with the range of meanings potentially present in Ecclesiastes. What I hope to add to the conversation on Ecclesiastes is a detailed description of what readers have seen when standing in certain places before this ancient text and by way of critique, point out what we do not see from those standpoints. What is particularly interesting about Ecclesiastes, and what the book you are reading now investigates, are the multiple ways this biblical book's author is presented in the text. This is because, in a way unique to the biblical texts, the book's own authorial voice is as open to multiple understandings as is any of the book's content. Not only is what Ecclesiastes says a place for interpretive work on the reader's part, but also who is believed to be saying it.[13]

Ancient Authors

Readers of Ecclesiastes have wondered about its author's identity and historical context, but this is true for most of the biblical books. Another author-related question that occurs to many readers of Ecclesiastes is less common: How did a book like this get into the Bible? This question deals with authorship because of two assumptions underlying it. There is the literary assumption that the books of the Bible, because they are a collected whole, must cohere into a thematic unity. There is also the religious assumption that, while the Bible has many human writers, they are all guided by a single divine author, and therefore ought to speak with one voice in theological matters. These assumptions are not unique to modern readers. In his defense of Judaism written at the end of the first century CE, Josephus sets forth arguments supporting the inspired nature of the Jewish sacred texts. When compared to the "thousands of inconsistent and contradictory books" (μυριάδες βιβλίων . . . ἀσυμφώνων καὶ μαχομένων) of the Greeks, the Jewish writings possess an unparalleled degree of reliability:

> ἅτε μήτε τοῦ γράφειν αὐτοεξουσίου πᾶσιν ὄντος μήτε τινὸς ἐν τοῖς γραφομένοις ἐνούσης διαφωνίας, ἀλλὰ μόνων τῶν προφητῶν τὰ μὲν ἀνωτάτω καὶ παλαιότατα κατὰ τὴν ἐπίπνοιαν τὴν ἀπὸ τοῦ θεοῦ μαθόντων, τὰ δὲ καθ' αὐτοὺς ὡς ἐγένετο σαφῶς συγγραφόντων.
>
> (*Ag. Ap.* 1.37)

> No one can write on their own authority and there is no disagreement in the writings. It is only prophets who have written both about the loftiest, most ancient things which they learned from God by inspiration, besides also having written clearly about the things that happened to them.

Josephus is using rhetorical overkill to critique Greek culture, because the idea of divine inspiration guaranteeing a storyteller's historical veracity is also a Greek idea as old as Homer. In book 8 of the *Odyssey*, Odysseus praises the blind bard Demodocus because he can recount the fall of Troy as if he had been there himself, due to the inspiration of the Muse or Apollo—the god of prophecy.

> Δημόδοκ', ἔξοχα δή σε βροτῶν αἰνίζομ' ἁπάντων.
> ἢ σέ γε μοῦσ' ἐδίδαξε, Διὸς πάϊς, ἢ σέ γ' Ἀπόλλων,
> λίην γὰρ κατὰ κόσμον Ἀχαιῶν οἶτον ἀείδεις,
> ὅσσ' ἔρξαν τ' ἔπαθόν τε καὶ ὅσσ' ἐμόγησαν Ἀχαιοί,
> ὥς τέ που ἢ αὐτὸς παρεὼν ἢ ἄλλου ἀκούσας.
> (*Od.* 8.487–91)

> I respect you, Demodocus, more than any man alive—
> surely the Muse has taught you, Zeus's daughter,
> or god Apollo himself. How true to life,
> all too true . . . you sing the Achaeans' fate,
> all they did and suffered, all they soldiered through,
> as if you were there yourself or heard from one who was.[14]

Authorship in Mesopotamia during the first millennium BCE similarly views the author as the recipient of divine inspiration, while also making clear that authors are but the first in a chain of other specialists (i.e., singers and copyists, who keep the text "alive" through time). This process of "preserving" the text also admits of regular updating and revision.[15] In Egypt, authors' names are associated with texts—often for centuries—and texts are seen as a way to guarantee their authors' immortality. A student text preserved in a 19th dynasty papyrus (ca. 13th century BCE) now in the British Museum reminds the scribe that, while the rich and powerful build for themselves great tombs, it is writers who truly possess immortality through their texts because writings are preserved by means of constant copying, unlike tombs that eventually fall into disrepair.[16] In both Mesopotamia and Egypt, texts have a power that they grant to their authors, whether it be evidence that the author has been the recipient of divine favor or preservation of the author's name beyond death. By the Hellenistic period the direction of influence goes the other way and there is widespread evidence of attributed authorship used to lend authority to texts.[17] When the libraries of Alexandria and Pergamum were established, their royal patrons were eager to collect (and pay for) a copy of every written text. Human nature being as it is, enterprising individuals offered up many pseudonymous works for purchase, using the authority of the author's falsely attributed name to lend validity, and value, to the text or to create literary output for an important figure in the tradition.[18] This connection between a writing's value, whether as art, prophecy, or law, and its author's identity is also prevalent in Jewish literary circles during the Hellenistic period (at least two or three centuries prior to Josephus's broadside discussed above), and can be seen in the proliferation of numerous pseudonymous Jewish writings, the attribution of the Pentateuch to Moses, and the translator's prologue to Sirach. The close conceptual link between a text's authority and its author lives on in both modern English and Romance languages, where the words "author" and "authority" are etymologically related. A look at their Latin parents, *auctor* and *auctoritas*, respectively, shows that an *auctor* was used in a literal sense to refer to a biological progenitor, and in metaphorical sense of a person initiating a variety of actions, the composition of a literary work being only one. *Auctoritas* not only referred to the *auctor*'s capacity for initiating action but often to the product of that action.[19]

The role of the author for ancient Jewish and Greco-Roman readers helps to put into relief some distinctive features about the book of Ecclesiastes. While the Hebrew Bible contains some three-dimensional characters who have challenged the creativity of rabbis, pastors, and theologians for centuries, Qohelet is distinct among biblical characters for a number of reasons. He is both a character and an author, but unlike Moses, he refers to himself in the first person. His words are not set in a narrative framework established by an omniscient narrator as in Job.[20] Unlike the prophets, Qohelet does not claim to speak for another as do the prophetic texts. Unlike Proverbs, Qohelet speaks almost entirely from his own experience. In his volume on the history of reception of Ecclesiastes, Eric Christianson notes,

> Readers have not "received" a coherent idea from Qoheleth. What they have received, in abundance, is the spirit of his persona, the whole distilled essence of his brooding presence. Qoheleth the man, therefore, has had greater impact than any one passage of Ecclesiastes.[21]

Christianson's point is spot-on: the voice of Qohelet, the persona readers construct from a polyvalent text, exerts a strong pull on how the book is read. But Christianson errs in his use of the singular. There is no one "spirit" of any one "persona," or any singular "presence," brooding or otherwise, in Ecclesiastes. We are instead confronted with a variety of partial, fragmentary authorial voices that often frustrate more than they clarify our attempts to read the text as a coherent unit. This makes Ecclesiastes a distinctive book in the Hebrew Bible. No other biblical text has the combination of such a strong authorial presence presented in such an elusive way.

The major divide in authorial voices in Ecclesiastes is that between the first-person text in 1:12–12:8 and the third-person voice that frames it in 1:1–11 and 12:8–14, with a brief appearance in 7:27. Some of the prophetic books and parts of the book of Proverbs (e.g., Jer 1:1; Amos 1:1, Prov25:1; 31:1) are also mostly first-person texts introduced by a third-person statement identifying the speaker. The prophetic texts assert that they are first-person narrations of the prophets, who themselves speak on behalf of God. Prov 25:1 introduces a collection of proverbs with the statement, "These are also proverbs of Solomon which Hezekiah's men copied." Prov 31:1 states that the following material comes from a king named Lemuel, who learned it from his mother. In contrast the first-person voice in Ecclesiastes identifies himself exclusively by means of titles (Qohelet, king in Jerusalem) rather than names. This creates multiple questions of identity that challenge the reader's relationship with the book's narrative voice. By way of example, take the rather simple statement in 1:12: "I, Qohelet, was king over Israel in Jerusalem." The statement's purpose is to identify the person behind the title, "Qohelet," and this is what it appears to do. But the phrase, "king over Israel in Jerusalem," does not help very much in identifying Qohelet, because the Hebrew Bible lists 21 kings (and one queen) from David to Zedekiah who ruled over Israel in Jerusalem. Which one is Qohelet? The reference to Qohelet as the "son of David" in the superscription of 1:1 may not offer much help, since it might be a guess of the scribe who added the superscription, or "son of David" may be understood as any king in the Davidic line. The patronymic בן דוד only occurs elsewhere in explicit reference to Solomon (Prov 1:1; 2 Chron 13:6, 30:26, 35:3) but in the plural (בני דוד) it is used to refer to the Davidic dynasty (2 Chron 23:3; 32:33). There is also the problem of the verb הייתי, which can express completed action. In both the Targum and the Talmud, the verb was read as reference to past completed action, raising another set of questions: Is the speaker now no longer king over Israel in Jerusalem? Or is he still king over Israel, but no longer in Jerusalem?

The combination of the third-person voice that frames the first-person text, which identifies the speaker as, "Qohelet, David's son, king in Jerusalem" with the "I" who calls himself "Qohelet" and speaks as if he were a great king in Jerusalem, magnifies interpretive possibilities. Jacqueline Vayntrub notes that the narrator could have used the name Solomon had he wished, but instead chose the more enigmatic, "Qohelet" because "indirect references and hints of connection . . . may accord with a work that resists stable interpretation."[22] Ecclesiastes also presents a complication not found in these other examples of royal superscription. This is because the narrative voice returns in an epilogue (not found in other such collections) to tell us that Qohelet was a teacher (and not a king), and perhaps not a very good one to boot. The narrator points out that Qohelet tried to find useful sayings for his pupils, but follows this with the warning that one should not stray from the traditional sources used to acquire wisdom. The epilogue also affirms divine justice and the necessity of religious duty, thereby undermining much of what Qohelet seems to have said. The result is that the voice of the epilogue's narrator and the voice of Qohelet can be read in mutually exclusive terms in which only one of them can be right. As is the case with Qohelet's elusive identity, the epilogue also raises questions for a reader: If the narrator seems to disapprove of the words of Qohelet, then why has he chosen to preserve them? Behind both the narrator and Qohelet lies the persona of whoever decided to group this book with the others that are now part of the Hebrew Bible and whose reasoning is opaque to us. What are we to make of these presences? With whom should we agree?

Added to this, the reader also finds contradictory statements on important matters inside the first-person narrative. Qohelet says that wisdom is the cause of sorrow but also that the wise are better than fools the way those who can see are better than the blind (1:18, 2:13–14). He affirms that God takes from the wicked to give to those who please him, and will judge the righteous and the wicked (2:26, 3:17), while also professing not to know if God will judge between the righteous and the wicked, knowing only that both die the same (9:1–2). He points out the futility of pleasure (2:1–2, 10–11) and also commends it as the only possible joy in life (8:15, 9:7–9). Besides having to judge the words of a sage whose teachings are perhaps refuted by the same person who preserved them, the reader must also make sense of a text that contains contradictory instructions on how to live life.

All of the questions raised in the preceding paragraphs have been asked, and a variety of answers proposed. Many of these answers are described and analyzed in this book, part of whose aim is to shed light on how these answers function for readers as ways making sense of the text. We also need to acknowledge that these are questions because of the way we think about authors and literary works. While the link between authors and texts dates back to first millennium BCE, the modern understanding of an author as an individual responsible for a work that is written, completed, and published is an anachronism for biblical texts. Biblical texts, like many of their ancient Near Eastern and Greco-Roman counterparts, did not originate as the complete product of an individual "author." The presence of a small writing class in a mostly oral culture influenced the way literary texts were produced and understood, most importantly in the fact that many literary texts deemed worthy of writing down were also recited in various settings.[23] Arising from and coexisting with an oral milieu, literary texts exhibit some of the qualities of oral compositions, for example the repetition of formulaic expressions or type scenes, and frequent wordplay.[24] They also show clear signs of being composite works that grew over time as the result of a long and mostly anonymous process of composition that includes multiple iterations of oral performance. In the same way that separate oral performances of works are discrete entities—sonic "incarnations" of a work, if you will—multiple manuscripts of an ancient work are each different textual incarnations of that written tradition that exists in each work without inhering completely in any. Brennan Breed refers to this phenomenon as a text's "differential identity."[25]

To sum up, the term "author" does not simply denote an individual who writes something, especially regarding ancient Near Eastern and classical texts, the Bible included. Authorship is often applied retroactively to texts whose compositions are unknown. It embraces many connotations that reveal how readers think about certain writings and how they are to be read. These connotations are at work in how readers have understood the author of Ecclesiastes, a text that presents readers with conflicting and vague statements about its author. Before proceeding, I need to spend a little more time in this introduction thinking about the idea of an author with the help of Michel Foucault.

Authors as Interpretive Aids

In his short but influential essay, "What Is an Author?" Foucault seeks to describe the author as a cultural function and not as an identity (i.e., a flesh-and-blood person who composes a piece of writing). The "author function" denotes "the singular relationship that holds between a author and a text, the manner in which a text apparently points to this figure who is outside and precedes it."[26] Foucault's essay makes several points germane to thinking about the author in Ecclesiastes, and I will refer to it throughout this book.

First, the "author" is a concept that both arises from and helps to define the genre of certain texts. Important texts are required to have authors, and authors are required to have a corpus of certain kinds of texts attributed to them. The idea of an author is a taxonomic device, an interpretive tool used to designate and group texts. Authorial attribution also gives texts normative force.[27] This is evident in how popular culture speaks of "classic" literature. While it is simply a matter of personal taste to dislike a current popular author such as John Grisham or Nicholas Sparks, saying that one does not enjoy (or "appreciate," as it is called) Homer, Shakespeare, Jane Austen, or James Joyce functions instead as a self-evaluative statement, revealing something about the speaker's education, background, and cultural capital.[28]

But the author function does not simply connect texts with names. It is ultimately a necessity for certain kinds of texts and is as creative an enterprise as the generation of texts itself, "a complex operation whose purpose is to construct the rational entity we call an author."[29] The author function provides a context for a writing, posits a creative will behind it, and constructs the historical and cultural circumstances that explain its origin. An author is not something "out there," discovered by readers; it is something made by them.

> We speak of an individual's "profundity" or "creative" power, his intentions or the original inspiration manifested in writing. These aspects of an individual, which we designate as an author (or which comprise an individual as an author), are projections, in terms always more or less psychological, of our way of handling texts: in the comparisons we make, the traits we extract as pertinent, the continuities we assign, or the exclusions we practice. In addition, all these operations vary according to the period and the form of discourse concerned.[30]

What Foucault means when he says that readers create authors is different than the concept of the implied author used in literary criticism. An implied author is one constructed completely on the basis of internal textual clues, without recourse to external cultural influence. When Foucault discusses the criteria used to determine the authorship of a work (i.e., those ways of reading a text that provide for the text a fully developed picture of its author), he is keen to show how a particular understanding of an author's thought and life serve to limit how a work is read. It marks the boundaries between acceptable and forbidden interpretations. It also resolves contradictions, whether these be with other works attributed to the same author or with the dominant discourse of the culture that reads the text. The author function can be a tool to prevent culturally normative texts from doing anything other than legitimize and reinforce that culture's values.

The author function does a good deal of heavy lifting in biblical studies, where scholars' stock-in-trade has long been the construction of authors from texts, whether it be "J," "P," "the Deuteronomist," "the Chronicler," or "Deutero-Isaiah," each complete with their own respective ideologies and historical contexts. Perhaps it is no surprise that the roots of academic biblical studies can be traced back through Richard Simon and Jean Astruc to Spinoza's claim that Ezra wrote the Pentateuch, behind that to Lorenzo Valla's exposure of the *Donation of Constantine* as a forgery, and finally to Porphyry's (correct) argument that the book of Daniel was written during the Maccabean revolt.[31] All of these critical milestones revolve around the issue of the author. In regard to Ecclesiastes, Foucault's work provides a theoretical language for understanding the different ways the author of Ecclesiastes has been constructed and articulated by readers through the centuries. Particularly relevant in this regard are those readings of Ecclesiastes that understand the book's author to be King Solomon, an attribution that is brought by readers to the text and is also the result of their making sense of it.[32] I will examine these interpretations in detail in chapter one.

Foucault offers a theoretical structure to clarify how readers play an active role in the construction of the author of a text. The recent work of Brennan Breed on biblical reception history provides an equally important method for understanding how a biblical text is read across time and cultures.

Reception Theory

Modern biblical scholarship, arising from the German model of *Wissenschaft*, has long demanded that scholars take into account how biblical texts have been interpreted in the past. A standard part of every doctoral dissertation is the review of scholarship (*der Stand der Forschung*) by means of which the doctoral candidate demonstrates her competence in the field to engage in the scholarly conversation. This kind of interpretive history is not reception history. Biblical reception history, the analysis of how a biblical text has been interpreted in different times by different readers, is founded on the hermeneutical thought of Hans Georg Gadamer. It emphasizes the impact that "classic" works have on a shaping a culture and thus sees influence as running both ways between a text and its readers. Gadamer uses the term *Wirkungsgeschichte* ("history of effect") to refer to a work's influence on readers throughout time.[33] Describing a text's *Wirkungsgeschichte*, or its reception history, in biblical studies is a rapidly expanding subfield in the discipline. It has become a favored reading strategy of those for whom it is essential that the Bible continue to support their theological claims. Craig Bartholomew, who has written a great deal on Ecclesiastes, sees Gadamer's hermeneutics as sympathetic to the project of reading it—and other biblical texts—from within a confessional tradition because "Gadamer refuses to set reason in opposition to tradition. Indeed understanding takes place as an event within a tradition."[34] The recently launched Ancient Christian Commentary on Scripture series is dedicated to "the revitalization of Christian teaching based on classical Christian exegesis" and seeks to "refrain from the temptation to fixate endlessly upon contemporary criticism." Contemporary criticism here means non-confessional approaches, and notice that they are described as a temptation—enticing but ultimately bad for you, and endless—with no purpose or final goal.[35] But reception history can do more than allow doctrinally informed readings to take their place alongside scholarly ones. It retrieves forgotten voices of the past, decenters historical-criticism from its long-held privileged perch, and explores the range of meanings at work in—and on—a given text.[36]

Brennan Breed's book, *Nomadic Text*, is one of the first attempts to articulate a theory and method of reception history for biblical studies. Rich in philosophical and theoretical discussion, Breed's work is necessary reading for anyone working with reception history of the Bible. I highlight here only a portion of his insights and methodological recommendations. In a deceptively simple definition, Breed states that reception history is nothing more than "people taking a text and doing something with it."[37] With a multiplicity of written iterations of the biblical text—the Bible's differential identity—Breed turns to how those texts are read. Corresponding to the idea of differential identity regarding the manuscript traditions of the biblical text, Breed uses the concept of "virtual multiplicity" from Giles Deleuze to show that a biblical text contains many potential meanings that are made virtual or explicit by different readers. Because potential meanings in a text exist in a reciprocal relationship with each other and with many different aspects of a reader's cultural context, the virtual multiplicity of meanings in the Bible is vast and changing.[38] Usually reception history focuses on readers and what they see in texts, in a manner similar to how an inkblot in a Rorhschach test is assumed to do nothing more than elicit what is already in a person's mind. Breed insists that reception history begins inside the text, with all its potentialities. When readers interpret a text, they are not merely seeing what they think is there. They are making real a potential interpretation that is already there in the text.[39] This does not alter the fact that readers can only see those things in a text by virtue of their own standpoint.[40] But when doing reception history the potentialities of the text, and not the contexts of the readers, guide the analysis. Thus writing the reception history of a text is more than cataloging different readings, and biblical reception history should not group readings into externally determined categories, such as pre-modern versus modern, or Jewish versus Christian, or textual interpretations versus those in the sonic or visual arts. Interpretations that cut across all of these categories can be found together. This is what Deleuze refers to as a text's "nomadic distribution." The text's potential cannot be readily boxed in by external categories that are alien to it. For Breed reception history of the Bible lets categories arise from the texts themselves, and these readings may then be traced in their trajectories through time.[41] He uses the helpful image of marbles rolling on an old wooden floor.

> Perhaps no two marbles would end up in exactly the same place, but the contours of the floor would herd the marbles into a general pattern of distribution . . . Say, for example, that some marbles congregated by the low point near the door and others clumped in a depression near the kitchen table . . . From this exercise, one might be able to locate the basic contours of the floor.[42]

The places where the marbles congregate are, for Breed, a text's "semantic nodes," certain potential readings of a text that are actualized by readers across many historical and cultural contexts. Of course, no reader has the bird's eye perspective to survey the entire old wooden floor from above. We ourselves a part of an intellectual landscape with its own topography and limits beyond whose horizons we cannot see. I mean everyone, and our place in the landscape shapes every reading of a text. This is along the lines of what Jacques Berlinerblau calls "sociohermeneutics," which he describes as study of the "interplay that exists between a polysemous sacred text and culturally positioned interpreters."[43] Sociohermeneutics is concerned with issues that "stand at the intersection of exegesis, hermeneutics, sociology and history,"[44] and is interested with the influences, biases, and issues at stake in a particular group's reading of a biblical text. Scholars engaged in reception history must also attend to these issues not only for the readings they examine but for themselves too, as Jonathan Morgan makes clear.

> The location of the reception historian in relation to the text and their own context, and their choices with regard to which sites [specific texts] have been privileged and which interpretations emphasized, are seen as operative in the ongoing process of reception.[45]

Combining Breed with Foucault requires some manipulation on my part. For Breed, semantic nodes are formed by looking at the readings in the text which readers uncover. For Foucault, authors are constructed out of texts and function as interpretive controls. I want to identify the semantic nodes of Ecclesiastes at this intersection of the readings arising from the text and the authorial norms being imposed on the text. The fragmented, multivalent nature of Ecclesiastes as a text and of Qohelet as a voice makes this a potentially fruitful avenue of inquiry. It is why I have written this book, although I make no claims to have exhausted the range of potential readings in my investigation. It is also important to state that this book is not a general reception theory of Ecclesiastes. Such works have already been written but they predate Breed's important methodological contribution. Some deserve mention here.[46] Over 150 years ago, Christian Ginsburg provided a 200-page "historical sketch of exegesis" by way of introduction to his book on Ecclesiastes that still proves useful.[47] More recently, Mary E. Mills has drawn on a wide range of philosophers and literary theorists to write a sophisticated analysis of how Ecclesiastes is read by modern commentators.[48] Katharine Dell's book divides readings of Ecclesiastes between ancient and modern interpreters. Among the latter, Dell distinguishes ecological, post-colonial, and feminist readings.[49] Suseela C. Yesudian-Storfjell aims for a representative cross-section of ancient and modern, Jewish and Christian readings in her study.[50] Finally, there is Eric Christianson's volume on Ecclesiastes in the Blackwell Bible Commentary, a series devoted to biblical reception history.[51] Christianson groups readings around certain specific ideas and texts, arranging his commentary sequentially following the order of the book. He looks at readings from all periods, both scholarly and pre-modern, in a largely chronological arrangement. In contrast, the following chapters of this book describe the semantic nodes that are revealed when examining how all sorts of readers of Ecclesiastes have understood the book's author.[52] So, on the one hand, this book engages in a reception history of the author of Ecclesiastes. But on the other, I also offer my own interpretations of the author in Ecclesiastes and include them in their appropriate semantic nodes. In other words, my own actualizations of the text will be described and placed alongside the others.[53] This will require my entering into dialogue with other readings and engaging in the critical give and take that is the staple of modern biblical studies. But in addition to that, I also want to make explicit the fact that my interpretations are part of the larger history of readers actualizing the potential meanings in Ecclesiastes. My voice is part of the chorus, and not a soloist's with a backing group of earlier readers. And just because one of the contexts from which I read is that of modern biblical scholarship, that does not necessarily mean that my readings have any greater claim toward "objectivity" than others.[54] Different readers approach texts with different goals.

On Riddles

The title of this book refers to the "riddle" of authorship in Ecclesiastes, and that term needs to be explained at the end of this introduction. Our default understanding of a riddle is that it is a enigmatic or trick question with one correct answer. We "solve" the riddle by discovering the answer. In J.R.R. Tolkien's, *The Hobbit*, two characters engage in a riddle game, a competition decided on who can correctly answer the most riddles.[55] There are riddles like this in the Hebrew Bible, the best known being those traded between Samson and the Philistines in Judges 14.[56] But another kind of riddle in the Hebrew Bible does not require one to find the right answer, but to create the best answer. These riddles are expressed as open-ended questions meant to evoke clever, playful, biting responses. Several occur in Proverbs, for example in Prov 30:18–19):

שלשה המה נפלאו ממני
וארבע לא ידעתים
דרך הנשר בשמים
דרך נחש עלי צור
דרך אניה בלב ים
ודרך גבר בעלמה

> There are three things too wondrous for me;
> four I do not understand:
> the way of an eagle in the sky,
> the way of a snake on a rock,
> the way of a ship in the heart of the sea,
> and the way of a young man with a girl.

The opening couplet of the riddle uses a familiar ancient Near Eastern linguistic device of "x + 1," and scholars refer to these biblical examples as numeric proverbs. The statements of the couplet are easily turned into questions: "What are three things too wondrous for you? What are four you do not understand?" The open-ended nature is deliberate and invites clever replies that show the respondent's ability to think quickly and speak gracefully.[57] A riddle's challenge often lies in its use of linguistic ambiguity to confuse. Take the old standby: "What's black and white and read all over?" The crux of this riddle is the homophony between "read" and "red" (which can only work in an oral setting). In the four responses of the riddle from Proverbs, the term, "way" (777) can mean both "how something moves" (snakes, ships, birds) and "how one goes about something" (men and women). This double meaning is the linguistic play at work in the answers. But these answers need not be the only ones to the question.[58] A variety of answers to such open-ended queries can be generated and the "best" ones remembered or written down. As with traditional riddles, these numeric sayings fit in a social atmosphere that mixes diversion with competition and runs the gamut from friendly play among peers to high stakes competition between rivals.[59]

When I refer to the "riddle of authorship in Ecclesiastes," I mean "riddle" in the biblical sense—an open-ended question that challenges our creativity as well as our analytical skills, and not an enigma with just one solution awaiting discovery.[60] In the chapters that follow, I will survey and analyze some of the many different answers to the question, "Who is Qohelet, the author of Ecclesiastes?" First I look at how those readers who understood Qohelet to be Solomon constructed a biography of that biblical figure from a variety of traditions and used it to read Ecclesiastes while at the same time creating a fixed place for the biblical book in a corpus of Solomonic writings. The relationship of these Solomonic works with each other have been used to interpret each individual work, Ecclesiastes included. In chapter two I examine those readings that both acknowledged that Ecclesiastes was not written by Solomon but see Qohelet as adopting either a Solomonic or royal persona. Chapter three addresses how the contradictory statements in Ecclesiastes have been resolved by recourse to one or more constructed authors otherwise invisible in the narrative. In chapter four I look at how Qohelet has been understood as saint, sinner, or repentant sinner turned saint. Chapter five groups readings that see Qohelet as a philosopher, or his thought as philosophical. Drawing on Breed's method of reception history, I group my discussion of these readings into nodes that cut across historical epochs and confessional commitments. Indeed, each chapter is itself a particular interpretive node insofar as it groups together readings with similar views of the author of Ecclesiastes. I make no claim to a comprehensive collection of all the readings that fit into these nodes. I am striving for enough of a representative grouping of marbles to reveal the shape of this particular old wooden floor from where I can see it and with the help of what others have seen.

To restate the questions I posed in the beginning of this introduction: Why have I written a book on Ecclesiastes when there are already so many? It is because Ecclesiastes is a particularly rich locus for how doctrinal, confessional, historical, philological, and literary concerns meet and combine in the book's reception history. What will my book add to the conversation? It will mark a beginning in the use of Brennan Breed's model of reception history and provide a helpful mapping of past readings, their relation to each other, and their blind spots. I hope that readers of my book come away from it not only with a greater knowledge of Ecclesiastes, its readers, and its "authors," but also with an awareness of the always complex and often-beautiful process of biblical interpretation.

Notes

1. A search of the American Theological Library Association database in EBSCO for all titles containing either "Ecclesiastes," "Qoheleth," or "Qohelet" in peer-reviewed publications appearing from 1995–2015 returns 346 discrete results (98 books, 134 peer-reviewed articles, and 114 essays/book chapters in edited volumes). By contrast, the book of Zechariah, a biblical text roughly the same length as Ecclesiastes, returns 162 discrete results in a search made with the same parameters. I will refrain from the obligatory citation of Eccl 12:12 in this regard.
2. Michael Legaspi, *The Death of Scripture and the Rise of Biblical Studies*, OSHT (New York: Oxford University Press, 2010) has a detailed and vivid discussion of the origins of modern biblical criticism. Stephen D. Moore and Yvonne Sherwood describe how the Enlightenment's attack on the Bible's morality led to biblical scholarship's diversion into questions of history (*The Invention of the Biblical Scholar: A Critical Manifesto* [Minneapolis, MN: Fortress Press, 2011]).
3. Ronald Hendel, "Mind the Gap: Modern and Postmodern in Biblical Studies," *JBL* 133 (2014): 440.
4. Described in John Collins, *The Bible after Babel: Historical Criticism in a Postmodern Age* (Grand Rapids: Eerdmans, 2005).
5. I want to begin by saying that I loathe the terms "maximalist" and "minimalist," but they are the most often used terms to characterize the parties in this debate, and so I use them under protest. Major "minimalist" works are Philip R. Davies, *In Search of "Ancient Israel": A Study in Biblical Origins*, JSOTSup 148 (Sheffield: Sheffield Academic Press, 1992); Thomas L. Thompson, *The Early History of the Israelite People: From the Written and Archeological Sources*, SHANE 4 (Leiden: Brill, 1992); Niels Peter Lemche, *The Israelites in History and Tradition*, LAI (Louisville, KY: Westminster John Knox, 1998). Samples of the polemics: Iain Provan, "Ideologies, Literary and Critical: Reflections on Recent Writing on the History of Israel," *JBL* 114 (1995): 585–606; Thomas L. Thompson, "A Neo-Albrightean School in History and Biblical Scholarship," *JBL* 114 (1995): 683–98; Philip R. Davies, "Method and Madness: Some Remarks on Doing History with the Bible," *JBL* 114 (1995): 699–705; William G. Dever, *What Did the Biblical Writers Know and When Did They Know It?: What Archeology Can Tell Us about the Reality of Ancient Israel* (Grand Rapids, MI: Eerdmans, 2001).
6. See Joel Baden and Candida Moss, "Can Hobby Lobby Buy the Bible?" *Atlantic Monthly* 317 (January-February 2016): 70–7, http://www.theatlantic.com/magazine/archive/2016/01/can-hobby-lobby-buy-the-bible/419088/.
7. Brennan W. Breed, *Nomadic Text: A Theory of Biblical Reception History*, ISBL (Bloomington: Indiana University Press, 2014) 15–74. "There is no original biblical text . . . We have always been thinking without the original text: now we just have to think without thinking about the original text" (57).
8. For a discussion of textual iterations in oral-literate cultures, see Raymond F. Person, Jr., "The Problem of 'Literary Unity' from the Perspective of Oral Traditions," in *Empirical Models Challenging Biblical Criticism*, eds. Raymond F. Person, Jr. and Robert Rezetko (Atlanta: Society of Biblical Literature, 2016) 217–36.
9. James Crenshaw, "Ecclesiastes: Odd Book In," *BRev* 31 (1990): 28–33; Elias Bickerman, *Four Strange Books of the Bible: Jonah, Daniel, Koheleth, Esther* (New York: Schocken, 1985).

10. David Carr, *The Formation of the Bible: A New Reconstruction* (New York: Oxford University Press, 2011) 451.
11. Jennie Barbour, *The Story of Israel in the Book of Qohelet: Ecclesiastes as Cultural Memory*, Oxford Theological Monographs (Oxford: Oxford University Press, 2012) 29.
12. For arguments both for and against, see the essays in *Was There a Wisdom Tradition? New Prospects in Israelite Wisdom Studies*, ed. Mark R. Sneed, AIL (Atlanta: SBL Press, 2015).
13. For a partial, similar, but shorter example of what I am doing in this book, see Patrick L. Miller, "What the Preacher Forgot: The Rhetoric of Ecclesiastes," *CBQ* 62 (2000): 215–25.
14. Translation is from Robert Fagles, *Homer: The Odyssey* (New York: Penguin, 1996) 207. For more discussion of this idea and its use by both Josephus and the Greeks, see Thomas M. Bolin, "History, Historiography, and the Use of the Past in the Hebrew Bible," in *The Limits of Historiography: Genre and Narrative in Ancient Historical Texts*, ed. Christina Shuttleworth Kraus (Leiden: Brill, 1999) 113–40.
15. Benjamin Foster, "On Authorship in Akkadian Literature," *Annali di Istituto Universitario Orientali di Napoli* 51 (1991): 17–32; several essays in *The Oxford Handbook of Cuneiform Culture*, eds. Karen Radner and Eleanor Robson (New York: Oxford University Press, 2011) and most recently Marc Van De Mieroop, *Philosophy before the Greeks: The Pursuit of Truth in Ancient Babylonia* (Princeton, NJ: Princeton University Press, 2016) 16–27.
16. P.Chester.Beatty 4 (P.BritishMuseum 10684) translation in *AEL* 2.175–8.
17. Not that this did not also happen in Egypt and Mesopotamia, particularly with cultic texts, as noted in Foster, "On Authorship," 18. Martin West argues for a similar process in 6th century BCE that led to creation of a poet called "Homer" seen as the author of the *Iliad* and *Odyssey* ("The Invention of Homer," *Classical Quarterly* 49 [1999]: 364–82).
18. Mentioned by the 2nd-century CE writer Galen in his treatise, *On Hippocrates, On Human Nature*, 15.105.
19. See Charlton T. Lewis, Charles Short, *A Latin Dictionary* (Oxford: Clarendon, 1879) s.v., "auctor" and "auctoritas."
20. But see the discussion in chapter three of readings that see a frame narrator in Ecclesiastes.
21. Eric Christianson, *Ecclesiastes through the Centuries*, Blackwell Bible Commentaries (Malden, MA: Wiley-Blackwell, 2007) 256.
22. Jacqueline Vayntrub, "Proverbs and the Limits of Poetry," (PhD diss., University of Chicago, 2015) 322.
23. "Literary" as contrasted with administrative texts, which appear to encompass the majority of the earliest writing; see the overview in Jean Bottèro, *Mesopotamia: Writing, Reasoning, and the Gods*, trans. Zainab Bahrani and Marc Van De Mieroop (Chicago: University of Chicago Press, 1992); trans. of *Mésopotamie. L'écriture, la raison et les dieux* (Paris: Gallimard, 1987).
24. The marked distinction between oral and written cultures and how they think argued by Walter Ong, in *Orality and Literacy: The Technologizing of the Word* (New York: Methuen, 1982) has been replaced by a more nuanced understanding of a predominantly oral culture that also contains a small group who can produce and consume literary texts. See, Susan Niditch, *Oral World and Written Word: Ancient Israelite Literature*, LAI. (Louisville: Westminster John Knox, 1996). For evidence of an oral-literate nexus, see Charles Halton, "Allusions to the Stream of Tradition of Neo-Assyrian Oracles," *ANES* 46 (2009): 50–61; and Nili Samet, "'The Tallest Man Cannot Reach Heaven; The Broadest Cannot Cover Earth'—Reconsidering the Proverb and Its Biblical Parallels," *JHebS* 10, Article 18 (2010). doi:10.5508/jhs.2010.v10.a18.
25. Cf. Breed, *Nomadic Text*, 72, borrowing the term from Saussure.

26. Michel Foucault, "What Is an Author?" *Professing the New Rhetorics: A Sourcebook*, trans. Donald Bouchard and Sherry Simon, eds. Theresa Enos and Stuart C. Brown (Englewood Cliffs, NJ: Prentice Hall, 1994) 178–93, 184; trans. of "Qu'est ce qu'un auteur?" *Bulletin de la société française de philosophie* 63 (1969): 73–104. Its influence is attested by the fact that the English translation has been anthologized numerous times.
27. "The function of an author is to characterize the existence, circulation, and operation of certain discourses within a society . . . it serves as a means of classification. A name can group together a number of texts and thus differentiate them from others. A name also establishes different forms of relationships among texts" ("What Is an Author?" 184).
28. Erroneously, Foucault claims that the necessity for the understanding of an author as an owner of a text is an exclusively modern phenomenon because it presupposes the development of organized and comprehensive means of social control and punishment. Equally problematic is the fact that he places religious texts outside of this activity because the "authors" of these texts (either mythological figures or individuals long dead) are beyond the reach of societal censure ("What Is an Author?" 184–5). But the case of Qohelet shows that even long-dead authors of religious texts are not immune from interrogation and censure.
29. Foucault, "What Is an Author?" 186.
30. Foucault, "What Is an Author?" 186.
31. Maurice Casey, "Porphyry and the Origin of the Book of Daniel," *JTS* 27 (1976): 15–33; Salvatore I. Camporeale, "Lorenzo Valla's 'Oratio' on the Pseudo-Donation of Constantine: Dissent and Innovation in Early Renaissance Humanism," *Journal of the History of Ideas* 57 (1996): 9–26.
32. "Neither Hermes nor Hippocrates existed in the sense that we can say Balzac existed, but the fact that a number of texts were attached to a single name implies that relationship of homogeneity, filiation, reciprocal explanation, authentification, or of common utilization were established among them . . . the author's name characterizes a particular manner of existence of discourse . . . its status and its manner of reception are regulated by the culture in which it circulates" ("What Is an Author?"184).
33. Hans-Georg Gadamer, *Truth and Method*, trans. Joel Weinsheimer and Donald G. Marshall, 2nd rev. ed. (New York: Crossroad, 1989) 300–6; trans. of *Wahrheit und Methode: Gesammelte Werke* 1, rev. and expanded ed. (Tübingen: Mohr Siebeck, 1986).
34. Craig Bartholomew, *Reading Ecclesiastes: Old Testament Exegesis and Hermeneutical Theory*, AnBib 139 (Rome: Pontifical Biblical Institute, 1993) 19. Bartholomew, in contrast to the historical analysis of Moore and Sherwood, Legaspi, and Hendel discussed above, sees historical criticism as hostile to Christian faith. "The historical critical method was shaped within an ethos of suspicion towards Christianity" (86). His ultimate goal is to argue: "that biblical interpretation is best served by a philosophy of history shaped by the Christian narrative" (88).
35. Quotation from the general series introduction in every volume. The dust jacket goes even further: "Today the historical-critical method of interpretation has nearly exhausted its claim on the biblical text and on the church."
36. Three new series, the Blackwell Bible Commentaries (published by Blackwell), Illuminations (published by Eerdmans) and Scriptural Traces (published by Bloomsbury) all are dedicated to reception history as is the journal, *Relegere* and De Gruyter's, *Encyclopedia of the Bible and Its Reception.*
37. Breed, *Nomadic Text*, 115.
38. Breed, *Nomadic Text*, 116–27.
39. Breed, *Nomadic Text*, 121.
40. "A text can also be thought of as a virtual multiplicity. The differential relations between lexemes, sentences, and paragraphs, for example, creates a potential field of reading that can be actualized in divergent ways. These differential relations within the text

must be set in play with the system of culture within which one reads the text, including the semantic, generic, and historical sets of relations that determine the context of reading. Together, these differential relations comprise the powers of a text. These powers include its hermeneutic potentials but also embrace all affectivity a text might create" (Breed, *Nomadic Text*, 122).

41. Breed, *Nomadic Text*, 141.
42. Breed, *Nomadic Text*, 149–50.
43. Jacques Berlinerblau, *The Secular Bible: Why Nonbelievers Must Take Religion Seriously* (New York: Cambridge University Press, 2005) 81.
44. Berlinerblau, *Secular Bible*, 80.
45. Jonathan Morgan, "Visitors, Gatekeepers, and Receptionists: Reflections on the Shape of Biblical Studies and the Role of Reception History," in *Reception History and Biblical Studies: Theory and Practice*, eds. Emma England and William John Lyons, LHBOTS (London: Bloomsbury, 2015) 63.
46. But by no means can I discuss all of them here. For example, the two detailed studies of Svend Holm-Nielsen are also worth noting: "On the Interpretation of Qoheleth in Early Christianity," *VT* 24 (1974): 168–77; "The Book of Ecclesiastes and the Interpretation of It in Jewish and Christian Theology," *ASTI* 10 (1975): 38–96. Roland E. Murphy's "Short Note" was ahead of his time "Qohelet Interpreted: The Bearing of the Past on the Present," *VT* 32 (1982): 331–7. Also deserving of mention is the invaluable bibliography in Stuart Weeks, *The Making of Many Books: Printed Works on Ecclesiastes 1523–1875* (Winona Lake, IN: Eisenbrauns, 2014).
47. Christian D. Ginsburg, *Coheleth, Commonly Called the Book of Ecclesiastes* (London: Longman, Green, Longman and Roberts, 1861) 27–223.
48. Mary E. Mills, *Reading Ecclesiastes: A Literary and Cultural Exegesis*, Heythrop Studies in Contemporary Philosophy, Religion, and Theology (Aldershot: Ashgate, 2003).
49. Katharine Dell, *Interpreting Ecclesiastes: Readers Old and New*, Critical Studies in the Hebrew Bible 3 (Winona Lake, IN: Eisenbrauns, 2013). See also her article, "Ecclesiastes as Wisdom: Consulting Early Interpreters," *VT* 44 (1994): 301–29.
50. Suseela C. Yesudian-Storfjell, "The Reception of Qoheleth in a Selection of Rabbinic, Patristic and Nonconformist Texts," (PhD diss., University of Sheffield, 2003).
51. Christianson, *Ecclesiastes through the Centuries*. Christianson is the most prolific scholar working in Ecclesiastes reception history. In addition to this commentary see also "Voltaire's *Precis* of Ecclesiastes: A Case Study in the Bible's Afterlife," *JSOT* 29 (2005): 455–84 and "Ecclesiastes in Premodern Reading: Before 1500 C.E.," in *The Words of the Wise Are like Goads: Engaging Qohelet in the 21st Century*, eds. Mark J. Boda, Tremper Longman III, and Cristian G. Rata (Winona Lake, IN: Eisenbrauns, 2013) 3–36.
52. In this regard, my book resembles parts of Christianson's arrangement of readings in his chapter entitled, "Testimonia," (*Ecclesiastes through the Centuries*, 1–16) specifically "Qoheleth the Philosopher" and "Preacher of Joy." There are also resemblances with Miller's taxonomy of interpretations of Ecclesiastes by scholars ("What the Preacher Forgot," 216–21). Bartholomew's survey separates "pre-critical" from "critical" readings (*Reading Ecclesiastes*, 31–52).
53. A point made by Breed, *Nomadic Text*, 205.
54. For further discussion on the relationship between historical criticism and reception history, see Robert Evans, *Reception History, Tradition, and Biblical Interpretation: Gadamer and Jauss in Current Practice*, LBHOTS (London: Bloomsbury, 2014) 26–52; James Harding, "What Is Reception History and What Happens to You If You Do It?" in *Reception History and Biblical Studies: Theory and Practice*, eds. Emma England and William John Lyons, LHBOTS (London: Bloomsbury, 2015) 31–44. Harding begins his essay with the provocative statement that "There is no such thing as Biblical Studies."

55. John Ronald Reuel Tolkien, *The Hobbit, or, There and Back again* (Boston: Houghton Mifflin, 1966). The chapter is entitled, "Riddles in the Dark."
56. In Judges 14 and elsewhere, the Hebrew term for riddle is חדה.
57. Van De Mieroop argues that the inherent ambiguity in the Babylonian writing system was the foundation of ancient Near Eastern critical thought (*Philosophy before the Greeks*, 59–84).
58. Decades ago, Harry Torczyner, argued that these numeric proverbs grew out of riddles ("The Riddle in the Bible," *HUCA* 1 [1924]: 125–49, 135). Hans-Peter Müller agrees that these riddles can have many different answers, but because he sees them originating in an educational setting, he also maintains that there is a "right" answer known to the teacher ("Der Begriff 'Rätsel' Im Alten Testament," *VT* 20 [1970]: 465–89, 487).
59. I disagree with the overly rigid distinction between play and competition in riddles and numeric proverbs made in Wolfgang. M. W. Roth, *Numerical Sayings in the Old Testament: A Form-Critical Study*, VTSup (Leiden: Brill, 1965) 95–9; and James Crenshaw, "Impossible Questions, Sayings, and Tasks," *Semeia* 17 (1980): 19–34, 22.
60. Compare Breed's discussion of the shift from biblical interpretation as solution-driven to problem driven (*Nomadic Text*, 124–5).

1 Qohelet as Solomon

The narrative voice of Qohelet states that he was David's son and king over Israel in Jerusalem. The longest and most widely held understanding of the author of Ecclesiastes understands this description literally, and reads the book as the composition of Solomon, the son of David and Bathsheba, who reigned over Israel in Jerusalem (1 Kgs 2:12). This interpretation is so pervasive that we even find it in the *Arabian Nights*. In recounting his first voyage, Sindbad says that while he had been born wealthy, he had squandered his wealth by the time he was a young man.

> I was stricken with horror and dismay at the gravity of my plight, and bethought myself of a proverb of our master Solomon son of David (may peace be upon them!) which my father often used to cite: "The day of death is better than the day of birth, a live dog is better than a dead lion, and the grave is better than poverty."[1]

The cited "proverb" is really three separate sayings. The first two are citations from Ecclesiastes (7:1 and 9:4). The third is attested in a collection of sayings, *Ghurar al-Hikam wa-Durar al-Kali* (*Exalted Aphorisms and Pearls of Speech*, compiled ca. 510/1116) attributed to Alī ibn Abī Ṭālib (d. 40/661) the companion of Muhammad and the last of the "rightly guided prophets" in Sunni Islam. The persistence of the name of Solomon, combined with the flexibility of the cited sayings—the two proverbs from Ecclesiastes occur two chapters apart in the book, and the third saying isn't in the Hebrew Bible at all—show how proverbial sayings and legendary sages can move across cultures and attract other sayings. The three sayings together do not offer a coherent worldview. The first assumes a world fraught with such suffering and injustice that death is to be preferred to life. The second takes the opposite tack: because the poor live longer than the powerful, and it is better to be poor and live. The third saying qualifies the first by limiting the preference of death only to poverty, and rebuts the second, saying that death is to be preferred to poverty.

The default belief for centuries prior to the rise of modern biblical scholarship was that Solomon was the book's author. In his reception history study of Ecclesiastes, Eric Christianson notes that "the significance of Solomon as author" grew "almost grotesquely out of proportion."[2] It is not clear exactly when the equation between Qohelet and Solomon arose. The earliest extant interpretations of Ecclesiastes, in the rabbinic literature, already assume Solomon to be the author.[3] There is a wide range of dates for the rabbinic texts, but even the earliest proposed (ca. 1st century CE) is still anywhere from 200 to 400 years later than the composition of Ecclesiastes. If we push further back, the Wisdom of Solomon, dating from the 2nd century BCE, refutes thoughts found in Ecclesiastes about the absence of an afterlife and the importance of enjoying life before death. Wis 2:1–9 describes as "ungodly" (ἀσεβεῖς) those who say: that people are born by chance (2:2); that upon death we return to dust while our spirit evaporates (2:2–3); that there will be no remembrance of people after they die (2:4); and so people ought to live a life of sensuous enjoyment "as in youth . . . because this is their portion and lot" (ὡς ἐν νεότητι . . . ὅτι αὕτη ἡ μερὶς ἡμῶν καὶ ὁ κλῆρος οὗτος [2:6,9]).[4] It is unclear whether the author of the Wisdom of Solomon is attacking Ecclesiastes in particular or those views in general but the parallels with Ecclesiastes, right down to the use of "portion" and "lot" to describe life, are striking. It would be significant if the Wisdom of Solomon were in fact giving a rebuttal of a viewpoint in Ecclesiastes, because the Wisdom of Solomon is also attributed to Solomon. Its author would therefore be asserting his own "Solomonic" authority against that of Qohelet, who is described here as "godless."[5]

As mentioned in the introduction, this book analyzes understandings of Qohelet as an author by means of Brennan Breed's use of semantic nodes in doing reception history. It is not a chronological reception history. But because Qohelet was equated with Solomon for such a long time, I need to address the issue of Solomonic authorship in this chapter before I proceed with revealing different semantic nodes for Qohelet in readings of Ecclesiastes. This chapter's discussion of Solomonic authorship is not the only place to look for all the pre-modern readings of Ecclesiastes that understood Qohelet to be Solomon. Doing so would remove these readings from the semantic nodes in which they would otherwise appear and create the impression that pre-modern and modern, critical readings of Ecclesiastes are essentially different. In many respects they are not. Instead, in the following chapters, pre-modern and modern readings will be grouped into their relevant semantic nodes, giving a vivid picture of the persistence and continuity of certain readings. In this chapter I want only to examine how ancient readers relied upon a constructed Solomonic biography and their belief that Solomon had written Ecclesiastes to help make sense of it.

On Coherence and Contradiction

In his description of the author function Foucault observes that contradictions in a text may be resolved by subsuming them under a larger unity, namely the author.[6] Solomonic attribution of Ecclesiastes is a prime example of this, and many readings of Ecclesiastes deal with the book's contradictions by appeal to the figure of Solomon delineated in the cultural norms of these other writings. One of the earliest discussions of the book centers on its contradictions. In the Talmud, b. Šabb. 30b, it is said that the wise (חכמים) tried to store or put aside (לגנוז) Ecclesiastes because its words contradicted each other (סותרן זה את זה). The rabbis resolve the problem by claiming that the presence of "words of Torah at its beginning and at its end" (שתחילתו דברי תורה וסופו דברי תורה; in reference to Eccl 1:2, 12:13) override any contradictions in the book.[7] This is a neat solution, relying as it does on the assumption that the beginnings and ends of books are normative for how one is to interpret the text in the middle and more importantly, that the words supporting the ideology of readers take precedence over any that challenge that ideology. Katharine Dell argues that contradictions were a greater obstacle to the acceptance of Ecclesiastes in early Judaism than the problem of Solomon having written something heterodox, but of course, the possibility that Solomon would have written something heterodox is itself a contradiction to those for whom Solomon is a paragon of wisdom.[8] That is to say that the idea of contradiction operates here on two levels: where a text contradicts itself, and where a text contradicts things outside of itself, such as views of the author that are drawn from other sources or what other normative texts say. It is important that Dell highlights the relationship between the authorship of Ecclesiastes and the book's theological content. It also points out how the belief in Solomonic authorship actually created a way out of the problem of any inconsistencies in Ecclesiastes. While the Talmud is clear that some saw contradictions in Ecclesiastes as a problem, it is not as if the remainder of the biblical texts are free of this phenomenon. This is why the last of Rabbi Ishmael's thirteen exegetical principles is that two contradictory texts are resolved by appeal to a third. The Midrash also notes that the rabbis wanted to put aside (גנז) Ecclesiastes (Ecclesiastes Rabbah 11:9). Unlike the Talmud, this is not because of internal contradictions but due to an external one, between Ecclesiastes and the Torah of Moses.

> א״ר שמואל בר׳ יצחק בקשו חכמים לגנוז ספר קהלת שמצאו בו דברים שמטין לצד מינות אמרו כל חכמתו של שלמה כך שאמר שמח בחור בילדותך ויטיבך לבך בימי בחורותיך והלך בדרכי לבך ובמראה עיניך ומשה אמר ולא תתורו אחרי לבבכם ואחרי עיניכם ושלמה אמר והלך בדרכי לבך ובמראה עיניך הותרה הרצועה לית דין ולית דיין כיון שאמר ודע כי על כל אלה יביאך האלהים במשפט אמרו יפה אמר שלמה
>
> R. Samuel b. Isaac said, "The sages wished to put away the book of Ecclesiastes because they found that its words tend toward heresy." They said that all of Solomon's wisdom is in his words, "Rejoice, young man, in your youth. Let your heart cheer you in the days of your youth. Walk according to the wishes of your heart and the desire of your eyes" [Eccl 11:9a]. But Moses said, "Do not follow after your hearts or your eyes" [Num 15:39] and Solomon said, "Walk according to the wishes of your heart and the desire of your eyes." Is the restriction removed? Is there judgment without a judge? But [Solomon] also said, "Know that for all of these God will bring you to judgment" [Eccl 11:9b]. And they said, "Solomon has spoken well."

The contradiction between a saying of Qohelet (Eccl 11:9a) and the Torah (Num 15:39) is resolved by means of appeal to a second text in Ecclesiastes (Eccl 11:9b).

A doctrinal conflict between Moses and Solomon is no contest. The king must be brought into agreement with the lawgiver. Note how the problem is resolved by appeal to another text from Ecclesiastes. The rabbis do not explicitly appeal to the greater authority of the Mosaic text in its contradiction with its Solomonic counterpart. Instead they find a text in Ecclesiastes that agrees with the Torah. The argument is not solved by appeal to authority, even though there is no doubt whatsoever that the rabbis held the works attributed to Moses to be of greater authority than those attributed to Solomon. Rather, because the Torah is more normative than Ecclesiastes, the rabbis find a way to bring the teaching of Ecclesiastes in line with that of the Torah by bringing into the discussion a third text—which necessarily needs to be from Ecclesiastes—that conforms with the injunction of Moses. If the rabbis had not believed that the text was written by Solomon, they would not have bothered with the interpretive strategies to explain the book's contradictions. This will not be the last time that the contradictions in Ecclesiastes appear in this book. Both ancient and modern readers struggle with them, and their resolutions of them appear in more than one semantic node discussed in chapter three.

Solomon's Biography

Foucault also points out that an author's biography both helps to interpret an individual text, giving it a context and limiting interpretive choices, and resolves tensions among a group of texts attributed to a single author.[9] Both of these uses of Solomon's biography are present in readings of Ecclesiastes. Most biographies of Solomon are based on the biblical material in 1 Kings and 1–2 Chronicles, which gives the following picture: Solomon was the son of David and Bathsheba. He succeeded to the throne on his father's death and reigned in Jerusalem for forty years. During that time, he engaged in massive building projects, most notably a sumptuous temple for Yahweh. He amassed such wealth that silver was as common as stone and counted for nothing (1 Kgs 10:21–27). Solomon was also the wisest man who ever lived because of a direct gift of wisdom from Yahweh. This only added to his prestige and power, and foreign rulers came to him for advice. This overview cannot do justice to the biblical accounts, which are filled with the hyperbole and plotlines that characterize folklore. But the Bible's own summary statement is to the point: "Solomon was greater in wealth and wisdom than all the rulers of the world" (ויתגדל המלך שלמה מכל מלכי הארץ לעשר ולחכמה [1 Kgs 10:23, 2 Chr 9:22]).

The fly in the ointment of this otherwise rosy portrayal is Solomon's sponsoring of the worship of gods other than Yahweh. In what seems like an edited variant of the typical story of the fantastically wealthy monarch, 1 Kings 11 mentions Solomon's huge harem, but diverges into a lengthy description of how Solomon both built shrines for the gods of his foreign wives and also worshipped these gods himself. The text says that Solomon "walked after" (וילך שׁלמה אחרי) Astarte and Milcom, and built altars and high places for Chemosh, Molech, and other gods not named. This violation of his agreement with Yahweh justifies the division of the kingdom after Solomon's death. The phrase "they [foreign wives] turned away his heart" (ויטו נשיו את לבו/נשיו הטו את־לבבו) used twice in verses 3–4 to describe the king's apostasy, both echoes and contrasts with Solomon's great wisdom. "Heart" in biblical Hebrew (לב/לבב) refers to intellectual capacity, or what we would call the mind. When God gives Solomon wisdom in 1 Kings 3, he specifically grants the king "a wise heart" (לב חכם v. 12). Now Solomon turns his mind away from the source of his wisdom and directs it toward other gods. While it is not surprising that the patriarchal author of 1 Kings 11 blames Solomon's wives for his apostasy from Yahweh, it is important that he states in verse 3 that this occurred when the king was old. The idea of the great king becoming feeble minded or weak in his old age and listening to women (which in a patriarchal culture would have been thought a sign of male weakness) parallels the biblical account of the end of David's life in 1 Kings 2. There the great king ends his days shivering in bed with a lovely maiden to warm him (and with whom he does nothing), and his final words to Solomon are instructions for the destruction of his enemies. Like his father, Solomon's old age is typified by a loss of patriarchal power vis-à-vis women, but with the added theme, widespread in the Hebrew Bible, of the foreign woman who leads the Israelite male into apostasy. The large harem of Solomon in 1 Kings is connected by readers of Ecclesiastes with Qohelet's boast in 2:8 that he had "the delights of humankind, concubines galore" (ותענוגת בני האדם שדה ושדות).[10]

Standard in the job description of monarchs across cultures is that they are to be wise, or to have at least one wise advisor close at hand. Rulers are often patrons of wisdom, which in the ancient Near East overlaps—but is not coterminous—with scholarship (i.e., mastery of the written tradition). A few ancient Near Eastern kings are portrayed as the authors of texts or scholars in their own right. This tradition dates as far back as Shulgi of Ur (21st century BCE), who presents himself as literate and fluent in multiple languages.[11] Ashurbanipal's founding of the great library at Nineveh in the 8th century BCE establishes his reputation as a ruler dedicated to scholarship and the scribal arts.[12] In the prologue to the Standard Version of the *Epic of Gilgamesh*, the eponymous main character is portrayed as a hero who learns wisdom from bitter experience and then writes it down to share with others. "He came a distant road and was weary but granted rest, [he] set down on a stele all [his] labors."[13] It comes as no surprise then that, added to Solomon's deeds as a king, the Hebrew Bible notes his achievements as a sage and scholar in another summary statement enumerating Solomon's intellectual prowess.

ויתן אלהים חכמה לשלמה ותבונה הרבה מאד ורחב לב כחול אשר על שפת הים
ותרב חכמת שלמה מחכמת כל בני קדם ומכל חכמת מצרים
ויחכם מכל האדם מאיתן ויהי שמו בכל הגוים סביב
וידבר שלשת אלפים משל ויהי שירו חמשה ואלף
וידבר על העצים מן הארז אשר בלבנון ועד האזוב אשר יצא בקיר וידבר על הבהמה ועל העוף ועל
הרמש ועל הדגים
ויבאו מכל העמים לשמע את חכמת שלמה מאת כל מלכי הארץ אשר שמעו את חכמתו

God gave Solomon wisdom, understanding, and insight[14] much greater than the sand on the seashore.
Solomon's wisdom surpassed the wisdom of the ancients[15] and all the wisdom of Egypt.

He was wiser than anyone else . . . and his name was known in all the surrounding nations.
He spoke three thousand proverbs and one thousand and five songs.
He spoke about trees, from the cedar of Lebanon to the reed[16] that grows out of a wall. He also spoke about cattle, birds, creeping things and fish.
People from every nation came to listen to Solomon's wisdom.

(1 Kgs 5:9–14 [Eng: 4:29–34])

In addition to Solomon's uttered wisdom, the Hebrew Bible attests to his literary output. An often-overlooked biblical reference to Solomon as an author—discussed by Eva Mroczek—occurs in the description of Josiah's religious reforms in 2 Chronicles 35. There, Josiah orders the people to prepare for the Passover according to written texts attributed to David and Solomon.

והכונו לבית אבותיכם כמחלקותיכם בכתב דויד מלך ישראל ובמכתב שלמה בנו

Establish the houses of your ancestors according to their divisions in the writing of David, king of Israel and in the writing of Solomon, his son.

(2 Chron 35:4)

The exact nature of this "writing of Solomon" (מכתב שלמה) is unknown, and Mroczek is right to say that it cannot refer to any known Solomonic text.[17]

The statement in 1 Kings 5 of Solomon's scholarly output quoted above was the catalyst for the creation of many Solomonic texts and legends. The "one thousand and five songs" spurred the writing of poems attributed to him, most notably the 1st century CE Odes of Solomon, which circulated in Greek, Syriac, and Coptic. Reference to Solomon's wisdom about trees and animals gave rise to the belief that he possessed magical powers and the ability to manipulate nature. In his expansive retelling of the 1 Kings 5 passage in the *Antiquities*, Josephus adds that God also gave Solomon knowledge of how to exorcise demons, and that the king composed both healing chants and exorcism spells.

οὐδεμίαν γὰρ φύσιν ἠγνόησεν οὐδὲ παρῆλθεν ἀνεξέταστον, ἀλλ᾽ ἐν πάσαις ἐφιλοσόφησε καὶ τὴν ἐπιστήμην τῶν ἐν αὐταῖς ἰδιωμάτων ἄκραν ἐπεδιξατο. παρέσχε δ᾽ αὐτῷ μαθεῖν ὁ θεὸς καὶ τὴν κατὰ τῶν δαιμόνων τέχνην εἰς ὠφέλειαν καὶ θεραπείαν τοῖς ἀνθρώποις. ἐπῳδάς τε συνταξάμενος αἷς παρηγορεῖται τὰ νοσήματα καὶ τρόπους ἐξορκώσεων κατέλιπεν, οἷς οἱ ἐνδούμενοι τὰ δαιμόνια ὡς μηκετ᾽ ἐπανελθεῖν ἐκδιώκουσι. καὶ αὕτη μέχρι νῦν παρ᾽ ἡμῖν ἡ θεραπεία πλεῖστον ἰσκύει.

There was nothing in nature [Solomon] did not know about, nor did he leave anything unexamined, but he investigated all of them and was knowledgeable about their different qualities. God handed over to him knowledge about demons in order to help and heal people. He wrote incantations that healed diseases and he left behind exorcisms that cast out possessing demons so that they will never return.

(*Ant.* 8.44–45)

Josephus is again engaged in a rhetorical exercise with his non-Jewish readers. He describes Solomon's knowledge of nature using a form of the verb φιλοσοφέω (ἐφιλοσόφησε). This is the root, of course, of the word, "philosophy," and Josephus thus puts Solomon's wisdom on a par with the Greek scientific tradition. Note too that Josephus mentions that Solomon's exorcisms were "left behind" (κατέλιπεν) and used even in his own day. This allows Josephus the chance to transition to an anecdote of how a Jewish exorcist named Eleazar performed an exorcism in the presence of the emperor Vespasian and his staff, thus demonstrating the fact that the ancient king's wisdom and power resides in the Jewish people still. But the tradition of Solomon's magical powers over demons neither begins nor ends with Josephus. It is found widely in early Jewish traditions and later in the *Qur'an.*[18] The Greek Testament of Solomon contains a number of Solomon's occult adventures, with the king defeating whole armies of demons in battle. Specifically connected to Ecclesiastes, the Targum of Eccl 2:5 mentions Solomon's powers of healing, exorcism, and Torah exposition.

> עבדית לי גנת שקיין ופרדסין וזרעית תמן כל מיני עיסבין מנהון לצרך מיכלא ומנהון לצרך משתייא ומנהון לצרך אסותא וכל מיני עיסבי בוסמין נציבית בהון אילני סרק וכל אילני בוסמין דאייתיו לוותי טלני ומזיקי מן הינדקא וכל אילני עבדי פירין ותחומיה מן שור קרתא דירושלם עד כיף מיא דשילוח
>
> I made for myself a garden of pools and parks. and there I planted all sorts of grasses among them some for eating and some for drinking, some of them for healing, and all sorts of sweet-smelling grasses. I planted in them fruitless trees and all the spice trees that the ghosts and demons brought to me from India[19] and all the trees that give fruit. [The garden's] border is from the wall of the village of Jerusalem up to the waters of Shiloah.

Ecclesiastes Rabbah 1:13 notes that Solomon's culinary/pharmacological knowledge extended even to "how to sweeten mustard or lupins, and how to prepare a hot brew consisting of a third part each of wine, water, and pepper" (היאך ממתיקין את החרדל וממתיקין את התורמסין והיאך שותין את החמין יין ומים ופלפלין בשליש). The Midrash also directly connects the book with the description of Solomon's wisdom in 1 Kings 5, using the phrase in Eccl 7:23, "all this I tested with wisdom" (כל זה נסיתי בחכמה) as a springboard into a lengthy commentary on 1 Kings 5. Among other items discussed there, the Midrash squares the claim that Solomon allegedly spoke 3000 proverbs with the fact that there are not that many attributed to him in the tradition.

> וידבר שלשת אלפים משל אמר רבי שמואל בר נחמני חזרנו על כל המקרא ולא מצינו שנתנבא שלמה אלא קרוב לשמנה מאות פסוקים ואת אמרת שלשת אלפים אלא מלמד שכל פסוק ופסוק שנתנבא שלמה יש בו שנים ושלשה טעים.
>
> "And Solomon spoke three thousand proverbs" [1 Kgs 5:12]. Rabbi Samuel bar Nachmani said, "We have searched all of scripture but we cannot find that Solomon prophesied anymore than eight-hundred verses. But you say three thousand." But it teaches that every verse that Solomon prophesied has two or three senses.

The complex web of allusions is worth untangling. In commenting on a line from Ecclesiastes where Qohelet speaks of testing everything with wisdom, the equation between Qohelet and the description of Solomon in 1 Kings 5 is made. Then, a claim about Solomon's wisdom from 1 Kings 5 is questioned when compared with the larger Solomonic corpus. The answer recasts Solomon as not just a wise king but an inspired sage. He no longer "speaks" (דבר) the proverbs, as 1 Kings 5 describes. He "prophesies" (נבא) them. And because these proverbs are prophetic utterances, each contains a surplus of meaning that allows for multiple interpretations. There is a constant interplay between texts that are used to create Solomon's biography and other texts that are then read through those biographical lenses. Importantly, any text can be in either category—as a source for biographical information, or as something interpreted through biographical information.

Solomonic attribution occurs elsewhere within the biblical canon. Two psalms have headings attributing them to Solomon. Psalm 72 is an enthronement psalm, with wishes for power and wealth for the king that resemble the descriptions of Solomon in Kings and Chronicles (including a reference to Sheba). Psalm 127 is more relevant because it relates more to Ecclesiastes than to the biblical description of Solomon.

אם יהוה לא יבנה בית שוא עמלו בוניו בו
אם יהוה לא ישמר עיר שוא שקד שומר
שוא לכם משכימי קום מאחרי שבת
אכלי לחם העצבים כן יתן לידידו שנא
הנה נחלת יהוה בנים שכר פרי הבטן

If Yahweh does not build a house, those who build it toil in vain.
If Yahweh does not guard a city, he who keeps watch guards in vain.
In vain is your early rising and your late rest,
Eating the bread of pain, because he gives sleep to his beloved.
Indeed sons are an inheritance from Yahweh, the fruit of the womb a reward.
(Ps 127:1–3)

This psalm opens with a rigid parallel structure in the first two lines. Both begin with אם יהוה לא, followed by a third-person masculine singular imperfect verb (יבנה/ישמר), a singular direct object that refers to human habitation (בית/עיר), the noun שׁוא, a third-person masculine perfect verb (שמלו/שקד), and a masculine participle (בוניו/שומר) from the same root as the masculine singular imperfect verbs at the beginning of the line (יבנה/ישמר). The third line is made of parallel halves formed by two participles (משכימי/מאחרי) followed by two infinitives (קום/שבת). The parallel grammatical structure is offset by the contrast between the meaning of the two phrases (early rising/late retiring) all governed by the initial word, שׁוא, which connects the third line back to the first two. From there the psalm's structure becomes more open, with connections drawn between the "bread of pain" (לחם העצבים) in line 4 and "the fruit of the womb" (פרי הבטן) in line 5. Finally, there is the possible subtle connection of the verb "sleep" (שׁנא) immediately following "beloved" with the identically written verb, "hate" (שׂנא).[20]

This psalm connects with Ecclesiastes in several respects. It speaks about the futility of human effort without divine favor and describes this situation as "vain." Although the Hebrew word for "vain" used in the Psalm (שׁוא) is different from the term in Ecclesiastes (הבל) there is a good deal of overlap in their respective semantic ranges. The Psalm tells the reader that those who do not have Yahweh's support rise early, retire late, and eat "the bread of pain" (or "toil" [עצב], used also in Gen 3:16 to refer to the pain of childbirth)[21] while Yahweh showers favors on those whom he loves. Eccl 2:26 is almost an exact parallel:

כי לאדם שטוב לפניו נתן חכמה ודעת ושמחה
ולחוטא נתן ענין לאסוף ולכנוס לתת לטוב לפני האלהים
גם זה הבל ורעות רוח

> To the one who pleases him, [God] gives wisdom and knowledge and joy.
> But to the sinner he gives the job of gathering and piling up so that he might give to the one who is good before God.
> This also is vain, a chasing after the wind.

The psalm ends by extolling the blessings of male offspring, expressing a sentiment akin to the complaint voiced more than once in Ecclesiastes 2–3 of the misery of the person who has no heirs. These significant thematic ties between Psalm 127 and Ecclesiastes make it no surprise that the psalm has a Solomonic superscription. Beyond that is guesswork. Was the superscription added to the psalm because it contained themes similar to Ecclesiastes, also believed to be a Solomonic work? Was the psalm deliberately written as a Solomonic text in the spirit of Ecclesiastes? Do the psalm and Ecclesiastes derive from other traditions about Solomon connected with vanity and divine favor now lost to us? The psalter as we now know it comes to be much later than has often been thought. Psalms were originally arranged in many different, smaller collections and used for a wide variety of purposes.[22]

The other main biblical texts attributed to Solomon are, of course, the Song of Songs and Proverbs. Strictly speaking, only sections of Proverbs are attributed to Solomon (see the superscriptions at 1:1, 10:1, and 25:1) but later readers make him the author of the entire collection. For example, in Ecclesiastes Rabbah, Rabbi Joshua identifies the names of all the wise in Proverbs (Agur, Jakeh, Lemuel, Ithiel) as other names for Solomon. Notably, each of these names has an etymological explanation that is connected to Solomon's sinfulness. Rashbam also uses etymology to equate Solomon with both Qohelet and Agur in Prov 30:1, connecting the name קהלת with קהל ("gather") and the name אגור with אגר ("collect").[23]

Texts and Biography Combined

Readers have used Proverbs, Song of Songs, Ecclesiastes, and the biographical data in 1 Kings to construct a life of Solomon. This constructed biography was then used to help interpret the works, mainly by placing them in a chronological order corresponding to events in Solomon's life. A lengthy passage in the Song of Songs Rabbah uses the three works (Proverbs, Song of Solomon, Ecclesiastes) to mark three different phases in Solomon's life. As is the norm in rabbinic texts, there are many different opinions raised without any single solution carrying the day. Rabbi Ḥiyya argues for the order Proverbs-Song of Songs-Ecclesiastes because the text from 1 Kings 5 refers to the proverbs written by Solomon before it mentions his songs. Another statement attributed to Ḥiyya says that Solomon wrote all three works in his old age. Contrasted to this is the claim in Ecclesiastes Rabbah that, after Solomon's dream at Gibeon—recounted in 1 Kings 3 and which occurred in Solomon's youth (1 Kgs 3:7)—a holy spirit (רוח הקדש) alighted on him and he wrote Proverbs, Song of Songs, and Ecclesiastes apparently in one go. In Song of Songs Rabbah 1:1, Rabbi Jonathan uses stages of human moral and cognitive growth in support of the order Song of Songs-Proverbs-Ecclesiastes. Young men write love songs; adult men compose sayings of advice, and old men think about the vanity of the world. Notice that all of these arrangements place Ecclesiastes last. The text itself does not want readers to miss this: the lengthy discussion of the order of these works in Song of Songs Rabbah 1:1 concludes with the observation that "everyone knows that Ecclesiastes was the last composed" (הכל מודין שקהלת בסוף אמרה). The Talmud (b. Sanh. 20b) uses this same order and the royal titles in each of the three biblical books to make the moral claim that Solomon was punished through his life by a steady diminishment of power. This text is discussed more in chapter four.

Placing Ecclesiastes last creates a convenient ambiguity that helps with the book's prickly contents. On the one hand, Ecclesiastes represents the mature thoughts of a wise man who in his age has only grown wiser. On the other, because it is assumed that the aged tend to be naturally bitter and morose, the darker parts of Ecclesiastes can be seen as the product of a once-great man in his senectitude, moral decay, or deathbed repentance. This connects with the portrayal of Solomon in 1 Kings who, like his father David, becomes more decrepit as he ages and also opens up the possibility for readers to imagine a later repentance on Solomon's part.

Among ancient Christian readers, the works of the Solomonic corpus were said to have been composed in the order of Proverbs first, Ecclesiastes in the middle, and the Song of Songs at the end. The earliest example of this is found in Origen, although he states that he is expressing an already widespread opinion.

> First, let us examine why it is, since the churches of God acknowledge three books written by Solomon, that of them the Proverbs is put first, the one called Ecclesiastes second, and the book Song of Songs has third place.[24]

For Origen, the primary criteria for this ordering of the books are intellectual and spiritual (which overlap for him). The three books form a philosophical curriculum corresponding respectively to moral (Proverbs), natural (Ecclesiastes), and contemplative (Song of Songs) philosophy. Ecclesiastes is a teaching of natural philosophy because the book reveals the true nature of material things to be vanity and shows us that the only worthwhile things are spiritual. This understanding isn't limited to Christian readers. The Jewish commentary on Ecclesiastes of Isaac Ibn Ghayyat notes how the book deals with wisdom regarding the natural world, with specific reference to the description of Solomon's wisdom in 1 Kings 5:

> The wise man who composed this book is described with a beautiful image [the name "Qohelet"] which comprises the classification of sciences: religious sciences, ethical sciences, mathematics, philosophy, astronomy, physics, medicine, and music, as is found in the verse "he was wiser than anyone else" (1 Kgs. 5:11). This book is named after 'collection', and it is [grammatically] feminine because it alludes to wisdom and philosophy. In consequence, there is nothing from the sciences which is not included in this book in a brief manner or alluded to.[25]

Origen, in an apologetic polemic similar to that of Josephus, claims that the Greek tripartite division of philosophy originates with wise King Solomon, and that the Greeks learned it from him

> Now it seems to me that certain wise men of the Greeks took these ideas from Solomon, since it was long before them in age and time that he first gave these teachings through the Spirit of God.[26]

Because Origen notes that this ordering is already customary in the churches that he knows, he is explaining and not instituting it.[27] Most likely the order is dictated by the fact that the Song of Songs was read as an allegory for spiritual union with God. As a theological pinnacle it was necessary to place it as the final book in the series. Ecclesiastes questions many of the values set forth in Proverbs, and this logically demands that it be placed after Proverbs. What is more important with this sequence is that, unlike the rabbinic texts, which ordered the books based on events in Solomon's life, the Christian ordering of the books corresponds to the chronology of a reader's life. There is a proper order in which one is to engage these books, depending on the reader's maturity. This sequence also implies that these are the order in which the books were composed, beginning with the simpler text and progressing to the more difficult. To read the texts in the same order of their composition, and implicitly at the same stage of life as their author, is thus to retrace the spiritual development of the great Solomon's life in one's own lifetime. Solomon is understood to be teacher in a dual sense. His writings contain wisdom for willing reader, and his life offers a pattern for others to imitate.

Origen was influential on later Christian authors, and this ordering of the Solomonic books becomes standard. Jerome, who was heavily indebted to Origen, says that while Proverbs is suitable for the young, Ecclesiastes is appropriate only for adult readers because it stresses the transience of human life.

> In Proverbiis parvulum docens, et quasi de officiis per sententias erudiens. Unde, et ad filium ei sermo crebro repetitur. In Ecclesiaste vero maturae virum aetatis instituens, ne quidquam in mundi rebus putet esse perpetuum, sed

caduca, et brevia universa, quae cernimus. Ad extremum iam consummatum virum, et calcato saeculo, praeparatum, in Cantico Canticorum sponsi jungit amplexibus.

(PL 23:1012b-c)

In Proverbs [Solomon] teaches a boy about his duties and instructs him through sayings. This is why he repeatedly addresses a son. In Ecclesiastes, he teaches a man of mature age not to believe that anything in this world is permanent but that everything we see is perishable and fleeting. When a man has been fully prepared and completed trampling on the world, he [Solomon] unites him to the embrace of the bridegroom in the Song of Songs.[28]

Note that, while Ecclesiastes contains what me might whimsically call "adult material," it is for Jerome but a prelude to the Song of Songs, which invites only the spiritually adept to a mystical divine union. Writing in Bethlehem, with access to Jewish interpretations, Jerome also notes that Jewish readers say that Ecclesiastes was written by a repentant Solomon after he had wrongly relied on his own wisdom and wealth, offending God by his attachment to women ("Aiunt Hebraei hunc librum Solomonis esse, poenitentiam agentis, quod in sapientia divitiisque confisus, per mulieres offenderit Deum" [PL 23:1021a]). Jerome does not follow this interpretation himself, but he mentions it in order to do two of his favorite things. First is to demonstrate his erudition, here by reference to Jewish biblical interpretation. Second is to express his abhorrence of sexuality. Jerome expands the biblical understanding of Solomon's sin—that he married *foreign* women who led him to worship alien gods—to refer simply to women ("per mulieres offenderit Deum"), implying that Solomon's sexual congress with any women of any kind was in itself sinful. But Jerome will not read Ecclesiastes through the interpretive lens that it is a composition of a penitent Solomon. Like many other readers, Jerome is reluctant for there to be any sinfulness or wrongdoing in the constructed Solomonic author he uses to read Ecclesiastes. This is explored in more detail in chapter four.

The influence of Origen in placing Ecclesiastes between Proverbs and Song of Songs is present also in Greek Christian writings. Didymus the Blind (313–398) puts Ecclesiastes after Proverbs and before the Song of Songs, but says that the book's content is for the "simple" (πτωχοῖς).[29] Conversely, Gregory of Nyssa says that Ecclesiastes can only be read after one has struggled with the "obscure words, wise sayings, riddles and many subtle words" (οἱ σκοτεινοὶ λόγοι καὶ αἱ σοφαὶ ῥήσεις καὶ τὰ αἰνίγματα καὶ αἱ ποικίλαι τῶν λόγων στροφαί, quoting Prov 1:3,6) in Proverbs.

πρόκειται ἡμῖν ὁ Ἐκκλησιαστὴς εἰς ἐξήγησιν ἴσον ἔχων τῷ μεγέθει τῆς ὠφελείας τὸν πόνον τῆς θεορίας. τῶν γὰρ παροιμιακῶν νοημάτων ἤδη προγυμνασάντων τὸν νοῦν, ὧν οἱ σκοτεινοὶ λόγοι καὶ αἱ σοφαὶ ῥήσεις καὶ τὰ αἰγίγματα, καὶ αἱ ποικίλαι τῶν λόγων στροφαὶ, καθὼς περιέχει τὸ τοῦ βιβλίου ἐκείνου

> προοίμιον, τότε τοῖς πρὸς τὰ τελειότερα τῶν μαθήματων αὐξηθεῖσιν, ἐπὶ ταύτην τὴν γραφὴν τὴν ὑψηλὴν ὄντως καὶ θεόπνευστον, ἡ ἄνοδος γίνεται. εἰ οὖν ἡ παροιμιακὴ μελέτη ἡ πρὸς ταῦτα ἡμᾶς ἑτοιμάζουσα τὰ μαθήματα, οὕτως ἐπιπονός τίς ἐστι καὶ δυσθεώρητος, πόσον χρὴ πόνον αὐτοῖς ἐνορᾶν τοῖς ὑψηλοῖς τούτοις νοήμασι τοῖς νῦν προκειμένοις εἰς θεωρίαν ἡμῖν;
>
> Ecclesiastes is offered for our study.[30] It offers as much benefit as the effort to think about it. The thoughts in Proverbs have already exercised our minds, containing "obscure words, wise sayings, riddles," [Prov 1:6] and many "subtle words" [Prov 1:3] according to the book's [Proverbs] own prologue. So there is an ascent to those progressing to perfect knowledge in this exalted, inspired book. Because if careful attention to Proverbs which prepares us for this teaching is already painful and hard to understand, how much pain is needed for us to contemplate the lofty thoughts which are presented for our consideration?[31]

Note the difference between Gregory of Nyssa, for whom Proverbs makes difficult reading—something he derives from the opening verses of Proverbs—and both Jerome, who sees Proverbs as an appropriate introductory text for the young, and Didymus, for whom Ecclesiastes is a book for the simple. This is the same phenomenon as in the rabbinic texts. Each tradition has a specific ordering of books that remains constant but for which different explanations are offered. Following Origen, Gregory of Nyssa sees the sequence of Proverbs-Ecclesiastes-Song of Songs as a philosophical curriculum corresponding to the age of the student. Proverbs speaks to a young man (although it is difficult for him to read) and inflames his passion to desire wisdom, while Ecclesiastes teaches the more mature reader that the things of the visible world are ultimately naught and that desire rightly guided must be directed toward higher realities.[32]

Conclusion

The concept of biography is used in more than one way to create and justify a certain ordering of the major Solomonic works in the Bible. For Jewish readers, the constructed life of Solomon structures the ordering of the works. Ecclesiastes is almost universally placed last because the book's content implies an old or repentant author and the biblical account of Solomon's life in 1 Kings notes that he sinned after achieving great wealth and wisdom.[33] The ordering of the books made in tandem with Solomon's biography is both a descriptive and a normative device in Jewish readings, explicitly tracking with the biblical account of Solomon and implicitly admonishing the reader not to follow the same path. For Christian readers, there is no hint of sinfulness on Solomon's part. Rather, he is seen as a great teacher and philosopher. The ordering of the books functions as a normative tool that casts Solomon as an ideal figure and invites readers to structure their intellectual lives around this sequence of the books. While Jewish and Christian readings of the ordering of these three books are different from each other in detail and rationale, all of these readings can be grouped together because they interpret the three major Solomonic works in the Bible through a biographical lens.

These ancient readings of Ecclesiastes and their use of a constructed biography of Solomon reveal the complexity and variety of interpretations available to creative readers. The constructed biography itself is subject to expansion, as in the stories of Solomon as exorcist or apothecary, or in the claim that he is the source of Greek philosophy. Seeing Solomon's life through the lens of his literary output as a model for the reader's own spiritual life of necessity is connected with a biography of Solomon that omits any flaws on his part. This biography is one-sided, omitting any mention of Solomon's sins recounted in the tradition and leaving only the portrait of an intellectual and spiritual guide. The placing of works in a chronological order can be related to either when they were written in Solomon's life, or when they should be encountered in the reader's life, or both.

Notes

1. *Tales from the Thousand and One Nights*, trans. Nessim Joseph Dawood, rev. ed. (London: Penguin, 1973) 115. Dawood's Arabic text is William Hay Macnaghten, *The Alif Laila, or Book of the Thousand Nights and One Night*, 4 vols. (London: W.H. Allen, 1839–42).
2. Eric Christianson, *Ecclesiastes through the Centuries*, Blackwell Bible Commentaries (Malden, MA: Blackwell, 2007) 90.
3. For example, in the Targum, the phrase הוא שלמה is included after קהלת in 1:1, and in 12:8–10 Qohelet is equated with Solomon three times.
4. Wis 2:1–9: εἶπον γὰρ ἐν ἑαυτοῖς λογισάμενοι οὐκ ὀρθῶς, Ὀλίγος ἐστὶν καὶ λυπηρὸς ὁ βίος ἡμῶν, καὶ οὐκ ἔστιν ἴασις ἐν τελευτῇ ἀνθρώπου, καὶ οὐκ ἐγνώσθη ὁ ἀναλύσας ἐξ ᾅδου. ὅτι αὐτοσχεδίως ἐγενήθημεν καὶ μετὰ τοῦτο ἐσόμεθα ὡς οὐχ ὑπάρξαντες· ὅτι καπνὸς ἡ πνοὴ ἐν ῥισὶν ἡμῶν, καὶ ὁ λόγος σπινθὴρ ἐν κινήσει καρδίας ἡμῶν, οὗ σβεσθέντος τέφρα ἀποβήσεται τὸ σῶμα καὶ τὸ πνεῦμα διαχυθήσεται ὡς χαῦνος ἀήρ. καὶ τὸ ὄνομα ἡμῶν ἐπιλησθήσεται ἐν χρόνῳ, καὶ οὐθεὶς μνημονεύσει τῶν ἔργων ἡμῶν· καὶ παρελεύσεται ὁ βίος ἡμῶν ὡς ἴχνη νεφέλης καὶ ὡς ὁμίχλη διασκεδασθήσεται διωχθεῖσα ὑπὸ ἀκτίνων ἡλίου καὶ ὑπὸ θερμότητος αὐτοῦ βαρυνθεῖσα. σκιᾶς γὰρ πάροδος ὁ καιρὸς ἡμῶν, καὶ οὐκ ἔστιν ἀναποδισμὸς τῆς τελευτῆς ἡμῶν, ὅτι κατεσφραγίσθη καὶ οὐδεὶς ἀναστρέφει. δεῦτε οὖν καὶ ἀπολαύσωμεν τῶν ὄντων ἀγαθῶν καὶ χρησώμεθα τῇ κτίσει ὡς ἐν νεότητι σπουδαίως· οἴνου πολυτελοῦς καὶ μύρων πλησθῶμεν, καὶ μὴ παροδευσάτω ἡμᾶς ἄνθος ἔαρος· στεψώμεθα ῥόδων κάλυξιν πρὶν ἢ μαρανθῆναι· μηδεὶς ἡμῶν ἄμοιρος ἔστω τῆς ἡμετέρας ἀγερωχίας, πανταχῇ καταλίπωμεν σύμβολα τῆς εὐφροσύνης, ὅτι αὕτη ἡ μερὶς ἡμῶν καὶ ὁ κλῆρος οὗτος ("For they [the wicked] did not reason rightly and said among themselves [saying]: 'Short and sorrowful is our life, and there is no remedy when a human being dies, and no one is known who has returned from Hades. Because we came into being by chance and hereafter we shall be as though we had never existed, because the breath in our nostrils is smoke and reason is a spark within the beating of our hearts, when it is extinguished, the body will turn to ashes, and the spirit will be dispersed as thin. And our name will be forgotten in time, and no one will remember our deeds; our life will pass away as the traces of a cloud and will be scattered as mist that is chased by the rays of the sun and weighed down by its heat. For our allotted time is the passing of a shadow, and there is no putting back of our death, because it has been sealed and no one turns it back. Come, therefore, let us enjoy the good things that exist, and let us make good use of the creation as in youth; let us take our fill of costly wine and perfumes, and let no flower of spring pass us by. Let us crown ourselves with rosebuds before they are withered. Let none of us be without

share in our revelry; everywhere let us leave signs of enjoyment, because this is our portion and this our lot.'" [NETS]).

5. So too Lester Grabbe, "Intertextual Connections between the Wisdom of Solomon and Qoheleth," in *Reading Ecclesiastes Intertextually*, eds. Katharine Dell and Will Kynes, LHBOTS (London: Bloomsbury, 2014) 201–13. Based on what we know of ancient Jewish literature, I assume the author of the Wisdom of Solomon to have been male.
6. Michel Foucault, "What Is an Author?" in *Professing the New Rhetorics: A Sourcebook*, trans. Donald Bouchard and Sherry Simon, eds. Theresa Enos and Stuart C. Brown (Englewood Cliffs, NJ: Prentice Hall, 1994) 184; trans. of "Qu'est ce qu'un auteur?" *Bulletin de la société française de philosophie* 63 (1969): 73–104.
7. There are other discussions of Ecclesiastes in both Talmuds. Some are treated elsewhere in this book. An overview can be found in David J. Halperin, "The 'Book of Remedies', the Canonization of the Solomonic Writings, and the Riddle of Pseudo-Eusebius," *JQR* 2/72 (1982): 269–92.
8. Katharine Dell, *Interpreting Ecclesiastes: Readers Old and New*, Critical Studies in the Hebrew Bible 3 (Winona Lake, IN: Eisenbrauns, 2013) 26–7.
9. "The author explains the presence of certain events within a text, as well as their transformations, distortions, and their various modifications (and this through an author's biography or by reference to his particular point of view, in the analysis of his social preferences and his position within a class or by delineating his fundamental objectives)" ("What Is an Author?" 187). Over half a century ago, the literary critics W. K. Wimsatt, and Monroe C. Beardsley exposed this interpretive strategy in modern literary criticism as a psychological analysis of an author, a method with Romantic roots, masquerading as criticism ("The Intentional Fallacy," in *The Verbal Icon: Studies in the Meaning of Poetry* [Lexington: University of Kentucky Press, 1954] 2–18).
10. The phrase, ותענוגת בני האדם שדה ושדות, is difficult to translate. While ותענוגת need not necessarily refer to sexual pleasures, it is used that way in Song 7:7, another text that interacts with the tradition of Solomon's sexual life. The phrase שדה ושדות has proven even more difficult. Following the LXX (οἰνοχόον καὶ οἰνοχόας) some translate it as "female cupbearers" (e.g., Antoon Schoors, *Ecclesiastes*, HCOT [Leuven: Peeters, 2013] 165) others as "women," referring to concubines, following Ibn Ezra (e.g., Thomas Krüger, *Qoheleth*, Hermeneia [Minneapolis: Fortress, 2004] 56–8; and the NRSV). Still others, following the meaning of שדה in the Mishnah as "chest," understand the phrase to refer to coffers of treasures (e.g., Choon-Leong Seow, *Ecclesiastes*, AB [New York: Doubleday, 1997] 131–2; NJPS).
11. See Eckart Frahm, "Keeping Company with Men of Learning: The King as Scholar," in *The Oxford Handbook of Cuneiform Culture*, eds. Karen Radner and Eleanor Robinson (New York: Oxford University Press, 2011) 508–32.
12. See the recent discussion in Marc Van De Mieroop, *Philosophy before the Greeks: The Pursuit of Truth in Ancient Babylonia* (Princeton, NJ: Princeton University Press, 2016) 19–26.
13. ([*u*]*r-ḫa ru-uq-ta il-li-kam-ma a-ni-iḫ u šup-šu-uḫ*, [*šá-k*] *in i-na* [na4]*narê*(na.rú.a) *ka-lu ma-ha-aḫ-ti*; I. 9–10); text and translation in Andrew R. George, *The Babylonian Gilgamesh Epic: Introduction, Critical Edition, and Cuneiform Texts*, 2 vols. (Oxford: Oxford University Press, 2003) 1.548–9.
14. Translating "breadth of heart" (רחב לב).
15 קדם can mean either "east" or "from before" (i.e., "antiquity"). The LXX understands it as the latter, translating the term with ἀρχαίων.
16. Translating אזוב, "hyssop."
17. Eva Mroczek, *The Literary Imagination in Jewish Antiquity* (New York: Oxford University Press, 2016) 37–8.
18. See 27.15 for Solomon's knowledge of animals' language and his encounter with an ant colony.

19. The translation of Peter Knobel, "The Targum of Qohelet," in Céline Mangan, John Healey, and Peter Knobel, *The Targum of Job, The Targum of Proverbs, The Targum of Qohelet*, ArBib (Collegeville, MN: Liturgical Press, 1991) 24.
20. This paragraph owes much to F. W. Dobbs-Allsopp, *On Biblical Poetry* (New York: Oxford University Press, 2015).
21. The verbal form of this term occurs once in Ecclesiastes, at 10:9.
22. Demonstrated by Mroczek, *Literary Imagination*, 25–50.
23. Sara Japhet and Robert B. Salters, *The Commentary of R. Samuel Ben Meir Rashbam on Qoheleth* (Jerusalem/Leiden: Magnes/Brill, 1985) 90. In the Talmud, (b. Baba Basra 15a) it is said that Ecclesiastes was compiled by the men of Hezekiah, another way of linking the book with Proverbs.
24. *Prologue to the Commentary on the Song of Songs*, in Rowan A. Greer, *Origen: An Exhortation to Martyrdom, Prayer, and Selected Works*, CWS (New York: Paulist, 1979) 231. Origen's Greek text of the *Prologue* does not survive. It is known in the Latin translation of Rufinus.
25. Translation and quotation in Mariano Gómez-Aranda, "The Influence of Isaac Ibn Ghayyat on Abraham Ibn Ezra's Commentary on Ecclesiastes," *JJS* 63 (2012): 100.
26. Greer, *Origen*, 231–2.
27. *Contra* Christianson who claims that "it was Origen who began the tradition of a 'Solomonic corpus.'" (*Ecclesiastes through the Centuries*, 92).
28. See the discussion and compare the English translation in Richard J. Goodrich and David J. D. Miller, *Jerome: Commentary on Ecclesiastes*, ACW (Mahwah, NJ: Paulist Press, 2012) 34.
29. *Commentary on Ecclesiastes*, 5.28 in Gerhard Binder and Leo Liesenborghs, *Didymos der Blinde: Kommentar zum Ecclesiastes (Tura-Papyrus) Teil I.1* (Bonn: Rudolf Habelt Verlag, 1979) 7–9.
30. ἐξήγησιν, literally, "exegesis."
31. *Homilies on Ecclesiastes*, 1.1; Greek text in Françoise Vinel, *Grégoire de Nysse: Homélies sur l'Ecclésiaste*, SC 416 (Paris: Éditions du Cerf, 1996) 106–8. Alternative English translation in Stuart George Hall, ed., *Gregory of Nyssa: Homilies on Ecclesiastes* (Berlin: de Gruyter, 1993).
32. *Homilies on the Song of Songs* 1.22, in Richard A. Norris, Jr., *Gregory of Nyssa Homilies on the Song of Songs* (Atlanta, GA: Society of Biblical Literature, 2012) 22–3. In a detailed study of Gregory's reading of the three Solomonic books, Martin Laird notes "The training found in Ecclesiastes is likewise specific. Whereas the philosophy contained in Proverbs exercises soul so it can desire not corporeal things but virtue, Ecclesiastes trains desire to long for what is beyond appearance, beyond the grasp of senses." ("Under Solomon's Tutelage: The Education of Desire in the Homilies on the Song of Songs," *Modern Theology* 18 [2002]: 512).
33. I disagree with Suseela C. Yesudian-Storfjell when she states that, because "Qoheleth's persona is a problematic one . . . rabbinic exegesis reinvents Qoheleth, as Solomon . . . a pious student and teacher of the Torah" (The Reception of Qoheleth in a Selection of Rabbinic, Patristic and Nonconformist Texts," [PhD diss., University of Sheffield, 2003] 28).

2 Qohelet the King

Not all readers have thought that Qohelet, the royal author of Ecclesiastes, is Solomon. Readings that see the author as someone other than Solomon stretch back to antiquity, although the majority of readers with this interpretation are modern biblical scholars. To look at the authorial voice of Ecclesiastes in this way requires collapsing the voice of Qohelet in the text with the book's now unknown speaker. Once the author is no longer understood to be Solomon, the text becomes a series of clues, or enigmas, whose decipherment is supposed to reveal the author's time and identity. At first glance this is different from the use of a constructed Solomonic biography to read Ecclesiastes that I described in chapter one. On second look, it can be seen as a similar process, but using different data. Scholars now rely on linguistic, literary, and historical information to try and place the author of Ecclesiastes instead of traditions and texts connected with an assumed author. But the contexts derived from this historical data are just as much constructed as the biography of Solomon that readers built out of ancient textual traditions. It is also, like the constructed Solomonic biography, used to interpret the text.

Foucault notes that the author function serves also to determine authenticity of disputed texts based upon what is "known" about an author based on study of their genuine texts.[1] For some readers, the tension between their theological interpretations of the biblical canon as a whole and the statements of "Solomon" in Ecclesiastes became so great that even before the advent of modern scholarship, one finds that the book is deemed pseudonymous. The ideological issues at stake in the question of Solomonic authorship are by no means limited to the pre-modern era. The connection between Solomon and Ecclesiastes, and its severing, has been problematic for both proponents and opponents of Solomonic authorship. The issue is both a meeting place for believers and scholars and a crossroads between theology and exegesis.[2] The interpretive nodes examined in this chapter reveal interesting groupings of readings when doctrinal divides or historical eras are not allowed to dictate the arrangement of the evidence.[3] The discussion begins with an examination of the dogmatic issues at work in the denial of Solomonic authorship. With the realization that Solomon did not write Ecclesiastes, a major divide opens in the reception history of the book and its author. Readers who believed in Solomonic authorship had other texts and traditions to rely on in their interpretation of Ecclesiastes. Solomon's role as a normative figure in authoritative texts shaped how Ecclesiastes, as the words of Qohelet, were read. The doctrinal authority of Ecclesiastes was related in part to Solomon as its author, and the normative view of Solomon gave Ecclesiastes greater heft among readers. This close relationship between the two meant that a questioning of one could easily lead to questioning of the other.

I begin with one of the earliest claims that Solomon might not have written Ecclesiastes, in the commentary by the second century Christian writer, Didymus the Blind. Part of the 6th century CE Tura Papyrus discovered in 1941, the commentary takes the form of a series of questions put to Didymus by an unnamed catechumen.[4] Concerning the superscription attributing the book to the son of David who was king in Jerusalem, the speaker asks Didymus whether the "words of Ecclesiastes" are those of the book's author (ῥήματα ἐκκλησιαστοῦ ἐκ προσώπου τοῦ συγραφέως;).[5] The simplest reading sees the question as asking whether the words of the first-person voice in the book are the same as those of the frame narrator who writes the superscription and epilogue. This is a question other readers have had and the following chapter examines readings that see multiple voices at work in Ecclesiastes. But Didymus's answer shows that he understands the question to deal with Solomonic authorship.

> κυρίως μὲν ἐπὶ τῶν θεοπνεύστων γραφῶν συνγραφεύς ἐστιν τὸ πνεῦμα τὸ ὑποβαλὸν αὐτὸ λαληθῆναι, ὑπηρετεῖται δὲ ὑπό τινος σοφοῦ. οὐδὲ γὰρ τὸ πνεῦμα ἀοράτως ἐχάραξεν τὰ γράμματα καὶ τὰς λέξεις ἔθηκεν, ἀλλ᾽ ἐνπνεῖ ψυχῇ τινι ταῦτα. καὶ ἤτοι αὐτός ἐστιν ὁ γράφων αὐτὰ ὁ Σολομὼν ἢ τῶν σοφῶν τινες ἔγραψαν αὐτά. καὶ τάχα μᾶλλου τούτῳ ἀρέσκομεν, ἵνα μὴ δοξῃ τις περὶ αὐτοῦ λἐγειν τὸν λέγουντα ταῦτα.[6]
>
> In regards to the divinely inspired scriptures, the prompting Spirit might be said to be a co-author, assisting some wise writer. The unseen Spirit has not written the letters and placed the words, but breathed life into them. Now either Solomon is its [Ecclesiastes] author or some other wise person has written it. Maybe it's better that we say that, so that [Solomon] not seem to be saying these things about himself.

There is much to examine in this answer. Note that Didymus is doing two things here. He is reiterating the standard theological claim that the Spirit is the true author of the biblical books. But he uses this doctrinal chestnut to distance Solomon from the content of Ecclesiastes. Given that Didymus's interlocutor is most likely a construct, the questions asked reflect what Didymus thinks the important theological issues in Ecclesiastes are for Alexandrian Christians. Didymus argues that the author of Ecclesiastes ought to be somebody other than Solomon because it would be inappropriate for Solomon to be speaking about himself. This is an odd claim, and no reason for it is given here or anywhere else in the commentary.[7] In fact, beyond this subtly expressed doubt, Didymus seems reluctant to discuss any further the relationship between the narrator's voice and

Qohelet's. The commentary ends at Eccl 12:6, before the narrator speaks again,[8] and Didymus proceeds throughout the commentary understanding Solomon to be the author of Ecclesiastes. But in his comments on the remainder of Eccl 1:1 (υἱοῦ Δαυιδ βασιλέως Ισραηλ ἐν Ιερουσαλημ) Didymus goes into a rather long digression about pseudepigraphic writings. He notes the presence of these writings in Christian literature, especially gospels, and the fact that earlier bishops (including Clement of Alexandria) kept such texts away from the people. At the end of this he assures the questioner that it is impossible (ἀδύνατον) for Ecclesiastes to be a forgery because Eccl 1:1 lists Solomon's lineage, ethnicity, and city.[9]

What does this very clear example of "the interpreter doth protest too much" tell us?[10] There is certainly a tension at work in thinking about Qohelet as both the author of Ecclesiastes and as King Solomon. For readers like Didymus, the potentially questionable content of Ecclesiastes may taint the figure of Solomon, and the book needs to be distanced from the biblical king. This is different from the rabbinic response to this problem described in the previous chapter. The rabbis salvaged Solomon's orthodoxy by finding theologically acceptable texts to counter the questionable ones. Chapter one also shows that for other readers the connection between Ecclesiastes and Solomon is what gives the book its authority to speak on matters of wisdom. These solutions act as two sides of a thoroughfare on which the connections between Ecclesiastes the text and Solomon as a sage pass in opposite directions. On one side, Solomon's authority lends credibility to a suspect text and the link is highlighted. On the other, elements of the text risk endangering Solomon's reputation and the king is distanced from the book.

The theological tension at work in Didymus's commentary is not what explicitly led to the denial of Solomonic authorship of Ecclesiastes in the modern period. It was philology.

In his 1644 commentary on the Old Testament, Hugo Grotius ruled out Solomonic authorship because some of the terminology in Ecclesiastes was similar to that found in post-exilic texts.[11] But philological analysis of the biblical text was not completely free from theological entanglements, which were, importantly, based on the issue of authorship. In his detailed account of the origins of philology, James Turner describes the constant interplay between scholarly advances in biblical philology and their doctrinal consequences in a 400-year period that begins in the Renaissance.[12] Following Thomas Hobbes, Baruch Spinoza denied Mosaic authorship of the Pentateuch in his posthumously published *Tractatus Theologico-Politicus* (1677). He has also been expelled from the Amsterdam Jewish community. In a book published the next year, Richard Simon, a Catholic priest, maintained Mosaic authorship for a core of the Pentateuch, but posited centuries of post-Mosaic editorial activity. He was expelled from his religious order.[13] A little over a hundred years later another priest, Alexander Geddes, would be censured by the Catholic Church for denying Mosaic authorship of the Pentateuch, and the Protestant philologist Wilhelm Gesenius attacked for the same reason.[14] Among those hostile to organized religion, Ecclesiastes was a biblical book in which a kindred spirit was seen and the scholarly denial of its putative Solomonic authorship offered a parade example to those critical of religion that academia could push back the ignorance of tradition. It is significant in this regard that the opening lines of Voltaire's 1759 verse translation of Ecclesiastes subtly points out the book's disputed authorship.[15]

By the 19th century, Turner notes, biblical philology had segregated itself from other philological disciplines with the establishment of seminaries and free-standing theological schools. This was a deliberate move meant to limit the threat of interdisciplinary work to doctrinal claims on biblical authority and this rift grew wider throughout the 1800s.[16] The second half of that century begins a period that Turner refers to as "the Bible Wars," in which the

> confused tendencies within the ranks of Old Testament philologists in particular became two opposing camps. The warriors fought not so much over philological techniques, but over what philology ultimately implied about the Bible's relation to its own history and historical contexts. The nature of scripture and its authority seemed at stake.[17]

These doctrinal stakes were much higher for Mosaic authorship of the Pentateuch than for Solomon's having written Ecclesiastes. By the 19th century biblical philology branched out from questioning traditional views of authorship to casting doubt on the historicity of some biblical texts. The situation as Turner describes it, with both those who challenged traditional doctrine and those defending it drawing on philology to buttress their claims, decided the outcome of the "Bible Wars" in favor of the challengers. Those defending the theological status quo began to engage in what can only be called a rearguard action, sacrificing some traditional positions that were clearly untenable. For example, by the turn of the 20th century, most exegetes acknowledged that Jonah was not swallowed by a fish, although recourse to Assyrian documents continued to be used well into the 20th century to support the historicity of Jonah's mission to Nineveh.[18] Like Jonah's "whale," Solomonic authorship of Ecclesiastes was another of these expendable claims.[19] Other historical and literary questions, notably the Mosaic authorship of the Pentateuch, were still open, hotly debated in print, and fought over ruthlessly in both academic and ecclesiastical politics.[20] This is no surprise, given the importance of authorship and authority that I discussed in the introduction. While there are many unbelievable things in the Pentateuch that rival the marvel of Jonah's survival in a great fish, the Pentateuch's authority depended in large part on the belief that Moses wrote it. Any attempt to impugn the historicity of its accounts or origins was understood as an attack on both the authority of Moses and the authority of the text. The issue of Solomonic authorship of Ecclesiastes took a different route from that of the Pentateuch, and not many theologically conservative scholars were willing to dig in their heels on this issue. Instead, they looked to theologically orthodox predecessors to sanitize their denial of Solomon's having written Ecclesiastes.

At Table with Luther

Since at least the 19th century, some scholars writing on Ecclesiastes cite this saying from Luther's *Table Talk* that supports the denial of Solomonic authorship:

> Ecclesiastes is a very good and pleasant book, although it is a fragment; it wants boots and spurs, and rides in sandals, as I used [to] when in the cloister. It has many a fine rule for domestic government. It is like a Talmud, compiled from many books, perhaps from the library of Ptolemy Euergetes in Egypt. So also the Proverbs of Solomon were collected by others from the mouth of the king, perhaps as he sat at table or elsewhere, and brought together.[21]

The quotation is taken from an English translation of the 1566 edition of the *Table Talk* published in Eisleben.[22] But this Lutheran logion is spurious. The Latin notes of Conrad Cordatus, another interlocutor of Luther's, show that Luther was referring to the book of Ecclesiasticus/Ben Sira, and not Ecclesiastes ("Ecclesiasticum puto tempore Machabaeorum esse scriptum").[23] This error was recognized in the 19th century but persists in Ecclesiastes scholarship to this day.[24] What makes it noteworthy is that the perceived authority of Luther on this question is used by those on both sides of the ideological divide of Turner's "Bible Wars." On the one hand, conservative scholars informed by philological analysis that ruled out Solomonic authorship relied on Luther's authority to give theologically orthodox support to the view that Ecclesiastes was not written by Solomon. A parade example is Franz Delitzsch, for whom the philological evidence was so clear that he could make the observation—itself proverbial in Ecclesiastes scholarship—that if Solomon had written Ecclesiastes the history of classical Hebrew made no sense ("Wenn das B. Koheleth altsalomonisch wäre, so gäbe es keine Geschichte der hebräischen Sprache").[25] Immediately prior to this he cites the pseudo-Lutheran *Tischrede*, prefacing it with the claim that critical scholarship is not only beneficial to Christian faith, but owes its existence to Reformation thinkers.[26] Among English-speaking scholars of the same period, Edward Plumptre also cites approvingly this apocryphal saying of Luther, noting it as evidence of the reformer's "bold insight," on a par with Luther's denial of Pauline authorship of Hebrews.[27]

But use of this "saying" of Luther's is not confined to the 19th century. Among theologically conservative publications on Ecclesiastes, Luther's "denial" of Solomonic authorship is still cited as recently as 2010.[28] On the other side, exegetes unaffiliated with conservative theological positions have not needed to appeal to Luther for a long time. But it is referred to in 19th- and early 20th-century works written with an apologetic edge supporting the value of historical-critical study of the Bible.[29] The 1861 study of Christian Ginsburg serves as a good example. While discussing the question of Solomonic authorship of Ecclesiastes, Ginsburg appeals to the theological idea of progressive revelation to argue that the thought of Ecclesiastes on the afterlife proves that the book cannot be Solomonic:

> With those who believe that the blessed Trinity is revealed in the first verse of the first chapter of Genesis; that the doctrine of justification by faith, the atonement, and all the other cardinal truths of Christianity, are set forth in the chapters immediately following, we do not intend to argue. We appeal to those whom a rational and reverential study of Holy Writ, and a due regard to the laws of language, have taught that God, who causes the natural light at first to break feebly upon our eyes, and to increase gradually in splendour till it attains to its meridian glory, also caused the light of the Sun of Righteousness, at first beaming faintly, to shine more and more unto the perfect day and we ask if such an explicit declaration about the return of the soul to God, who shall hereafter judge not only every action but every secret of man, whether it be good or evil, can be assigned to the early dawn of Revelation? Let the dim intimations respecting a future state, given under the types and figures prior to the exile . . . be compared with the naked truth, as declared after the exile by Daniel, in the Book of Wisdom, Tobit, 2 Macabees, and especially in the New Testament; and we submit that the gradual development of this doctrine will be fully recognized; and hence it will also be conceded, that the distinct reference of Coheleth to a future judgment, precludes the idea of the Solomonic authorship of the book.[30]

Citing Luther's spurious logion, Ginsburg refers to him as "the sagacious Reformer," who arrived at the critical insight of non-Solomonic authorship of Ecclesiastes by dint of his "sheer penetration" and without access to the tools of modern scholarship.[31] In Ginsburg's discourse, modern critical scholarship—philology—tracks smoothly with liberal theological ideas (note, however, that progressive revelation is crudely supersessionist), and both find their source in the religious giants of the past.

I take pleasure in the irony that, to support the claim that Solomon didn't write something he was thought to have written, appeal was made to something Luther was thought to have said that he didn't say. This diversion into Luther's dining room sheds light on the controversy surrounding Solomonic authorship of Ecclesiastes, a view that has been dominant for 90 percent of the book's interpretive life. In the debate over this question in the Western, Protestant, world it was never so much about Solomon or Ecclesiastes as it was about biblical authority, the nature of inspiration, the role of scholarship in theology, and the relationship between faith and reason.

A Solomonic Mask

The move away from Solomon as author creates new interpretive challenges for readers. The author's "Solomonic" self-description (wise, powerful, wealthy) demands an explanation. What is Qohelet's motive for presenting himself as

Solomon? How does this literary conceit influence how readers made sense of the content in Ecclesiastes? The need to answer the question of Qohelet's intention in his self-presentation, coupled with the partial liberation of academic biblical studies from theological orthodoxies, allowed readers a wider range of interpretive choices in constructing Qohelet's identity and in making sense of his words.

For some the author was not Solomon, but pretending to be. In his lectures on Hebrew poetry published in 1753, Robert Lowth obliquely brings up the disputed authorship of Ecclesiastes when he notes that the book is written, "sub persona Salomonis," a phrase most easily rendered, "in the guise of Solomon."[32] It is noteworthy that the English translation of Lowth's lectures renders "sub persona" as "in the character *of a person*" [italics mine]. In other words, not that the author of Ecclesiastes plays the role of Solomon but that the author of Ecclesiastes (i.e., Solomon, plays the role of somebody asking these kinds of questions).[33] This is certainly one meaning of the Latin phrase, "sub persona," and it is also an old interpretation, found as far back as Jerome's commentary.[34] But the possibility remains that the ambiguity of Lowth's original Latin text is deliberate.[35]

In Eccl 1:12, Qohelet introduces himself: "I, Qohelet, was king over Israel in Jerusalem." It is Qohelet's most revealing statement about his identity in the book, and as I discussed in the introduction, it is frustratingly obscure because no known king in Jerusalem can be connected with the name. In the Midrash to Ecclesiastes, Rabbi Samuel b. Isaac asks why this verse wasn't placed at the beginning of the book as a superscription—a question asked by modern scholars as well.[36] The answer is that "there is no before and after in the Torah" (לא שאין מוקדם ומאוחר בתורה). Rabbi Samuel's question points to the fact that the statement is also an introduction to a section of Ecclesiastes that quite a few scholars have called the "royal autobiography." In 1:12–2:23, Qohelet boasts of his wealth, power, and wisdom; he describes his experiment in hedonistic living and concludes with the complaint that human effort is ultimately meaningless in the face of our mortality. If Qohelet is hiding behind a Solomonic mask, then this self-description is a reflection of the biblical picture of Solomon. This is the opinion of the majority of modern biblical scholars, ably captured in C.L. Seow's claim that "it is probably the intent of the author to evoke memory of Solomon, the wise king *par excellence* and the best example of one who has it all."[37] In this node are readings that see parallels between Qohelet's boasts of great wisdom (1:16), opulent wealth (2:4–10), and sexual excess (2:8) and the description of Solomon in 1 Kings that I discussed in the previous chapter. Qohelet is assumed to have constructed his own Solomonic biography and used that in his self-portrayal in Ecclesiastes. Modern scholars in effect make Qohelet the author into a reader of the Solomonic tradition in the same way that many readers of Ecclesiastes read that tradition to make sense of Qohelet. The most extensive example of this is Jennie Barbour's reading of Ecclesiastes, in which the entire book draws upon earlier biblical traditions, what Barbour terms "the echo-chamber of [Qohelet's] own literary culture."[38] Consequently, Qohelet's royal self-description in 1:12–2:23 is "not only the literary archetype of Solomon, but . . . the afterlife of that archetype in the Bible."[39]

It is safe to assume that Qohelet would be aware of some of the Israelite literary tradition that is now in the Hebrew Bible. But we must admit that we have no clear idea exactly how much of that tradition existed in Qohelet's day, and in what form. That the biblical authors had access to the canon as we know it, but not much else, is also a problematic assumption. Eva Mroczek eloquently exposes the flaw in this view when she notes that "the imaginative world of early Jews cannot be assumed to be an inner-biblical one."[40] By way of example, she points out that 2 Chron 35:4 refers to a Solomonic text (מכתב) that contextually cannot be any of the biblical texts traditionally attributed to Solomon. Mroczek also demonstrates that pseudonymous authorship in antiquity is not motivated exclusively by the desire to deceive the reader or to claim a false authority for a text.

> Besides claiming authority, linking a text to a figure also extends and enriches narratives about him, transforming the character to make him speak to a new audience. Writing in the name of an ancient hero can also be a kind of spiritual exercise of self-effacement, in which the figure that the author emulates becomes an exemplar and literary guide for both him and his audience.[41]

Because these readings attribute to Qohelet a self-assumed Solomonic persona, the motives implied for this portrayal are important in the reception history of Ecclesiastes's author. For many readers, Qohelet presents himself as Solomon for radical or polemical reasons, for example, to attack the idea of "traditional" ancient Israelite wisdom and the picture of Solomon as its paragon. Thomas Krüger argues that "the teaching authority of King Solomon is 'deconstructed' and repudiated" by Qohelet's use of a Solomonic persona, and that the royal autobiography of 1:12–2:23 is a "caricature" and a "royal travesty."[42] Norbert Lohfink speaks of "the literary technique of a royal make-believe, a masquerade in which [Qohelet] assumes the image of the philosopher-king of Jerusalem, the famous Solomon," whose purpose is akin to what Aristotle says about tragic characters: that for their suffering to generate true pathos they have to fall from a great height.[43] For others, Qohelet hides behind a Solomonic façade in order to be ironic. Proof of this is the fact that Qohelet's repeated claim (1:16, 2:7, 2:9) to be greater in both wisdom and riches than all his predecessors in Jerusalem cannot make sense if he is Solomon, because David was the only prior king to reign in Jerusalem. Qohelet must, of course, know this, and so his boast is deliberately ridiculous. But this reading overlooks a similar statement made about Solomon in 1 Chron 29:25:

> יגדל יהוה את שלמה למעלה לעיני כל ישראל ויתן עליו הוד מלכות אשר לא היה על כל מלך לפניו על ישראל
>
> Yahweh exalted Solomon highly in the eyes of all of Israel and he gave to him royal glory which no other king over Israel before him had ever had.

This reference to Solomon's greatness over all of his implied many predecessors shows that Qohelet's use of this claim is not necessarily for ironic or satirical purposes. Nobody would ever accuse the Chronicler of having a sense of humor. What it shows is the use of a stock phrase denoting greatness, a use that is not concerned with an exact correspondence to the details of the Davidic dynasty. This is not ignorance of those details on the part of 1 Chronicles, because it also recounts them. To interpret Qohelet's use of this reference ironically effectively marginalizes him in relation to the tradition, which perpetuates the idea of Ecclesiastes as an "outsider" book in the canon. Irony and Ecclesiastes have long gone hand-in-hand in biblical scholarship.[44] In one of the more nuanced studies of irony in Ecclesiastes, Carolyn Sharp draws attention to the irony at work in the figure of Qohelet himself and not his use of the tradition. Qohelet is not simply using Solomon to ironically allude to the famous king's wisdom and wealth. Qohelet himself is an object of irony. His miserable life renders meaningless his exhortations to the reader to enjoy life because it is something a reader cannot imagine him ever doing. This inability to enjoy life undercuts the validity of his wisdom.[45] I examine in more detail readings that understand Qohelet to be a radical in chapter six.

What Kind of King?

Related, but not identical, to the issue of Qohelet's self-presentation as Solomon is the question of the cultural context that informs this description of a king's life. While Qohelet *may* have wanted readers to think of him as Solomon, his way of describing himself as a king would be informed by the traditional or dominant ideologies of kingship available to him. This is for some readers a genre question, either of the royal autobiography in Eccl 1:12–2:23 or of the book as a whole, depending upon the cultural contexts used to interpret the text. In the following paragraphs, I look at each particular context in turn: Mesopotamian/Northwest Semitic, Egyptian, Persian, and Greek.

Many readers who focus exclusively on Eccl 1:12–2:23 see a Mesopotamian or Northwest Semitic context for Qohelet's royal ideology. The opening phrase, אני קהלת הייתי מלך על ישראל בירושלם ("I, Qohelet, was king over Israel in Jerusalem") appears to model itself on a number of Northwest Semitic royal inscriptions spanning the 9th to 5th centuries BCE:

'nk mš' bn kmš[yt] mlk m'b
I am Mesha, son of Chemosh[*yt*] king of Moab.

'nk pnmw br qrl mlk y'dy . . .
I am Panammu, son of *qrl*, king of *y'dy* . . .

'nk 'šmn'zr mlk ṣdnm bn
I am Eshmunazar, king of the Sidonians, son of[46]

The most extensive recent study of this question is by Y.V. Koh, who argues that, not only does 1:12 deliberately mimic these royal inscriptions, but that the entire section of 1:12–2:23 is "rooted in ancient Near Eastern royal and literary practice," specifically in its boasting of great deeds and claim of greatness over any royal predecessor.[47]

The match between these inscriptions and the opening of the royal autobiography in Eccl 1:12 does not quite join. There is first a problem with titles. In the examples above, each of the kings identifies himself both as the king of a particular region or people and by his patronymic.[48] Qohelet, on the other hand, only notes that he was king over Israel, saying nothing about his father. It is only in the superscription of Eccl 1:1, which does not present itself as the voice of Qohelet, where he is called "David's son." There is also a problem with verbs. While it is true that extant West Semitic royal inscriptions use the perfect form of verbs in referring to the king's reign, none does so with the verb "to be." Grammatically speaking, the implied copula is present in all of these inscriptions—including Eccl 1:12—by the juxtaposition of the first person singular pronoun and the monarch's proper name. If the author of Qohelet wanted to imitate these inscriptions, we should expect an introductory statement without the verb הייתי, something like אני קהלת מלך על ישראל בירושלם ("I am Qohelet, king over Israel in Jerusalem"). Commentators are aware of this problem and have tried to address it. Seow argues that "there is no semantic difference between the idiom *hyyty mlk* 'I have been king' in Ecclesiastes and *mklty* 'I have reigned' or *yšbt(y) 'l ks'/mšb* 'I have sat on the throne/seat' in the West Semitic royal inscriptions."[49] But there is no consensus on this. Schoors maintains that the use of הייתי "leaves open" the question of "whether [Qohelet] is presenting himself to the reader as an ex-king."[50] Qohelet's choice to connect the first-person singular pronoun and the name/title "Qohelet" by explicit use of the perfect form of היה allows for the possibility that he is describing a situation that once was, but is no longer the case.

In addition to the perceived links between Eccl 1:12 and the introductory statements in these inscriptions, some readers see parallels between the two in Qohelet's proud enumeration of his building projects and possessions. But again, these parallels do not smoothly correspond. As Koh acknowledges, all of the building projects Qohelet names are for his own enjoyment (houses, vineyards, gardens, orchards, pools). In contrast, kings in Mesopotamian and Northwest Semitic inscriptions almost exclusively speak of large "public" building projects (e.g., walls, temple restoration).[51] What is also noteworthy is that Qohelet's royal perks do not give him pleasure. He ends his inventory of goodies with a long and detailed observation that the knowledge of his inevitable death robs all delights of their savor (Eccl 2:11–23). This regret on the part of the king is something that is not found in the royal inscriptions. Instead, they are consistent in extolling the military virtues, religious devotion, or building activities of the monarch. Any boasts of wisdom on a king's part are exclusively limited to the king's ability to rule or wage war; any expressions of faults or sinfulness on the king's part are equally limited to actions exclusive to a king, and their remedy is also included in the text.[52]

These attempts to equate Qohelet with a historical Mesopotamian or Northwest Semitic king overlook the royal ideology found in ancient narratives—as opposed to inscriptions—which includes both the king's wisdom and his regret. I discussed in chapter one the portrayal of the king as a sage. While it does occur in texts referring to historical kings, it is more at home in the narrative or epic tradition. The composition history of the *Epic of Gilgamesh* is the best example of this. The Old Babylonian form of the epic tells the story of how a bad king learns how to be a good one, and in this version Gilgamesh's wisdom centers around learning how to rule over his subjects in Uruk. The Standard Version takes the epic and expands the narrative to transform Gilgamesh into a heroic figure who must learn to accept the divinely ordained limits placed on all human beings. Gilgamesh's scholarly acumen is noted in the prologue to the Standard Version, which states that he wrote his experience down to teach the reader this great existential lesson. Gilgamesh the king in the Old Babylonian version only becomes Gilgamesh the sage in the Standard Version, when he both has a universal lesson to communicate and has written it down to do so.[53]

More important to my discussion is that, while there are no convincing parallels between Ecclesiastes and Mesopotamian or Northwest Semitic royal inscriptions, such parallels do exist between Ecclesiastes and the Old Babylonian version of the *Epic of Gilgamesh*. In an Old Babylonian fragment reportedly from Sippar, Šiduri counsels Gilgamesh to give up his quest for Uta-napishti:

> You, Gilgameš, let your belly be full,
> keep enjoying yourself, day and night!
> Everyday make merry,
> Dance and play day and night!
> Let your clothes be clean!
> Let your head be washed, may you be bathed in water!
> Gaze on the little one who holds your hand!
> Let a wife enjoy your repeated embrace![54]

Very similar advice is found in Ecclesiastes:

לך אכל בשמחה לחמך
ושתה בלב טוב יינך
כי כבר רצה האלהים את מעשיך
בכל עת יהיו בגדיך לבנים
ושמן על ראשך אל יחסר
ראה חיים עם אשה אשר אהבת
כל ימי חיי הבלך
אשר נתן לך תחת השמש

> Go, eat your bread with joy
> and drink your wine with a happy heart,
> because God has long ago approved of your deeds.
> At all times let your garments be white
> and never let oil be lacking from your head.
> Enjoy life with the woman whom you love
> all the days of your empty life
> that God has given to you under the sun.
> (Eccl 9:7–9).

Scholars have been puzzled trying to explain this overlap.[55] Koh avoids the question altogether. Instead she devotes her attention to the parallel between line 157 of the "autobiographical narration" of King Naram Sin and the counsel in Eccl 9:9 to enjoy oneself in the embrace of a wife. For Koh, the Naram Sin text recounts the thoughts of a "despondent royal narrator," which connects with Ecclesiastes because both texts present a wise and repentant king.[56] The question of how the *Epic of Gilgamesh* relates to Ecclesiastes is made particularly difficult because the parallel exists only in the Old Babylonian version of the epic, which dates to the middle of the second millennium BCE. It is not found in the Standard Version, which is a thousand years younger (and therefore closer in time with Ecclesiastes) and which continued to be copied up to and after the time that Ecclesiastes was written. Plausible scenarios for a Jerusalem author writing in Hebrew sometime in the 4th to 3rd centuries BCE to have had access to a 17th-century BCE Akkadian composition are hard to come by.[57] The most recent attempt by Nili Samet draws upon evidence demonstrating that variant versions of the *Epic of Gilgamesh* still circulated long after the writing of the "Standard Version" (a scholarly nomenclature, betraying modern ideas about canonical texts that do not apply in antiquity). The linguistic barrier is more of a challenge, which Samet attempts to surmount by recourse to a hypothesis—the Babylonian text of the *Epic of Gilgamesh* had been translated into Aramaic, and a hotly contested claim—that Qohelet was a native speaker of Aramaic.[58] This is the same problem for those who would argue that Ecclesiastes is mimicking Mesopotamian or Northwest Semitic royal inscriptions. No one has offered a plausible reconstruction of how Qohelet could have known these texts. Koh simply asserts that Qohelet "undoubtedly" knew and read these texts without any elaboration. Coming at the problem from the other side, Martin Shields goes against linguistic analysis that extends back to Hugo Grotius (discussed above) and claims a pre-exilic date for Qohelet, thus making him a contemporary of the inscriptions.[59]

Qohelet's use of הייתי in 1:12 has been read by some as not only referring to past completed action, but as evidence that Qohelet is speaking from beyond the grave in imitation of Egyptian royal instructions.[60] Among the group of Egyptian wisdom instructions (known in Egyptian as *sebayit*) the Old Kingdom, *Teaching for Merikare*, and the Middle Kingdom, *Teaching of Amenemhet*, are both presented as royal instruction from a king to his son. But neither text makes clear that the pharaoh who instructs in the text is dead; it has been assumed by scholars.[61] Apart from that, there is no significant overlap in content between either text and Ecclesiastes. The superscription in Eccl 1:1 is another point of contact readers have seen with Egyptian royal instructions.[62] And while it is true that Eccl 1:1 is similar to the superscriptions of both the *Teaching of Amenemhet* and the *Teaching for Merikare*, it is also practically identical to fifteen prophetic books in the Hebrew Bible. The fact of the matter is that many ancient texts contain superscriptions, and arguments for imitation or literary dependence must rely on more than this common trait.

Unlike the Mesopotamian and Northwest Semitic texts, there are no real verbal parallels between Ecclesiastes and Egyptian instructions.[63] But there is evidence for some kind of cultural contact between Egypt and Israelite scribes. There is a cluster of Egyptian loanwords in Hebrew that deal with the scribal occupation (e.g., the words for "pen," "ink," "palette," and different units of measurement), and Iron Age Hebrew inscriptions use hieratic numerals.[64] It has long been recognized that

Prov 22:17–24:22 is dependent upon the Egyptian *Instruction of Amenemope*. But the overlap in content in this instance makes some kind of relationship between these texts undeniable. That being said, there is still no plausible scenario for how *Amenemope* wound up in Proverbs. Knowledge of literary dependence of one text on another is significantly different than knowledge of the process that led to it.

Standard operating procedure for biblical scholars is to look for connections between the biblical texts and data from the surrounding cultures of the ancient Near East. It also often happens that some of these connections are forced or highly artificial.[65] It is important to note that some readers see dependence of Ecclesiastes on *both* Mesopotamian/Northwest Semitic and Egyptian royal texts.[66] This not only compounds the problem of cultural contact at work in trying to relate Ecclesiastes with either of these other cultures but underscores the multifaceted portrait Qohelet presents of himself. These different ways of reading Qohelet's autobiography are not solely reliant on the biases or predilections of exegetes. They are part of the text's range of possible meanings. Regardless of what the historical person writing behind the name "Qohelet" knew or did not know about royal ideology in the centuries before him, the text possesses the potential to see Qohelet's royal description in ways that appear to connect with Mesopotamian, Northwest Semitic, or Egyptian texts. My critique of those connections does not intend to say that they are completely illusory, but that the fit between Ecclesiastes and the extra-biblical data is rough.

It has long been known that Qohelet's worldview is influenced by that of the Persian empire. Both Persian loanwords in Ecclesiastes are from the realm of royal prerogative. In 2:5, Qohelet uses פרדסים to describe his royal gardens and in 8:11 he refers to a decree of punishment with פתגם. Qohelet also describes God and the divine-human relationship with ideas and imagery from Persian royal ideology. God for Qohelet, as C. L. Seow notes, rules the world in a manner similar to the Persian king, "who arbitrarily gives grants to favorite friends and courtiers, while others are left out."[67] Qohelet describes other divine actions in ways that resemble those of the Great King, specifically in how the Persian king's power was manifest in his great wealth and conspicuous largesse to those in his favor. The most frequent and obvious way the king showed favor to some lucky subjects was in allowing access to his daily table. Notably, the king would feast with his courtiers and guests while sitting behind a curtain, so that the diners could be seen by the king, while he himself remained unseen.[68] Persian royal ideology reserved all privileges exclusively to the king. He could give whatever to whomever he would but conversely was not bound to reciprocate any service or honor done to him.[69] This is all similar to Qohelet's understanding of the divine-human relationship. First there is the image of the all-seeing, but unseen, absolute ruler whose subjects eat and drink at his pleasure and under his watchful eye, which parallels Qohelet's constant refrain for humanity to eat and drink while they can, given that such things are no guarantee. It is significant that every time Qohelet urges the reader to eat and drink, he mentions either divine generosity or approval (2:24–26; 3:13–14; 5:18–19; 8:15; 9:7).

Since it is established that Qohelet knows Persian royal ideology, and draws on it in his description of God, there is a fair chance that his royal self-description also draws on Persia. The majority of extant Persian royal inscriptions are brief and among the repeated, salient ideological features in them is the use of the phrase "great king, king of kings, king of the lands/countries," and a boasting of the king's lineage.[70] The former is a long-standing royal title in ancient Near Eastern inscriptions. The latter is due in large part to the complicated and often violent succession history of the Achaemenids for whom the repeated affirmation of legitimacy was important. Looking at other writings that describe the Persian kings reveals descriptions of their opulent lifestyles. Herodotus (1.188) notes that whenever the king travels, he drinks only water from the river in Susa transported with him in silver jars. Plutarch (*Alex.* 20.12–13) describes the richness of the king's battle tent—golden vessels, rich spices, an elaborate banquet laid out—which Alexander occupies after defeating Darius III in battle. The king's large harem appears in many authors, both Greek (Plutarch, *Art.* 26–27; Athenaeus, *Deipn.* 13) and Jewish (Esther 1–2). Xenophon mentions the parks/game preserves of Persian kings and governors (*Anab.* 1.4.10; *Hell.* 4.1.15–16) using the Greek variant (παράδεισος) of the same Persian loanword found in the Hebrew Ecclesiastes (פרדס).[71]

Given the similarities between Qohelet's description of his royal wealth and Greek descriptions of the Persian kings, Greek literary traditions about kings also warrants attention in interpreting Qohelet's royal identity. Of significance here is the Greek literary trope that concerns *former* rulers—Croesus and Sardanapallus—who, after their rule, become renowned as teachers of wisdom, specifically a wisdom that emphasizes the finality of human death and the need to live one's life always with death in mind.

The story of Croesus begins with another ruler Solon, who held the office of chief archon of Athens in the late 6th century BCE. By the 4th century BCE, literary traditions about Solon's wisdom and skill in poetry are prevalent in Greek writers. Writing in the 5th century BCE, Herodotus (1.30–32) tells of Solon's visit to Croesus, the wealthy Lydian king. Eager to impress Solon, Croesus's servants, on the king's orders "led him [Solon] through the treasuries and showed him all the wonderful and rich things" (κελεύσαντος Κροίσου τὸν Σόλωνα θεράποντες περιῆγον κατὰ τοὺς θησαυρούς, καὶ ἐπεδείκνυσαν πάντα ἐόντα μεγάλα τε καὶ ὄλβια [1.30.1]). Complimenting Solon on his reputation for wisdom—specifically on the fact that Solon's life has been a ceaseless quest for wisdom—Croesus asks Solon to tell him whether, "of everyone you have seen, there is one who is the most blessed?" (εἴ τινα ἤδη πάντων εἶδες ὀλβιώτατον [1.30.1]). Of course, Croesus fully expects he himself to be the most blessed of men, due to his great wealth, and of course, Solon disappoints him. This is standard folktale morality, but what's interesting is how Solon justifies the richest man in the world *not* being the happiest. Solon's most blessed person is a man who died in battle and left behind healthy sons. Then, when pressed by Croesus to name the *second* most blessed man in the world, Solon names a pair of brothers who died after performing an act of religious devotion. When rudely challenged by Croesus about how such men could be considered more blessed than he when they are dead, Solon notes that the gods are jealous and send sorrow into the lives of people, so much so that "all a person is depends upon chance" (πᾶν ἐστὶ ἄνθρωπος συμφορή [1.32.4]). Consequently, the only way a person can be happy is *after* they have lived their life and made a good death, "but before [a man] has died, don't call him 'blessed'—but rather 'lucky'" (πρὶν δ' ἂν τελευτήσῃ, ἐπισχεῖν, μηδὲ καλέειν κω ὄλβιον ἀλλ' εὐτυχέα [1.32.7]).[72] Croesus is not impressed with Solon's wisdom—not at first anyway—but as Herodotus relates later on in Book 1, after Croesus's kingdom is lost to Cyrus and the former king is placed on a pyre to face his death, Croesus remembers the teaching of Solon, which Herodotus expresses succinctly, "that nobody among the living is blessed" (τὸ μηδένα εἶναι τῶν ζωόντων ὄλβιον [1.86.3]). Calling out Solon's name in anguish from the pyre, Croesus is spared by Cyrus the Great after he displays to the Persian king his new and dearly won wisdom. Croesus goes on to offer Cyrus sage advice on governing the newly conquered Lydians.

Sardanapallus is a legendary figure appearing in a variety of Greek sources spanning several centuries. In the most common version of the legend, he is the incredibly wealthy and licentious last king of Nineveh,[73] whose gross excesses lead to the revolt of his subjects. When the end comes, Sardanapallus piles all of his wealth into a great heap, climbs atop, and has himself burned to death. His epitaph, which is said to have been placed on the ruins of his city, is quoted in several authors, and reads:

> εὖ εἰδὼς ὅτι θνητὸς ἔφυς σὸν θυμὸν ἄεξε, τερπόμενος θαλίῃσι. θανόντι σοι οὔτις ὄνσις.
>
> (Athenaeus, *Deipn.* 8.336)
>
> Knowing well that you are mortal, lift up your heart; take delight in feasts. You will have no more pleasure when dead.

These examples from the Greek literary tradition show a wise king whose wisdom is manifest only after or at the end of his reign. This wisdom consists in a hard-won realization that human mortality casts its shadow over the entirety of human life. It serves to remind human beings that, because death is the only place one can be free from woe—as in the passages about Solon and Croesus from Herodotus—we ought to live enjoying all the pleasures life has to offer—as in the stories of Sardanapallus. This is, of course, identical to the advice Qohelet gives throughout Ecclesiastes. Both Qohelet and Greek traditions have the king describe his fabulous wealth from the vantage point of a time after his reign. These observations are then directly connected to the king's teaching that humanity's inescapable fate relativizes the value of riches while at the same time exhorting the reader to enjoy whatever goods lay to hand. There are no similar descriptions of kings in Mesopotamian or Egyptian royal texts. The *Epic of Gilgamesh* might be the most approximate example of an ancient Near Eastern king who learned this kind of wisdom. But remember that Gilgamesh *ignores* the advice of Šiduri that is found almost verbatim in Ecclesiastes in favor of continuing his fruitless quest to Uta-napishti and eternal life. The similarity between Qohelet and Greek royal traditions, combined with the difference between the biblical book and ancient Near Eastern or Egyptian texts, makes a case for a point of contact between Qohelet and this Greek literary trope.

This connection also offers another explanation for Qohelet's use of הייתי in Eccl 1:12. Reading the verb as reference to an experience entirely in the past, to a time when Qohelet once was "king over Israel in Jerusalem," but is now no longer, makes him the former king sharing his similar wisdom with the reader. This was how the verse is read in Ecclesiastes Rabbah (1:12)

> אני קהלת הייתי מלך על ישראל . . . שלשה עולמות ראה בימיו ובחייו . . . מלך והדיוט ומלך חכם טפש וחכם עשיר עני ועשיר ומאי טעמא את הכל ראיתי בימי הבלי . . . הדיוט מלך והדיוט טפש וחכם וטפש עני עשיר ועני ומה טעם אני קהלת הייתי מלך על ישראל בירושלים
>
> "I, Qohelet, was king over Israel in Jerusalem" [Eccl 1:12] . . . He saw three worlds during the days of his life . . . as king, commoner, and king; as wise, foolish, and wise; as rich, poor, and rich. Where is this shown? "I have seen everything in my empty days [Eccl 7:15] . . . He had been a commoner, king, and commoner; foolish, wise, and foolish; poor, rich, and poor. What is the proof? "I, Qohelet, was king over Israel in Jerusalem" [Eccl 1:12].

Finally, it is important to note that these Greek texts that resemble Qohelet's royal self-description are ideologically charged. Greek gender constructions shape their portrayals of Persian kings as decadent, soft, undisciplined, unmanned by their wealth. The books of Daniel and Esther have similar descriptions of Persian kings. Similarly, Qohelet's self-loathing, despite all of his kingly wealth, and his equating himself with a fool, are parallels to the satiric portrayals of Darius and Ahasuerus in the Hebrew Bible and to the descriptions of Croesus and Sardanapallus in the Greek texts. Does this mean that the presence of orientalism in biblical texts is evidence of Greek influence? Johannes Haubold's analysis of Berossus's *Babyloniaca* demonstrates that Berossus, a Babylonian priest writing about Mesopotamian history and religion for a Greek audience, "taps into orientalizing Greek fictions about Mesopotamia" in his account.[74] A similar process might be argued for ancient Jewish authors, including Qohelet.

Conclusion

Once readers understand Qohelet as somebody other than Solomon, different interpretive challenges and opportunities arise. To read Qohelet as adopting a Solomonic guise raises questions about ancient authors and their use of irony and pseudonymity that still disturb modern readers for whom the biblical texts carry religious authority. If there is one aspect of how readers have read Qohelet as the author of Ecclesiastes that demonstrates the complexity of the book's authorial voice, it is his royal self-portrayal. Readers are not simply constructing an author out of a text but are trying to interpret how an author constructed a separate, but related, voice to present to readers. This strategy places a barrier between Qohelet the author and Qohelet the king. It also opens up a rich vein of interpretation as readers try to bridge the intentional gap between Qohelet the 4th to 3rd century BCE Jewish author and Qohelet the rich and powerful king who is unhappy with both his riches and his power. Echoes of ancient Near Eastern, Persian, and Hellenistic royal ideologies in Qohelet's self-description raise issues of cultural influence, and challenge readers to imagine a plausible process for such contact to occur.

Notes

1. Michel Foucault, "What Is an Author?" trans. Donald Bouchard and Sherry Simon in Theresa Enos and Stuart C. Brown, eds., *Professing the New Rhetorics: A Sourcebook* (Englewood Cliffs, NJ: Prentice Hall, 1994) 178–93, 184; trans. of "Qu'est ce qu'un auteur?" *Bulletin de la société française de philosophie* 63 (1969): 73–104.
2. I am aware that there are many scholars who are also believers, and that theology and exegesis often overlap.
3. For the discussion in these next few paragraphs I am treading a similar path as Eric S. Christianson (*Ecclesiastes through the Centuries*, Blackwell Bible Commentaries [Malden, MA: Blackwell, 2007] 95–8). I will note those places where we diverge and where I am indebted to him.
4. See the discussion in Marc Hirshman, "The Greek Fathers and the Aggada on Ecclesiastes: Formats of Exegesis in Late Antiquity," *HUCA* 59 (1988): 143–7.
5. *Commentary on Ecclesiastes*, 7.9 in Gerhard Binder and Leo Liesenborghs, *Didymos der Blinde: Kommentar zum Ecclesiastes (Tura-Papyrus) Teil I.1* (Bonn: Rudolf Habelt Verlag, 1979) 16.
6. *Commentary on Ecclesiastes*, 7.9–32 in Binder and Liesenborghs, *Didymos der Blinde*, 16–19.
7. Compare Christianson (*Ecclesiastes through the Centuries*, 95) who reads Didymus as denying Solomonic authorship.
8. The commentary ends midway on the recto of page 362 of P. Köln Theol. Inv. 51 with no evidence that there is anything missing.
9. διὰ τὴν δυναμένην οὖν ἐκ ψευδεπιγραφιάς ἀπάτην γενέσθαι κεῖται καὶ τὸ γένος καὶ ἡ ἀρχὴ καὶ τὸ ἔθνος καὶ ἡ πόλις. συνδραμεῖν δὲ ἅμα πάντα ἀδύνατον ἐστιν. (Binder and Liesenborghs, *Didymos der Blinde*, 24, at the end of the discussion of pseudepigraphy on 20–4).
10. With apologies to all who love Shakespeare.
11. "Ego tamen Solomonis esse non puto, sed scriptum serius sub illius Regis, tamquam poenitentia ducti, nomine. Argumentum eius rei habeo multa vocabula, quae non alibi quam in Daniele, Esdra et Chaldaeis interpretibus reperias" (*Annotationes in Vetus Testamentum* in *Hugonis Grotii Opera omnia theologica, in tres tomos divisa, ante quidem per partes, nunc autem conjunctim et accuratius edita, curis Petri Grotii*, 4 vols. [London: Moses Pitt, 1679] 1.258).
12. James Turner, *Philology: The Forgotten Origins of the Modern Humanities* (Princeton, NJ: Princeton University Press, 2014). This attention I have given to Turner's analysis is important because it offers necessary and helpful context to many of the readings I describe in this chapter.
13. The theses of Spinoza and Simon did not come out of the blue, but relied upon earlier Jewish and Catholic exegesis, respectively (Jean-Louis, Ska, *Introduction to Reading the Pentateuch*, trans. P. Dominique (Winona Lake, IN: Eisenbrauns, 2006) 101–2; ET of *Introduzione alla lettura del Pentateuco. Chiavi per l'interpretazione dei primi cinque libri della Bibbia* (Edizioni Dehoniane: Rome, 1996). Interestingly, Spinoza says nothing about the Solomonic authorship of Ecclesiastes.
14. Discussion of Geddes and Gesenius in Turner, *Philology*, 214–16. In describing biblical studies during this period (the first half of the 19th century), Turner notes the problem

of focusing on philology "insofar as one can untangle philology and theology" (210). For more on Geddes, see Andrew Landale Drummond, "Alexander Geddes 1737–1802: Roman Catholic Priest and Higher Critic in the Age of Reason," *Historical Magazine of the Protestant Episcopal Church* 35 (1966): 73–85.

15. "Whether Ecclesiastes was, in fact, written by Solomon or whether another inspired author made the wise man speak . . ." Translation by Terry McWilliams and analysis by Eric Christianson in Eric Christianson, "Voltaire's *Precis* of Ecclesiastes: A Case Study in the Bible's Afterlife," *JSOT* 29 (2005): 455–84. In a letter from March 1761, Voltaire refers to Qohelet as "the good Jewish deist who took the name of Solomon." (Christianson, *Ecclesiastes through the Centuries*, 124).
16. *Philology*, 218, 231, 357–9. By1900 "the Bible *merited* study mainly because of its religious significance . . . The place of biblical philology in the changing institutional structure of universities reflected this increasingly awkward fit with other studies descended from philology. Biblical criticism gradually floated away from secularizing centers of academic research, into separate theological faculties, divinity schools, even stand-alone theological seminaries . . . Thus, as biblical criticism itself became discipline-like, methods that once bound it to other forms of textual philology no longer linked it to humanistic disciplines with the same ancestry" (359).
17. *Philology*, 226.
18. This didn't prevent some from arguing for the historicity of Jonah's visit to Nineveh and the city's subsequent repentance (Thomas M. Bolin, *Freedom beyond Forgiveness: The Book of Jonah Re-Examined*, JSOTSup 236 [Sheffield: Sheffield Academic Press, 1997] 33–6).
19. Some still argued over Solomonic authorship of Ecclesiastes. For some quotations from these scholars, see Christianson, *Ecclesiastes through the Centuries*, 97.
20. See the history in John Rogerson, *Old Testament Criticism in the Nineteenth Century: England and Germany* (London: SCM, 1984). For a discussion of these conflicts in Catholic circles, see Thomas M. Bolin, "The Biblical Commission's Instruction, *On the Historical Truth of the Gospels* (*Sancta Mater Ecclesia*) and Present Magisterial Attitudes Toward Biblical Exegesis," *Gregorianum* 93 (2012): 765–85.
21. George A. Barton, *A Critical and Exegetical Commentary on the Book of Ecclesiastes*, ICC (Edinburgh: T & T Clark, 1908) 21.
22. Joannes Aurifaber, *Tischreden; oder, Colloquia Doct. Mart. Luthers mit einem Nachwort von Johannes Adler* (Eisleben: Gaubisch, 1566) 128.
23. The tradition history of the *Tischreden* would fascinate any biblical scholar. Christian Ginsburg quotes the German as "So hat Salomo selbst das Buch den Prediger, nicht geschreiben sondern es ist zur Zeit der Macabbäer von Sirach gemacht . . . Dazu so ist wie ein Talmud aus vielen Büchern zusammengezogen, vielleicht aus der Liberei des Königs Ptolemäus Euergetes in Aegypten" (*Coheleth, Commonly Called the Book of Ecclesiastes* [London: Longman, Green, Longman and Roberts, 1861] 113). Ginsburg cites the German edition of the *Tischreden* of K. E. Förstemann and H. E. Bindseil, based on the Aurifaber edition cited in the previous note (*D. Martin Luthers Tischreden oder Colloquia nach Aurifaber's erster Ausgabe*, 4 vols. [Berlin: Gebauer'sche Buchhandlung,1844–1848]. The St. Louis edition of the *Tischreden* (Johannes Georg Walch, *Dr. Martin Luther's Sämmtliche Schriften* [St. Louis: Concordia Publishing House, N.D.] 22:1411) contains a corrected version. But the critical edition of the *Tischreden* known as the Weimarer Ausgabe omits the logion altogether (*Dr. Martin Luthers Werke: Kritische Gesamtausgabe, Tischreden*, 6 vols. [Weimar: Hermann Bohlaus, 1912–1921] 2:653) as does the standard English translation (Theodore Tapett, *Table Talk*, Luther's Works 54 [Philadelphia: Fortress Press, 1967]). Compare the discussion in Christianson, *Ecclesiastes through the Centuries*, 95 and the detailed description of the problem in Gottfried Wachler, "The Inspiration and Inerrancy of Scripture: An Examination of Hermann Sasse's Sacra Scriptura Based on the History

of Doctrinal Theology and Dogmatics," *Wisconsin Lutheran Quarterly*, 81 (1984): no pages. Compare the discussion in Christians, *Ecclesiastes through the Centuries*, 95.

24. William Hamilton Bart, *Discussions on Philosophy and Literature: Education and University Reform* (New York: Harper and Brothers, 1861) 493. A modern citation of this logion is Dominic Rudman, *Determinism in the Book of Ecclesiastes*, JSOTSup 316 (Sheffield: Sheffield Academic Press, 2001) 12.
25. Franz Delitzsch, *Biblischer Commentar Über Die Poetischen Bücher des Alten Testaments Vierter Band: Hoheslied und Koheleth* (Leipzig: Dörffling and Franke, 1875) 196–7. Discussion of Delitzsch's scholarship in the context of 19th-century exegesis is in Rogerson, *Old Testament Criticism in the Nineteenth Century*, 111–20.
26. "Erst die Reformation rief mit der Kritik der dogmatischen Traditionen zugleich auch die biblische Kritik ins Dasein und erhob diese zu einem wesentlichen Bestandtheil der Schriftwissenschaft" (Delitzsch, *Hoheslied und Koheleth*, 196).
27. Edward H. Plumptre, *Ecclesiastes, or the Preacher*, Cambridge Bible for Schools and Colleges (Cambridge: Cambridge University Press, 1888) 22–3. Earlier than either Plumptre or Delitzsch, Carl Peter Wilhelm Gramberg dated Ecclesiastes to the Hellenistic period (*Kritische Geschichte der Religionsideen des alten Testaments*, 2 vols. [Berlin: n.p., 1830] discussed in Rogerson, *Old Testament Criticism in the Nineteenth Century*, 58–9).
28. For example, J. Stafford Wright, "Interpretation of Ecclesiastes," *EvQ* 18 (1946): 18–34; Derek Kidner, *The Wisdom of Proverbs, Job and Ecclesiastes: An Introduction to Wisdom Literature* (Downers Grove, IL: InterVarsity, 1985) 106; Craig Bartholomew, *Reading Ecclesiastes: Old Testament Exegesis and Hermeneutical Theory*, AnBib 139 (Rome: Editrice Pontificio Istituto Biblico, 1998) 38; *idem*, *Ecclesiastes* (Grand Rapids, MI: BCOTWP, 2009) 44; Sidney Greidanus, *Preaching Christ from Ecclesiastes* (Grand Rapids, MI: Eerdmans, 2010) 7; August Konkel and Tremper Longman, III, *Job, Ecclesiastes, Song of Songs*, Cornerstone Biblical Commentary 6 (Carol Stream, IL: Tyndale House, 2006) 254.
29. The most recent extensive discussion of Solomonic authorship is Tremper Longman's. Writing for an evangelical readership, Longman goes to the effort of listing all of the exegetes of "impeccably conservative credentials" who also denied the Solomonic authorship of the book (*The Book of Ecclesiastes*, NICOT [Grand Rapids, MI: Eerdmans, 1998] 4).
30. Ginsburg, *Coheleth*, 252–3. The 1908 commentary of Barton, *The Book of Ecclesiastes* is another such example.
31. Ginsburg, *Coheleth*, 113.
32. "Etenim una est universi operis forma, unum et simplex argumentum, de rerum humanarum vanitate, sub persona Salomonis, in perdifficili quaestione dubitantis, in utramque partem disputantis, et ex ancipiti cogitandi cura sese tandem expedientis." (*De sacra poesi hebraeorum* [Oxford: Clarendon, 1753] 239).
33. "For the whole work is uniform, and confined to one subject, namely, the vanity of the world exemplified by the experience of Solomon; who is introduced in the character of a person investigating a very difficult question, examining the arguments on either side, and at length disengaging himself from an anxious and doubtful disputation." (*Lectures on the Sacred Poetry of the Hebrews Translated from the Latin by G. Gregory to Which Are Added the Principal Notes of Professor Michaelis and Notes By the Translator and Others*, 4th ed. [London: Thomas Tegg, 1849] 270).
34. Lewis and Short render "sub persona" as: "a personage, character, part, represented by an actor . . . the part or character which any one sustains in the world" (Charlton T. Lewis and Charles Short, *A Latin Dictionary* (Oxford: Clarendon Press, 1879) s.v., "persona").
35. Y. V. Koh reads Lowth as outright denying Solomonic authorship of Ecclesiastes (*Royal Autobiography in the Book of Qoheleth*, BZAW 369 [Berlin: De Gruyter, 2006] 10).

36. Oswald Loretz, *Qohelet und der Alte Orient: Untersuchungen zu Stil und theologischer Thematik des Buches Qohelet* (Freiburg: Herder, 1964) 144.
37. *Ecclesiastes*, AB 18C (New York: Doubleday, 1997) 37. Elsewhere in the same volume Seow writes: “There can be no doubt that the text intends to evoke the memory of the king . . . It is clear, too, from Qoheleth’s self-portrait in 1:12–2:11 that he had Solomon in mind” (*ibid.*, 97–8). The shift from Seow’s use of “probably” in the quotation from page 37 to his use of “no doubt” and “clear” in the second quotation is noteworthy. Anton Schoors is also certain of Qohelet’s Solomonic mask, writing that the superscription in 1:1 “no doubt, signifies Solomon” (*Ecclesiastes*, HCOT [Leuven: Peeters, 2013] 29). Schoors will go farther and state that he is certain that the ancient readers of Ecclesiastes would have noticed and understood this role-play (*ibid.*, 105).
38. Jennie Barbour, *The Story of Israel in the Book of Qohelet: Ecclesiastes as Cultural Memory*, Oxford Theological Monographs (Oxford: Oxford University Press, 2012) 169.
39. Barbour, *The Story of Israel in the Book of Qohelet*, 28.
40. Eva Mroczek, *The Literary Imagination in Jewish Antiquity* (New York: Oxford University Press, 2016) 38.
41. Mroczek, *The Literary Imagination in Jewish Antiquity*, 56.
42. Thomas Krüger, *Qoheleth*, Hermeneia (Philadelphia: Fortress Press, 2004) 11, 62. Schoors also uses the phrase “royal travesty” (*Ecclesiastes*, 105).
43. Norbert Lohfink, *Qoheleth*, trans. Sean McEvenue, CC (Minneapolis, MN: Fortress Press, 2003) 44 trans. of *Kohelet*, NEchtB (Würzburg: Echter Verlag, 1980). “Through use of this masquerade in which a person is presented in a higher social level, it is possible, without forfeiting the advantages of narrative presentation, to base an anthropology not on the experiences of people who fail to grow or achieve anything in life, but rather on the experiences of the highest human possibility, in the most fortunate world situations, joyfully lived. This makes only more devastating what then appears” (ibid.)
44. For an overview, see Izak Spangenberg, “Irony in the Book of Qohelet,” *JSOT* 72 (1996): 57–69.
45. Carolyn Sharp, “Ironic Representation, Authorial Voice, and Meaning in Qohelet,” *BibInt* 12 (2004): 37–68. Regarding Qohelet’s royal autobiography, Sharp notes: “‘Qohelet’ grounds his authority to speak, to teach, concretely in his personal identity and experience. He is a ‘son of David,’ a ‘king over Israel in Jerusalem’ (1:12) and has done all that a king can do, from constructing a magnificent court to amassing riches to indulging in pleasures of the flesh. In fact, he has done ‘more than all the kings who were before’ him in Jerusalem (2:9). Ah—more than all one of them (or all two of them, if one allows Saul into the lineage, construing ‘in Jerusalem’ more loosely)?” (51).
46. *KAI* 181, 214, and 14, respectively. These and other examples in Koh, *Royal Autobiography*, 74–7.
47. Koh, *Royal Autobiography*, 37, and also 28–9. See also Martin Shields, “Qohelet and Royal Autobiography,” in *The Words of the Wise Are like Goads: Engaging Qohelet in the 21st Century*, eds. Mark J. Boda, Tremper Longman III, and Cristian G. Rata (Winona Lake, IN: Eisenbrauns, 2013) 117–36.
48. Of the three examples in Koh (*Royal Autobiography*, 74–6) that I have not cited, only one (Zakkur, *KAI* 202) matches Eccl 1:12 with mention only of the land over which the king rules: *ʾnh zkr mlk ḥmt*.
49. *Ecclesiastes*, 119, so too Bo Isaksson, *Studies in the Language of Qoheleth, with Special Emphasis on the Verbal System*, Studia Semitica Upsaliensia (Uppsala: University of Uppsala Press, 1987) 50; and Koh: “Read against the background of West Semitic royal inscriptions, the verb הָיִיתִי in Qoheleth’s opening self-introduction should be understood to indicate a present state which has its beginning in the past” (*Royal Autobiography*, 78).

50. Schoors, *Ecclesiastes*, 61; see also Schoors, "The Verb *hāyâ* in Qoheleth," in *Shall Not the Judge of All the Earth Do What Is Right? Studies on the Nature of God in Tribute to James L. Crenshaw*, eds. David Penchansky and Paul L. Redditt (Winona Lake, IN: Eisenbrauns, 2000) 230.
51. Koh, *Royal Autobiography*, 79.
52. This leads Koh to attempt some tenuous connections, for example, the claim that "wisdom might be said to be implied in the king's successful administration of the land" to explain the lack of specific mention of wisdom in royal inscriptions (*Royal Autobiography*, 87).
53. For the growth and development of the epic, see the discussion in Andrew R. George, *The Babylonian Gilgamesh Epic: Introduction, Critical Edition, and Cuneiform Texts*, 2 vols. (Oxford: Oxford University Press, 2003) 1. 3–70.
54. *at-ta* ^{d}GIŠ *lu ma-li ka-ra-aš-ka, ur-ri ù mu-ši ḫi-ta-ad-dú at-ta,* $_{u}$*4-mi-ša-am šu-ku-un ḫi-du-tam, ur-ri ù mu-ši su-ur ù me-li-il, lu ub-bu-bu ṣú ba*!(KU)*-tu-ka, qá-qá-ad-ka lu me-si me-e lu ra-am-ka-ta, ṣú-ub-bi ṣe-eḫ-ra-am ṣa-bi-tu qá-ti-ka, mar-ḫi-tum li-iḫ-ta ad-da-a-am i-na su-ni-ka* (George, *The Babylonian Gilgamesh Epic*, 1. 272–86, transliteration and quotation on 1. 278–9).
55. See discussion of arguments both for and against influence in Christoph Uehlinger, "Qohelet im Horizont mesopotamischer, levantinischer und ägyptischer Weisheitsliteratur der persischen und hellenistischen Zeit," in *Das Buch Kohelet: Studien zur Struktur, Geschichte, Rezeption, und Theologie*, ed. Ludger Schweinhorst-Schönberger, BZAW 254 (Berlin: De Gruyter, 1997) 155–247; Johan Y.-S. Pahk, "Qohelet e le Tradizioni Sapienziali del Vicino Oriente Antico," in *Il Libro Del Qohelet: Tradizione, redazione, teologia*, eds. Giuseppe Bellia and Angelo Passaro, Cammini nello Spirito Biblica 44 (Milan: Paulist, 2001) 117–43. For an extended dialogue between the *Epic of Gilgamesh* and Qohelet see William P. Brown *Ecclesiastes*, IBC (Louisville, KY: John Knox Press, 2000) 1–7 and see the discussion in Thomas M. Bolin, "Rivalry and Resignation: Girard on Qoheleth and the Divine-Human Relationship," *Bib* 86 (2005): 245–59.
56. Koh, *Royal Autobiography*, 117. Reference to the *Epic of Gilgamesh* is relegated to a footnote on page 123.
57. See discussion in Joseph Ryan Kelly, "Sources of Contention and the Emerging Reality Concerning Qohelet's *Carpe Diem* Advice," *Antiguo Oriente* 8 (2010): 117–34.
58. Nili Samet, "The Gilgamesh Epic and the Book of Qohelet: A New Look, *Biblica* 96 (2015): 375–90. Eva Mroczek argues that the presence of Aramaisms in Ecclesiates has been overstated ("'Aramaisms' in Qohelet: Methodological Problems in Identification and Interpretation," in *The Words of the Wise Are like Goads*, 343–63.
59. Koh, *Royal Autobiography*, 143; Shields, "Qohelet and Royal Autobiography," 134–5.
60. First argued in Kurt Galling, "Koheleth-Studien," *ZAW* 50 (1932): 276–99.
61. Text and discussion for both writings are in *AEL* 1.97–109, 135–9. Discussion in Koh, *Royal Autobiography*, 123–39.
62. For example, Seow, *Ecclesiastes*, 98; Krüger, *Qoheleth*, 11, Michael V. Fox, *A Time to Tear Down and a Time to Build Up: A Rereading of Ecclesiastes* (Grand Rapids, MI: Eerdmans, 1999) 153–5.
63. In discussion and critique of this approach, Shannon Burkes lists as points of contact "royal authorship, a dialogue with one's heart, pessimism, carpe diem advice, references to female singers, ideas of the time and season, social injustice, counsel to keep one's words few when in worship, reversal of social positions, and the description of old age" (*Death in Qoheleth and Egyptian Biographies of the Late Period*, SBLDS 170 [Atlanta, GA: Society of Biblical Literature, 1999] 90).
64. William M. Schniedewind, *A Social History of Hebrew: Its Origins through the Rabbinic Period*, ABRL (New Haven, CT: Yale University Press, 2013) 56–60.
65. This is, I think, at bottom the problem in Koh's otherwise able assembly and discussion of a large set of texts.

66. For example, Krüger will argue that Ecclesiastes is drawing upon the Egyptian *sebayit* and the Mesopotamian ideology of a king boasting that he is greater than predecessors (*Qoheleth*, 11, 64). Seow also compares the Eccl 1:1 to Egyptian *sebayit* and Eccl 1:12 to West Semitic royal introductions (*Ecclesiastes*, 98, 119).
67. Seow, *Ecclesiastes*, 25–6. I have discussed this in detail in Thomas M. Bolin, "Qohelet and the Covenant: Some Preliminary Observations," in *Covenant in the Persian Period: From Genesis to Chronicles*, eds. Richard J. Bautch and Gary N. Knoppers (Eisenbrauns, 2015) 357–67, and the following remarks draw on that.
68. Pierre Briant, *From Cyrus to Alexander: A History of the Persian Empire*, trans. Peter T. Daniels (Winona Lake, IN: Eisenbrauns, 2002) 307–15; trans. of *Histoire de l'Empire perse: de Cyrus à Alexandre* (Paris: Fayard, 1996).
69. Briant, *From Cyrus to Alexander*, 317–18.
70. The title, "great king, king of kings, king of all the lands" is used as far back as neo-Assyrian kings in the 9th century BCE and adopted by Cyrus the Great in his Babylonian cylinder inscription. Examples of Persian kings' use of it in Amélie Kuhrt, *The Persian Empire: A Corpus of Sources from the Achaemenid Period* (New York: Routledge, 2007), 71 (Cyrus), 141 (Darius I) 244 (Xerxes I), 406–7 (Artaxerxes III).
71. All of these texts cited and discussed in Kuhrt, *The Persian Empire*, 576–614.
72. Compare the final choral verses from Sophocles, *Oedipus the King*: ὥστε θνητὸν ὄντα κείνην τὴν τελευταίαν ἰδεῖν | ἡμέραν ἐπισκοποῦντα μηδέν' ὀλβίζειν, πρὶν ἂν | τέρμα τοῦ βίου περάσῃ μηδὲν ἀλγεινὸν παθών (*Oed. tyr.* 1528–30; see the translation by Robert Fagles: "Now as we keep our watch and wait the final day | count no man happy till he dies, free of pain at last" [*Sophocles: Three Theban Plays*, rev. ed. [New York: Penguin, 1984] 251).
73. For a more detailed description of the Sardanapallus traditions, see Thomas M. Bolin, "'Should I Not also Pity Nineveh?'—Divine Freedom in the Book of Jonah," *JSOT* 67 (1995): 109–20.
74. Johannes Haubold, *Greece and Mesopotamia: Dialogues in Literature* (Cambridge: Cambridge University Press, 2013) 16, 142–77.

3 Qohelet and Contradiction

In "Song of Myself," Walt Whitman famously boasts, "Do I contradict myself? Very well then, I contradict myself."[1] With this statement Whitman deliberately thwarts his reader's expectation that the poem about "myself" will be free from contradiction. On the contrary, Whitman revels in contradiction, and in pointing that out to the reader in a singular, powerful voice that remains a constant presence in the poem, he creates yet another.[2] Readers expect authors to be coherent, even though that is not often the case. This expectation lies behind Horace's famous remark about when Homer "nods."

> Indignor quandoque bonus dormitat Homerus.
> I find it unseemly when good Homer sleeps.
>
> (*Ars* 358)

Horace's use of "indignor" embraces a range of meanings at work in the line. It can express the idea of finding something unworthy, as I have rendered it here. Read this way, Horace finds the contradictions in Homer (places in the poems where he has "slept") to be unworthy of the great poet. "Indignor" can also mean to be outraged or offended at, so Horace can also be read as expressing anger at having Homer thwart his expectations as a reader by contradicting himself.[3] In chapter one I touched on the contradictions in Ecclesiastes in the course of my discussion of how readers use an externally constructed biography of Solomon to interpret the book. In this chapter I examine the various interpretive nodes realized by readings of Ecclesiastes intended to directly address its contradictions.

On Coherence and Contradiction Once More

Among the uses Foucault gives for the author function is that of acting "as a principle of unity in writing," which explains "unevenness of production" and "neutralizes the contradictions" in texts. This is based on

> the belief that there must be—at a particular level of an author's thought, of his conscious and unconscious desire—a point where contradictions are resolved,

> where the incompatible elements can be shown to relate to one another or to cohere around a fundamental and originating contradiction.[4]

Foucault is referring in particular to contradictions in a body of works attributed to one author. But because contradictions in a single work strike readers as odd, given that readers assume a single, coherent presence to lie behind texts, Foucault's observation applies equally to how contradictions within a single work are addressed by appeal to the author.

I want to begin by revisiting in more detail the discussion in the Babylonian Talmud (b. Šabb. 30b) about contradictions in Ecclesiastes.

> אמר רב יהודה דרב שמואל בר שילת משמיה דרב בקשו חכמים לגנוז ספר קהלת מפני שדבריו סותרין זה את זה ומפני מה לא גנזוהו מפני שתחילתו דברי תורה וסופו דברי תורה תחילתו דברי תורה דכתיב מה יתרין לאדם בכל עמלו שיעמול תחת השמש ואמרי דבי ינאי תחת השמש הוא דאין לו קודם שמש יש לו סופו דברי תורה דכתיב סוף דבר הכל נשמע את אלהים ירא ואת מצותיו שמור כי זה כל האדם . . . ומאי דבריו סותרין זה את זה כתיב טוב כעס משחוק וכתיב לשחוק אמרתי מהלל כתיב ושבחתי אני את השמחה וכתיב ולשמחה מה זה עושה
>
> Rab Judah son of R. Samuel b. Shilath said in Rab's name, "The sages wished to put away the book of Ecclesiastes because its words contradict each other." So why didn't they put it away? Because its beginning and end contain words of Torah. Its beginning contains words of Torah where it is written, "What does a person gain from all the toil with which he toils under the sun?" [Eccl 1:3]. The students of R. Jannai said, "Under the sun there is none, but before the sun there is." Its end contains words of Torah where it is written, "The end of the matter; all has been heard. Fear God and keep his commandments for this is everything for everyone" [Eccl 12:13] . . . And how do its words contradict each other? It is written, "Sorrow is better than laughter" [Eccl 7:3] but it is written, "I say of laughter that it is praiseworthy"[5] [Eccl 2:2]. It is written, "Then I commend joy" [8:15], but it is written "And joy, what good is it?" [Eccl 2:2]

Notice that the resolution of *all* potential contradictions precedes the examples of specific contradictions. As I mentioned in chapter one, for the rabbis the placement of "words of Torah" at the beginning and end of Ecclesiastes suffices to neutralize any problems with the contents in between. These "words of Torah" function as a fence or boundary, limiting any potential harmful meanings of the words they enclose.[6] Nevertheless, in the continuation of the text (not quoted here) the contradictions cited are resolved anyway by means of equivocation: Qohelet is really talking about two different kinds of laughter and joy respectively, one being good while the other is bad. I discuss this further in chapter four.

Modern scholars of biblical wisdom literature might say that coherence is an unreasonable expectation of proverbial literature. The very nature of proverbs—short and of necessity, widely applicable—means that any written collection of them will be an artificial arrangement, made often for ease of access or memorization. Evidence for this in the Bible is in the placement of two proverbs side by side that argue the exact opposite course of action

אל תען כסיל כאולתו פן תשוה לו גם אתה
ענה כסיל כאולתו פן יהיה חכם בעיניו

> Do not answer a fool according to his folly, lest you look like him.
> Answer a fool according to his folly, lest he think himself to be wise.
> (Prov 26:4–5)

On one level, there is a Janus-style parallelism at work in these two proverbs. In the first, responding to the fool makes you seem similar to him. In the second, not responding to the fool will lead him to think that he is like you. It's a clever juxtaposition and exactly the kind of thematic arrangement that is found elsewhere in Proverbs. But that does not change the fact that the actual advice being given is contradictory. Returning to b. Šabb. 30b, after resolving the contradictions in Ecclesiastes, the rabbis turn their attention to this very text.

> ואף ספר משלי בקשו לגנז שהיו דבריו סותרין זה את זה שמפני מה לא גנזהו אמרי ספר קהלת לאו עיינינן ואשכחינן טעמא הכא נמי ליעיינן ומאי דבריו סותרים זה את זה כתיב אל תען כסיל כאולתו וכתיב ענה כסיל כאולתו
>
> They also wished to put away the book of Proverbs because its words contradict each other. So why didn't they put it away? They said, "We searched the book of Ecclesiastes and uncovered sound reasoning. Let us search here." And how do its words contradict each other? It is written, "Do not answer a fool according to his folly" [Prov 26:4] but it is written, "Answer a fool according to his folly." [Prov 26:5][7]

The contradictory statements in Prov 26, like Whitman's open confession of contradiction, demand our attention as readers and challenge us to address them head on. But even when contradictions in a text are not as explicit—or even intentional—readers notice them. In b.Šabb. 30b the cited contradictions in Ecclesiastes are between 2:2a and 7:3, and between 2:2b and 8:15.[8] The distance between these contradictory statements, while granted not great, demonstrates that the rabbis read Ecclesiastes with the expectation that the entire book ought to cohere in some way. At the same time, their unease at the fact that the book does not easily seem to cohere is evident in the appeal to the normative "words of Torah" that frame the potentially problematic text.

The contradictions in Ecclesiastes have not only exercised ancient readers. A good number of modern biblical scholars have also struggled with them.[9] More than any other chapter in this book, the nodes I describe in this chapter show the importance of Brennan Breed's method of reception history, which reveals how modern, scholarly interpretations are similar to those of the past. The most obvious proof of this is the fact that readings that thought Solomon to have written

Ecclesiastes are grouped with those that deny Solomonic authorship. The issue of Solomonic authorship is the distinguishing characteristic of modern, scholarly readings of Ecclesiastes, but here it plays little, if any, role in how the text itself is read.

Many attempts to resolve incoherence posit multiple speakers for the multiple voices of a text's contradictions so that contradictory elements are sorted and assigned to different voices, each of which is consistent. Three different ways of doing this are prevalent among readers of Ecclesiastes.[10] One is to claim that the text has been amended by other writers. A second is to classify contradictory statements as quotations by Qohelet that he refutes. Closely related to this approach is a reading that sees Qohelet assuming the identity of somebody else for rhetorical purposes.

There Are Editors

One of the earliest readers to see more than one author at work in Ecclesiastes is the 12th-century CE Jewish commentator Rashbam, who notes that the book's opening and final verses are not by Qohelet.

> שתי מקראות דברי קהלת הבל הבלים לא אמרן קהלת כי אם אותו שסידר הדברים כמות שהן
>
> These two verses [Eccl 1:1–2], "The words of Qoheleth," [and] "Vanity of vanities," were not said by Qoheleth but by the person who edited the words as they stand.
>
> הבל הבלים עכשיו נשלם הספר ואותן אשר סידרוהו אמרו מיכאן
>
> "Vanity of vanities" [Eccl 12:8]. Now the book is completed. Those who edited it speak from now on.[11]

Rashbam's term translated as "editor" (סידר) includes the idea of arranging the sequence of material and not just collecting and adding an opening. As I discussed in the introduction, Breed's understanding of reception history problematizes the neat distinction biblical scholars have long made between a text's composition and its history of interpretation.[12] This is something modern readers cannot easily imagine because we think of a literary piece as a single work with a single author. For example, one glorious day in the near future, I will type the last mark on the manuscript of this book, and it will be "finished."[13] Ancient literary works were not produced in this way, even when they are connected with an author who can be historically identified in time and place.[14]

Martin Luther also described Ecclesiastes as an edited work, here in his 1524 preface to the book:

> As they [the scholars who recorded Solomon's statements] themselves admit at the end of the book where they say, "These words of the wise are like goads and nails, fixed by the masters of the congregation and given by one shepherd" [Eccl 12:11]. That is to say, certain persons were at that time appointed to fix and arrange this and other books that were handed down by Solomon, the one

> shepherd. They did this so that not everyone would have to be making books as he pleased, as they also lament in that same place "of the making of books there is no end" [Eccl 12:2]; they forbid the acceptance of others.[15]

Like Rashbam, Luther reads the epilogue as the words of someone other than the author of the book and that they did more than preserve they book. They "fixed and arranged" it, editing in the same way denoted by Rashbam's use of סידר.

It is modern biblical scholarship that engages the most in finding evidence of editorial activity in the Bible. The field's roots lie in the questioning of the traditional authorship of biblical books. The entry points were the contradictions, specifically in the Pentateuch. These were resolved by sorting out doublets and assigning them to different, hypothetical authors based on the specious assumption that each author would only use one particular term for things in the narrative, such as the deity (Yahweh or Elohim) or the mountain of the god (Sinai or Horeb). This assumption is founded upon a more basic one that authors are individuals who create singular works and that individuality admits no contradiction. Whitman laughs. Because this method appeared to work with the Pentateuch, it was applied to practically every text in the Hebrew Bible, Ecclesiastes included.[16] Representative examples of elaborate redactional hypotheses for Ecclesiastes are the works of Paul Haupt and George Barton, both writing in the first decade of the 20th century CE.

Haupt's introduction to his verse translation of Ecclesiastes is a tour de force.[17] He identifies the original author as "a prominent Sadducean physician in Jerusalem," who ascribed to Epicurean philosophy.[18] The original form of Ecclesiastes was left unfinished at the author's death, but his friends completed it and out of fear of religious opprobrium, published it under Solomon's name. However, the book was deemed too dangerous by "Pharisaic authorities" who both added material to the text and rearranged it. Additions were made because, "several of the most objectionable statements are less offensive if preceded or followed by orthodox glosses and scattered through the less questionable sections."[19]

Barton first separates all the third-person material (1:1, 7:27, 12:8–12:13) from the first-person texts. With what is left, he follows Haupt in isolating three different hands. His method illustrates perfectly the issue of consistency under discussion in this chapter:

> Are there any utterances so contradictory they could not have been uttered by the same mind? . . . Through the first two chapters the thought flows on connectedly . . . until we come to 2:26, when we suddenly come upon a sentiment which is in direct contradiction to most of the statements which have preceded it in the chapter, and which contains the orthodox Jewish doctrine of rewards and punishments. *It is inconceivable* that a writer should say in the same chapter, that the wise man and the fool have the same fate and that there is no good but eating and drinking and enjoying one's self and also say that God punishes the sinner and rewards the good. *We accordingly are compelled to*

> *conclude* that 2:26 comes from the hand of a Chasid or Jewish orthodox glossator, whose philosophy of life was that of the Pharisees. (italics mine)[20]

Significantly, only one writer in Barton's reconstruction—Qohelet—is a *bona fide* author. The other two hands are "glossators," one a sage who added proverbs to the text and connected Qohelet with Solomon, the other a Pharisee who sought to undermine Qohelet's thought and bring it more in line with "orthodox" teaching.[21] The ideological biases of Barton and Haupt are hard to overlook. Authors are singular, creative geniuses whose work can be in no way culturally derivative or reflective of religious norms. Note that Barton extols Qohelet's text as "an original development of Hebrew thought," similar to philosophical breakthroughs in Greece such as Epicureanism. But at the same time, Qohelet is for Barton, "thoroughly Semitic," and hence, not dependent upon the Greeks.[22] "Glossators," in contrast to authors, are uncreative and tied to hidebound cultural structures (the wisdom tradition, "orthodox" religion). Barton's distinction between what is original and what is editorial is not based on evidence so much as it is on his own assumptions about what authors do and his own vulgar anti-Judaism.[23]

My discussion of Haupt and Barton is not intended to point out that redactional analysis of biblical texts is fraught with cultural and theological bias. It certainly is, and this has long been obvious. Examining their readings of Ecclesiastes brings to light the interpretive range of the text. For all the biases and assumptions Haupt and Barton bring to Ecclesiastes, they are not exclusively forcing an external meaning onto the text. The elements they use to construct their flawed editorial histories are there in the text. So too is the voice of Qohelet, which influences their reconstruction.

Haupt and Barton represent the high-water mark of readings that argue for multiple writers to account for the contradictory statements in Ecclesiastes, but this kind of reading does not entirely disappear. In standard works of the mid-20th century, Eccl 2:26, 3:17, 7:26b, 8:5b, 8:12b-13, 11:9b, and 12:7b are marked as "pious additions" added by someone with the intent to soften the sting of Qohelet's own thought.[24] With the exception of 12:7b, every one of these putative glosses expresses belief in a just God who punishes the evil/foolish and rewards the good/wise:

> כי לאדם שטוב לפניו נתן חכמה ודעת ושמחה ולחוטא נתן ענין לאסוף ולכנוס לתת לטוב לפני האלהים גם זה הבל ורעות רוח
>
> To the person who is good before him, [God] gives wisdom, knowledge, and joy. But to the sinner he gives the chore of gathering and piling up to give to the one who is good before God. This also is vanity, and a chasing after the wind. (2:26b)

> אמרתי אני בלבי את הצדיק ואת הרשע ישפט האלהים כי עת לכל חפץ ועל כל המעשה שם
>
> I said in my heart, "God will judge the righteous and the evil because there is a time for every pleasure and every task there."
> (3:17)

טוב לפני האלהים ימלט ממנה וחוטא ילכד בה

> The one who is good before God escapes her, while the sinner is captured by her.
>
> (7:26b)

שומר מצוה לא ידע דבר רע ועת ומשפט ידע לב חכם

> The one who keeps a commandment will not know any evil, and the heart of the wise knows the time and the judgment.
>
> (8:5b)

כי גם יודע אני אשר יהיה טוב ליראי האלהים אשר ייראו מלפניו
וטוב לא יהיה לרשע ולא יאריך ימים כצל אשר איננו ירא מלפני אלהים

> Because I know that it will be good to those who fear God, who are in reverence before him. But it will not be good for the evil who have no reverence before God, and they will not lengthen their days like a shadow.
>
> (8:12b-13)

ודע כי על כל אלה יביאך האלהים במשפט

> Know that for all of these things God will bring you to judgment.
>
> (11:9b)

Eccl 12:7b implies (for some readers) the idea of an afterlife:

והרוח תשוב אל האלהים אשר נתנה

> And the breath returns to God, who gave it.

The logic here is no different from that of Haupt and Barton. Authors are expected to be coherent. When they are not, redactional foul play is suspected. But notice also the ideological trajectory of editing described by these readings. A text deemed to be subversive by the *reader's* standards is determined to have been edited with the aim of reducing the text's challenge to the status quo. In contrast with authors who are daring and creative, editors are not true composers of texts because they dwell comfortably in their traditional cultural worldview.[25] The sum total of their activity is to temper or hedge in the creative genius of the author. But of course, true genius and development in thought—characterized by what a reader resonates with—can never be stifled forever. In the case of Ecclesiastes, an example of orthodox thinking is belief in a just deity, while deviations from it are read as challenges or attacks on the status quo. The latter viewpoint is accordingly assigned to an author and the former to an editor. A significant problem with this method is that it is difficult to determine what constitutes "orthodoxy" in the Hebrew Bible. Prophetic texts have Yahweh critique the efficacy of the very worship that he commands the Israelites to observe in the Pentateuch. Divine freedom takes precedence over justice throughout the biblical corpus, and not just in Ecclesiastes.[26]

While it makes sense to posit a dynamic tension among and within biblical texts in which competing theological positions engage in debate and polemic, it must be acknowledged that this is a reading strategy aimed at resolving contradictions. Another way of putting this is to say that, despite the dichotomy at work in the distinction between authors and editors, the net effect of positing one or more editors to a text is nothing less than to create new "authors" for it. I mean this in the sense that Foucault articulates: readers create personalities out of the text and then assign values to these personalities based on their own cultural assumptions. Nowhere is this more evident in Ecclesiastes than in regard to the book's epilogue, to which I now turn.

While recent scholarship in Ecclesiastes read the majority of the book as a whole, the exception is the last six verses.[27]

ויתר שהיה קהלת חכם עוד למד דעת את העם ואזן וחקר תקן משלים הרבה
בקש קהלת למצא דברי חפץ וכתוב ישר דברי אמת
דברי חכמים כדרבנות וכמשמרות נטועים בעלי אספות נתנו מרעה אחד
ויתר מהמה בני הזהר עשות ספרים הרבה אין קץ ולהג הרבה יגעת בשר
סוף דבר הכל נשמע את האלהים ירא ואת מצותיו שמור כי זה כל האדם
כי את כל מעשה האלהים יבא במשפט על כל נעלם אם טוב ואם רע

[9]In addition to being wise, Qohelet also taught the people knowledge.
He pondered, studied, and corrected many sayings.
[10]Qohelet sought to find pleasant words and he wrote the words of truth clearly.
[11]The words of the wise are like goads. Like fixed nails are the masters of collections[28] given by one shepherd.
[12]Beyond these things, my son, beware.[29] There is no end to the making of many books and in much study is the flesh wearied.
[13]The end of the thing. All has been heard. Fear God and keep his commandments because this is the whole thing for humankind,
[14]For God will bring to judgment every deed, every hidden thing, whether good or evil.

(Eccl 12:9–14)

Much as the verses within Ecclesiastes discussed above are seen as additions tacked on immediately after a theologically suspect saying of Qohelet's, and intended to counter or otherwise weaken them, for many readers the epilogue—in particular the final two verses[30]—functions as a repudiation of the entire work. Norbert Lohfink's observation is representative. The epilogue's final words advising the reader to observe the commandments "reduce the book of Qoheleth to a simple orthodox formula, which originates in Deuteronomy."[31] Notice Lohfink's value-laden language here: orthodoxy is simple and formulaic and its expression is a reduction of Qohelet's thought.[32] The recent article by Nili Samet contains a good deal of this loaded language. It refers to "the contradiction between the subversive ideas of vanity . . . and pious or conservative statements"; the epilogue's "strict religious agenda"; and Qohelet's attack on "conservative authoritative" religious answers. It characterizes the epilogue as "extremely conservative" and equates it with "traditional values." These normative qualifiers are asserted, not argued.[33] The epilogist and Qohelet are set at odds with each other. One represents conservatism or orthodoxy, the other a dangerous free thinker who needs to be neutralized. Both of these personalities and their tacit conflict in the pages of Ecclesiastes are created out of the text by readers who bring to it their own views regarding religious authority and control.

Not only does the epilogue tame Qohelet's thinking; for some readers, it is the reason the book was included in the canon. J.A. Loader claims:

> This redactor also unintentionally served the cause of his opponent, for his words at the end of the scroll formed one of the factors that contributed to the book's acceptance and retention in the list of holy Scriptures.[34]

The claim that the epilogue put Ecclesiastes in the canon creates a delicious historical irony for readers who equate orthodoxy with editors and theological daring with authors, because the pious editor's attempt to tame the book unwittingly allowed it to be preserved and its brilliant, unorthodox message to be admired. But the claim, without that particular ideological explanation, is found in Jerome, who notes in his commentary on Eccl 12:13–14

> Aiunt Hebraei cum inter caetera scripta Salomonis quae antiquata sunt, nec in memoria duraverunt, et hic liber oblitterandus videretur, eo quod vanas Dei assereret creaturas, et totum putaret esse pro nihilo, et cibum, et potum, et delicias transeuntes praeferret omnibus, ex hoc uno capitulo meruisse auctoritatem, ut in divinorum voluminum numero poneretur.
>
> The Hebrews say that, while it would appear that this book [Ecclesiastes] ought to be forgotten like those other writings of Solomon which have become obsolete and are no longer remembered, because it asserts the emptiness of God's creation, considers everything to be worthless, and prefers food, drink, and transitory pleasures to everything else, the power of this one passage [Eccl 12:13–14] makes it worthy to be numbered as one of the divine books.[35]

Jerome appears to be referring to a tradition similar to that in b. Šabb 30b discussed above,[36] and this reading in modern scholarship can be read as that ancient rabbinic debate reinscribed as historical data. The epilogue functions for modern readers as it did for the rabbis—a fence or wall that seeks to contain the dangerous contents behind it. But this retrieval of the rabbinic reading misunderstands it. There is no evidence that the epilogue played any role in the inclusion of Ecclesiastes in the canon. The rabbinic texts that speak of "putting away" (גנז) writings are not about their canonical status. The fact that the rabbis discuss Proverbs in b. Šabb. 30b is proof of that. No modern scholar would argue on the basis of that rabbinic text that the canonical status of Proverbs was in doubt, as they often do with Ecclesiastes.[37] The purpose of the rabbinic discussion is to model how one resolves contradictions in texts already accepted as authoritative. Historically, there is no evidence of a time when Ecclesiastes was not canonical, but because readers see parts of the book as theologically problematic—or groundbreaking—they construct literary and historical contexts with "orthodox" guardians pitted against Qohelet.

While many readers see the epilogue as the work of a hidebound traditionalist determined to counter Qohelet's challenge to the orthodox ancient Jewish religious belief (whatever that might be), others take the side of the epilogue's author and view him as the winner in a literary struggle with Qohelet. The book's final words act as a strong rebuke to all that has preceded it. In Martin Shields's jarring imagery:

> In essence, Qohelet is the epilogist's "straw man." But the epilogist does not go to great lengths to knock down the straw man, for—to employ a different illustration—the epilogist has given Qohelet sufficient rope, and he has hung himself. To the reader familiar with the remainder of the Old Testament, it is clear that the wisdom of Qohelet has gone astray . . . and is ultimately incompatible with the message of the remainder of the canon.[38]

For Shields, the epilogue's author is the normative voice in the book and any competent reader (i.e., "familiar with the remainder of the Old Testament") will see that it is "clear" that Qohelet is in the wrong. In his book-length treatment of Ecclesiastes, Shields goes so far as to say that the epilogist "is effectively the author of the work," thus moving him from the second-class status of redactor or "glossator" and to the exclusive company of a biblical author.[39]

The Author Quotes Himself

Shields's claim that the epilogist is the author of the entire work allows me to turn now to examine readings that do not rely on multiple writers to explain the contradictions in Ecclesiastes.[40] Several readings resolve the contradictions by classifying them as quotations of differing viewpoints cited by Qohelet, which he then refutes. For some readings, these are Qohelet's self-citations, where he looks back on how he once thought and realizes that he is wrong. The LXX makes this reading strategy a part of the text in Eccl 2:15, where Qohelet questions the worth of wisdom, only to immediately repent of the negative thought. The text in bold is not in Hebrew manuscripts of Ecclesiastes:

> καὶ εἶπα ἐγὼ ἐν καρδίᾳ μου, Ὡς συνάντημα τοῦ ἄφρονος καί γε ἐμοὶ συναντήσεταί μοι, καὶ ἵνα τί ἐσοφισάμην; **ἐγὼ τότε περισσὸν ἐλάλησα ἐν καρδίᾳ μου, διότι ἄφρων ἐκ περισσεύματος λαλεῖ**. ὅτι καί γε τοῦτο ματαιότης.
>
> And I said in my heart, "What happens to the fool will also happen to me. Why was I so wise? **Then had I spoken rashly in my heart, because a fool speaks with exaggeration**, so that this too is vanity.[41]

The LXX's phrase makes Solomon/Qohelet immediately repentant of his questioning of wisdom. The belief in Jewish tradition that Solomon wrote Ecclesiastes in his old age was often tied to the claim that it contained his later reflections on his youthful indiscretions, as discussed in chapter one. Jerome reads this way as well and sees in Eccl 3:22 Qohelet's repentance of his earlier statement in 3:18–20 that human beings are no different from beasts.

> Superiori errore turbatus, quod putarem inter homines et bestias nihil interesse, in hanc sententiam prava opinione ductus sum, ut nihil aliud boni dicerem, nisi praesentem carpere voluptatem.[42]
>
> I was confused by my mistake above, where I thought that there was no difference between people and beasts. I had been led by perverse thinking to state the opinion that there is no other good other than enjoying present pleasures.

In his challenge to Solomonic authorship, Hugo Grotius surmised that the book had been written to make it look as if Solomon had repented of his sins ("sed scriptum serius sub illius regis, tamquam poenitentia ducti, nomine").[43] An influential modern scholar who reads Ecclesiastes this way is Michael V. Fox. In a direct rebuttal to the decades of scholarship that found multiple writers in the book, Fox argues that Ecclesiastes is "a single, well-integrated composition, which uses interplay of voice as a deliberate literary device for rhetorical and artistic purposes."[44] Fox's critique is simple and effective: anything that can be said of editors in a text can just as readily be attributed to authors. Fox refuses to buy into the rigid distinction between an author and an editor, with the former understood as being more creative than the latter. Once freed from this presupposition, so-called editorial additions can be interpreted as the work of the same writer of the "original" text. In a 1977 article and two subsequent books, Fox offers a reading of Ecclesiastes that distinguishes three voices in the text, all of which are the product of the same author:

> Level 1. The frame-narrator, who tells about
> Level 2a. Qohelet-the-reporter, the narrating "I," who speaks from the vantage point of old age and looks back upon
> Level 2b. Qohelet-the-seeker, the experiencing "I," the younger Qohelet who made the fruitless investigation introduced in 1:12.[45]

To read the contradictions or tensions in the text as a later Qohelet citing and refuting himself is also what the LXX does with Qohelet's refutation in Eccl 2:15 discussed above. The "then I had spoken" (ἐγὼ τότε ἐλάλησα) in the Greek can refer to any point in time before the previous statement, whether moments or decades. It allows us to imagine Qohelet as the protagonist in an ancient Jewish production of Samuel Beckett's, *Krapp's Last Tape*, a one-act play consisting of nothing but an old man listening to recordings of himself from his youth.[46] The older and younger Qohelet occupy the second level in Fox's reconstruction, which is why I have Fox included in this set of readings. The first, or outer shell of this matryoshka doll belongs to the "frame-narrator," the author of the third-person superscription and epilogue. This inverts the standard reading of the epilogue discussed above. The epilogist is no longer a later writer adding words to the end of a text written by Qohelet. He is now the only writer, and his text preserves the spoken words of

Qohelet. This difference does not yield too much interpretive novelty compared to the older view of the epilogist as a redactor. The epilogist is still a later voice and is still read as critiquing Qohelet's thought. It is as historically unprovable as the older view that sees an author as a redactor at work. Fox's reading of Qohelet as the work of a single author whose voice is directly accessible in the prologue and epilogue has been influential.[47] For the most part, it allows readers to still set the contents of the epilogue against that of Qohelet without recourse to editors or redactors. Fox himself does this in a nuanced way. The voice of the frame narrator quotes the words of Qohelet and then speaks for himself in the epilogue in order both to distance himself from Qohelet's thought and to make that thought more palatable to his readers.[48] Other, more overtly theological readings are more one-sided. Tremper Longman appeals to the idea of a frame narrator in order to claim that the epilogist is the true author of Ecclesiastes (i.e., the inspired biblical author). This author has cited the first-person voice of Qohelet as "a foil, a teaching device . . . concerning the dangers of speculative, doubting wisdom in Israel."[49] Longman's use of the frame narrator to neutralize theological dangers in the first-person text is what the rabbis do in b. Šabb. 30b,[50] and his view of orthodox and "speculative" faith in ancient Israel is identical to readers on the opposite side of the ideological spectrum, such as Barton. The ways in which theological commitments generate readings of Ecclesiastes form their own interpretive node that I discuss further in chapter four.

The Author Quotes Others

In chapter two I discussed those readings that saw Qohelet as assuming the persona of either Solomon or another ancient king. Similar interpretations are offered by readers addressing the contradictions in Ecclesiastes. For some, the book engages in the rhetorical exercise of citing opposing comments in order to refute them. In an inversion of the readings above that see an orthodox editor refuting Qohelet, Ibn Ezra read Ecclesiastes as the work of Solomon in which the king quotes the opinion of sinners in order to show the evil of their ways.[51] Christian authors also use this reading. Gregory the Great says that Solomon in Ecclesiastes speaks "in impersonation of the weak . . . criticizing what he has just recommended." ("quia illa quasi ex desiderio carnali verba intulit . . . qui dum hoc postmodum vanum esse redarguit quod prius admonuisse videbatur patenter indicat").[52] Gregory the Great's treatment of Ecclesiastes occurs in his *Dialogues*. Like Didymus the Blind, discussed in chapter two, Gregory's use of the dialogue format allows him to discuss difficult parts of Ecclesiastes. When asked by his interlocutor about Eccl 3:18–19, where Qohelet compares humans to animals. Gregory explains the verse as a quotation of a wrong opinion by Solomon:

> Salomonis liber in quo haec scripta sunt, Ecclesiastes appellatus est. Ecclesiastes autem proprie "concionator" dicitur. In concione vero sentential promitur, per quam tumultuosae turbae seditio comprimatur. Et cum multi diversa sentient, per concionantis rationem ad una sententiam perducuntur.

> Hic igitur liber idcirco "concionator" dicitur, quia Salomon in eo quasi tumultuantis turbae suscepit sensum, ut ea per inquisitionem dicat, quae fortasse per tentationem imperita mens sentiat. Nam quot sententias quasi per inquisitionem movet, quasi tot in se personas diversorum suscipit. Sed concionator verax velut extensa manu omnium tumultos sedat, eosque ad unam sententiam revocat, cum in eiusdem libri termino ait, "Finem loquendi omnes partier audiamus. Deum time, et mandata eius observa. Hoc est enim omnis homo."
>
> Solomon's book in which these words appear is called Ecclesiastes. Translated this name means "Preacher." Now, in preaching one expresses sentiments that tend to quiet a noisy crowd. And when there are many people holding opinions of various kinds, they are brought into harmony by the reasoning of the speaker. This book, then, is called "the Preacher" because in it Solomon makes the feelings of the disorganized people his own in order to search into and give expression to the thoughts that come to their untutored minds perhaps by the way of temptation. For the sentiments he expresses in his search are as varied as the individuals he impersonates. But, like a true preacher, he stretches out his arms at the end of his address and calms the troubled spirits of the assembled people, calling them back to one way of thinking. This we see him do at the close of the book, where he says, "Let us all hear together the conclusion of the discourse. Fear God and keep his commandments: for this is the whole duty of man." [Eccl 12:13–14][53]

Gregory takes advantage of the standard Latin translation of "Qohelet" (via the Greek) as "preacher" (concionator) to create a specific context that demands particular rhetorical strategies. Preachers aim to persuade, and they can do that effectively by empathy, showing their flock that they both understand their struggles and can offer relief. Solomon, as preacher in Ecclesiastes, can express an incredible variety of others' opinions in his teaching and, like any great preacher, makes sure to end his discourse with an orthodox exhortation—this being the epilogue, which Gregory quotes. Olympiodorus, in his commentary on Ecclesiastes, notes that the wisdom of Solomon/Qohelet consists in his ability to adopt two different personae:

> Ἰστέον δὲ καὶ τοῦτο, ὡς ὁ σοφὸς Ἐκκλησιαστὴς ποτὲ μὲν ἐξ οἰκείου προσώπου τὸν λόγον φέρει, ποτὲ δὲ ἐκ προσώπου τοῦ περὶ τόνδε τὸν κόσμον ἐπτοημένου.
>
> One must know that Ecclesiastes, as a wise man, sometimes wears the mask of the one speaking the words, while at others times he wears the mask of one who is dismayed at the world.[54]

Olympiodorus's use of πρόσωπον can refer to an actor's mask or an assumed identity (or "persona," as the Latin translates πρόσωπον). This is also a practice of

Greek rhetoric and Jerome even refers to the Greek rhetorical term for this strategy, προσωποποιΐαν in commenting on Eccl 9:8.

> Nunc quasi errorem humanum et consuetudinem, qua se ad fruenda hujus saeculi bona invicem hortantur, inducit, et προσωποποιΐαν facit more rhetorum et poetarum.
>
> In order to best display the error of this human habit which continually exhorts us both to enjoy the goods of this world, he creates a προσωποποιΐαν after the manner of the rhetoricians and the poets.[55]

Gregory of Nyssa, in his 5th homily on Ecclesiastes, also describes the words of Qohelet/Solomon using Greek rhetorical terms.

> Τὰς οὖν τοιαύτας ἀντιθεσείς ὡς ἐξ ἰδίου προσώπου ποιούμενος πάλιν καθάπτεται τῆς ἀτόπιας τῶν προφερόντων ἐκεῖνα, ὡς ἀνεπισκέπτως ἐχόντων τῆς τῶν ὄντων φύσεως, καὶ διδάσκει τὴν διαφορὰν ἐν τίνι τὸ πλέον ἔχει ἡ ἀρετὴ τῆς κακίας, ὡς οὐχι διὰ τῆς τοῦ θανάτου κοινότητος ὁμοτιμίας τινὸς ἐν αὐτοῖς ἐλπιζομένης, ἀλλὰ διὰ τῶν εἰς ὕστερον ἀναμενόντων καλῶν ἢ κακῶν τῆς διαφορᾶς εὑρισκομένης. Ἔχει δὲ ἡ λέξις τῆς ἀντιθέσεως οὕτως, ἔγνων ἐγώ ὅτι συνάντημα ἓν συναντήσεται τοῖς πᾶσιν αὐτοῖς. καὶ εἶπα ἐγὼ ἐν καρδίᾳ μου ὡς συνάντημα τοῦ ἄφρονος καί γε ἐμοὶ συναντήσεταί καὶ ἵνα τί ἐσοφισάμην; ἐγὼ τότε περισσὸν ἐλάλησα ἐν καρδίᾳ μου, διότι ἄφρων ἐκ περισσεύματος λαλεῖ. ὅτι καί γε τοῦτο ματαιότης.
>
> These objections [Ecclesiastes] makes as from his own person, attacking again the absurdity of those who argue while paying no attention to the nature of things and he teaches how great the difference of how virtue is better than evil, so that death cannot be regarded as the same for all those awaiting it. We can expect a distinction between good and evil at the end. This is his rebuttal, "I know that the same fate happens to them all and I said in my heart, 'What happens to the fool is what will also happen to me. So why have I been so wise?' Then had I spoken rashly in my heart, because a fool speaks with exaggeration, so that this too is vanity" [Eccl 2:15].[56]

Françoise Vinel, the editor of the Greek text, notes that Gregory of Nyssa uses the formal rhetorical term ἀντιθέσις (translated above as "objection" and "rebuttal") which is used to designate one side of a debate in Greek rhetoric.[57] Gregory of Nyssa also cites a variant of the LXX of Eccl 2:15, which, as I discussed above, explicitly states that Qohelet is making a quotation here. But Gregory reads that verse differently. Unlike the LXX, Gregory argues that Qohelet is not refuting his own prior quotation, but that of a generic person who speaks foolishly. Like some other readers, Gregory does not want to impute any kind of sinful thoughts or deeds to Qohelet, even ones long since repented of. I take this up in detail in the following chapter.

Modern scholars, too, have read the contradictions in Ecclesiastes as an author quoting the opposing positions of others. R. Norman Whybray finds in Ecclesiastes quotations of traditional wisdom that are not rejected outright, but qualified or relativized. Whybray has constructed an author who is schooled in ancient Israelite wisdom and critical of it. The contradictions reflect the author's cognitive dissonance between what traditional wisdom teaches about the world and the author's own experience.[58] In this regard, Whybray's reading also belongs with those in the preceding section that see Qohelet citing himself. Along these lines, Fox's frame narrator, the author of Ecclesiastes who quotes the words of Qohelet, also belongs to this group of readings, just as his claim that the older Qohelet quotes the younger Qohelet belonged in the preceding section. This is because Fox also argues that both of Qohelet's voices—young and old—are fictional constructs of the frame narrator.[59] Theodore Perry's *Dialogues with Kohelet* is one of the most extensive versions of this reading. Perry, like Fox, reads a frame narrator (whom he calls P, for "Presenter") who constructs a wisdom teacher, Kohelet (K) for the purpose of having a dialogue between faith and skepticism. P, therefore, is not only present in the superscription and epilogue, but also quotes K and then offers a counterpoint throughout Ecclesiastes.[60]

Perry's reading of Ecclesiastes as a dialogue, rather than the more simplistic citation of an opposing viewpoint simply to be refuted, understands the author as more than a rhetorical assassin. Wisdom texts from Egypt, Mesopotamia, and Greece all include dialogues. Some of these dialogues are complex (e.g., Job), refraining from caricature of opinions. Some readers of Ecclesiastes see more than two voices in dialogue. For Michael Payne three debaters, whom he calls "Vanity, Vitality, and Piety," engage in a complex interplay that in the end reconciles the contrast between the hedonistic and pious statements in the book.[61] Kyle Greenwood also sees three voices at work, each with a distinctive perspective, theology, vocabulary, and method of discourse.[62] These readings stand in sharp contrast to those discussed above, which see many editorial hands at work in Ecclesiastes. For someone like Barton, Haupt, or Longman, different kinds of thoughts in the text demand different writers to have produced them. These constructed writers are one-dimensional ideologues. The readings of Fox, Greenwood, Perry, Payne, and Whybray envision an author who can hold contrasting ideas in tension and seek resolution without exclusion. In these readings, none of the voices is viewed negatively. The problem these readings must address is the fact that quotations and different speakers in Ecclesiastes are not explicitly marked as they are in Job, where each speaker is introduced by name and a verb denoting speaking or replying. For Perry, in a revival of Barton's method discussed above, "the perception of abruptly juxtaposed contradictory opinions" is the means to distinguish the different voices. Whybray relies on vocabulary and Greenwood verb conjugations to unweave the strands of the dialogue.[63] If these methods seem strained it is because they are driven by the multiple voices these readers see at work in Ecclesiastes.

The Text Is a Collection of Smaller Statements

Martin Luther protests strongly against readings of multiple voices in Ecclesiastes because he found it beneath Solomon's dignity to be "speaking in the manner of foolish men or dressing up in the mask of a foolish man as some interpreters say."[64] Luther nevertheless also relied upon his own construction of Solomon/Qohelet to help him deal with the book's contradictions. In the opening remarks of his *Notes on Ecclesiastes*, Luther engages in a brilliant imaginative exercise that describes the kind of setting where Solomon might have composed the words of Ecclesiastes:

> In my opinion, the title "Ecclesiastes," or "Preacher," should be applied to the name of the book itself rather than to that of the author, so that you understand that these are words that Solomon spoke publicly in some address to his princes and others. For, since he was a king, it was not part of his duty of office to teach; this belonged to the priests and Levites. Therefore, I think these words were spoken by Solomon in some assembly of his retinue, perhaps after dinner or even during dinner to some great and prominent men who were present . . . Then he poured this out to those who were present, as usually happens, and afterwards what he said was put down and assembled by the leaders of the community or of the church . . . In the same way, it could happen that one of us would discourse about human affairs while seated at table and others would take it down.[65]

Luther distances Solomon from any contradictory (or otherwise difficult) words in Ecclesiastes by denying that Solomon is the book's author in the literal sense. The words were spoken by Solomon, to be sure, but written and compiled by an unknown and anonymous number of note-takers. The final form of Ecclesiastes is therefore not the result of Solomon's authorship but of his *anamnuenses*. Contradictions can be explained as the result of their errors or of a lack of proper context in collection of the notes. In some ways, Luther's reading resembles that of Fox in that the words of Qohelet in Ecclesiastes have been written by somebody else. But Luther's claim that Qohelet's words came through different writers into Ecclesiastes is also similar to how Haupt and Barton see many editorial hands at work in the book's conflicting statements. The clear similarity between what Luther imagines Ecclesiastes's *Sitz im Leben* to have been and his own practice, exemplified in the *Tischreden* ("In the same way, it could happen that one of us"), is no doubt deliberate on Luther's part.[66] That Luther himself would be misquoted in the *Tischreden* on the very question of Ecclesiastes's authorship, as I described in the preceding chapter, is another enjoyable irony in the relationship between the reformer and Ecclesiastes.

I include Luther here among other readings that deal with the contradiction in Ecclesiastes by appeal to the text's nature as a collection of smaller sayings—much like Proverbs—as opposed to a consciously structured composition. This view is exemplified by William P. Brown, who describes Ecclesiastes as "the distillation of an investigative journal, the notebook of a resigned cynic."[67]

Like Whitman, Qohelet Contradicts Himself

For some readers, albeit a minority in the text's reception history, Qohelet's contradictions are simply that: deliberate contradictions whose tension is meant to challenge how readers think about the world and their place in it. This makes Qohelet into an ancient Israelite version of Whitman, a writer and poet who contains multitudes. But tensions are difficult to maintain, and so even though J.A. Loader argues that the contradictions in Ecclesiastes are deliberate "patterns of tension," he resolves them by arguing that Qohelet is citing traditional wisdom in one statement, only to critique it with its contradiction.[68] On the opposite side, Mark Sneed uses Derrida's philosophy to show how Qohelet cannot maintain the balancing act of contradictions and therefore deconstructs himself. The book's contradictions only appear to challenge traditional ideas when in fact they unwittingly maintain and affirm them.

> To give Qohelet credit, he attempts to transcend contemporary notions of retribution, which would cast him in a somewhat dissident role. However, his solution to this problem is quite traditional. Instead of questioning the whole notion of cosmic moral retribution, which would be truly deconstructive, he does something rather conservative—he employs an old dichotomy and gives it a new twist.[69]

The old dichotomy is the idea of "the fear of God" (יראת אלהים), which, Sneed notes, Qohelet never questions.

> Qohelet's new use of an old dichotomy unfortunately suffers from all the weaknesses associated with dichotomous thinking. God-fearing/non-God-fearing is nothing more than a revamped wise/righteous vs. foolish/wicked dichotomy.[70]

Sneed's use of Derrida and deconstruction to read Ecclesiastes is an effective way to actualize a potential at work in a seemingly contradictory text. Along these lines, in what I think is one of the most brilliant readings of Ecclesiastes I have found, John Jarick uses the Chinese practice of *I Ching* to demonstrate that the tensions in Qohelet are part of an endless repetition of antitheses whose only unity lies in their eternal destruction of each other.[71]

Conclusion

Because readers cannot tolerate ambiguity on the part of authors—especially authors of authoritative texts—they employ a variety of strategies to create multiple voices and authors. These created voices are nothing more than shards of the author of the entire text, who is also constructed by readers. For someone like Gregory the Great, wise king Solomon must adopt the guise of others because it is impossible for the king to have really believed some of the things he says in Ecclesiastes. This is also the case for Barton. This chapter, as much as any other in this book, makes an important point that I owe to Brennan Breed. The rationales at work in pre-modern readings of the Bible are not simply relics of a pre-critical past. These rationales persist in modern exegesis. Modern biblical scholars actualize the same kinds of potential readings in a text that earlier readers did. Even though modern readers do not feel the need to preserve the shine on Solomon's halo, like Gregory the Great or Luther did, their need for an "author" with an essential and unified religious outlook compels them to construct one by multiplying the voices in Ecclesiastes in order to allot contradictory viewpoints to them. Regardless of whether one sees problematic verses in Ecclesiastes as references or quotations made by the author, or glosses added by an editor, the interpretative motivation is the same: some of these words cannot be claimed by the voice in the text that the interpreter identifies as the author, an identification driven by values external to the text.

Notes

1. Ezra Greenspan, *Walt Whitman's "Song of Myself": A Sourcebook and Critical Edition* (New York: Routledge, 2005) 193.
2. For discussion of the connection between Whitman's poetry and biblical poetry, See F. W. Dobbs-Allsopp, *On Biblical Poetry* (New York: Oxford University Press, 2015) 95–9, 176–7.
3. Charlton T. Lewis and Charles Short, *A Latin Dictionary* (Oxford: Clarendon Press, 1879) s.v., "idignor."
4. Michel Foucault, "What Is an Author?" *Professing the New Rhetorics: A Sourcebook*, trans. Donald Bouchard and Sherry Simon, eds. Theresa Enos and Stuart C. Brown (Englewood Cliffs, NJ: Prentice Hall, 1994) 187; trans. of "Qu'est ce qu'un auteur?" *Bulletin de la société française de philosophie* 63 (1969): 73–104.
5. The Talmud reads מהלל < הלל I ("praise") rather than הלל III ("act foolishly").
6. The idea of Torah as a fence or barrier is found elsewhere in ancient Judaism, for example in the Letter of Aristeas.
7. The debate over contradictions in Prov 26 is mentioned also in Michael V. Fox, *A Time to Tear Down, a Time to Build Up: A Rereading of Ecclesiastes* (Grand Rapids, MI: Eerdmans, 1999) 1. Despite the fact that Proverbs presents itself as an anthology of once-separate collections, readers have long attributed the entire book to Solomon, even to the point of seeing the names of other sages in Proverbs as aliases for him. This is discussed in chapter one.
8. This use of a wide semantic range to interpret Ecclesiastes is something I will discuss in chapter four in relation to allegorical reading.
9. Most notably in two monographs devoted to the issue: James A. Loader, *Polar Structures in the Book of Qohelet*, BZAW 152 (Berlin: De Gruyter, 1979); Michael V. Fox, *Qohelet and His Contradictions*, JSOTSup 71 (Sheffield: Almond Press, 1989).
10. Compare with Fox's discussion in his chapter, "On Reading Contradictions" (*A Time to Tear Down*, 1–26) and James L. Crenshaw, "Qoheleth in Current Research," *HAR* 7 (1984): 41–56, repr. in *Urgent Advice and Probing Questions: Collected Writings on Old Testament Wisdom* (Macon, GA: Mercer University Press, 1995) 520–34. Writing in 1984, Crenshaw notes that "Unless I am mistaken the essential issue for more than

fifty years has been the search for an adequate means of explaining inconsistencies within the book" (522).

11. Sara Japhet and Robert B. Salters. *The Commentary of R. Samuel Ben Meir Rashbam on Qoheleth* (Jerusalem/Leiden: Magnes/Brill, 1985) 92–3, 212–13.
12. Brennan W. Breed, *Nomadic Text: A Theory of Biblical Reception History*, ISBL (Bloomington: Indiana University Press, 2014) 15–74.
13. But even then, I will have the opportunity to amend the text when I review the page proofs. There are also second editions and revised reprints.
14. As Eva Mroczek decisively demonstrates in her treatment of Ben Sira (*The Literary Imagination in Jewish Antiquity* [New York: Oxford University Press, 2016] 86–113.
15. Preface to Ecclesiastes in E. Theodore Bachmann, *Word and Sacrament I*, Luther's Works Volume 35 (Philadelphia: Fortress Press, 1960) 263.
16. So prevalent was this approach that in the early 20th century, Johns Hopkins Press printed a "Polychrome Edition" of the Hebrew Bible: "A critical edition of the Hebrew text, printed in colors . . . Exhibiting the composite structure of the books." In 1905 there were volumes for sixteen different biblical books.
17. Paul Haupt, "Ecclesiastes," *The American Journal of Philology* 26 (1905): 125–34; George A. Barton, *A Critical and Exegetical Commentary on the Book of Ecclesiastes*, ICC (Edinburgh: T & T Clark, 1908).
18. Haupt, "Ecclesiastes," 125. "The genuine portions of Ecclesiastes are Sadducean and Epicurean" (126).
19. Haupt, "Ecclesiastes," 128.
20. Barton, *Ecclesiastes*, 44–5.
21. "One was an editor deeply interested in the Wisdom Literature, and the other who came after him was deeply imbued with the spirit of the Pharisees. The first edited the book because it formed an important addition to the Wisdom Literature . . . The second, finding such a work attributed, as he supposed, to Solomon, added his glosses, because he thought it wrong that the great name of Solomon should not support the orthodox doctrines of the time" (Barton, *Ecclesiastes*, 46).
22. Barton, *Ecclesiastes*, 43.
23. Anti-Judaism is present in Haupt's reconstruction as well.
24. For example, Otto Eissfeldt, *The Old Testament: An Introduction*, trans. Peter Ackroyd (New York: Harper and Row, 1965) 499; trans. of *Einleitung in das Alte Testament*, 3 Auflage (Tübingen: Mohr Siebeck, 1964).
25. As Carolyn Sharp notes: "The traditional redaction-critical view postulates an earlier skeptical corpus that was perceived as in need of correction (the older, usually pejorative scholarly view of redaction) or responsive reinterpretation (the newer, more appreciative scholarly view of redaction influenced by canonical criticism) by another party, a later editor with different interests at heart" ("Ironic Representation, Authorial Voice, and Meaning in Qohelet," *BibInt* 12 [2004]: 62–3).
26. Extended discussion in Thomas M. Bolin, *Freedom beyond Forgiveness: The Book of Jonah Re-Examined*, JSOTSup 236 (Sheffield: Sheffield Academic Press, 1997).
27. For example, Choon Leong Seow, *Ecclesiastes*, AB 18C (New York: Doubleday, 1997) 39–40; Thomas Krüger, *Qoheleth*, Hermeneia (Minneapolis, MN: Fortress Press, 2004) 16. A rare exception is Norbert Lohfink, who argues for the presence of an editorial gloss only at 11:9b (*Qoheleth*, trans.Sean McEvenue, CC [Minneapolis, MN: Fortress Press, 2003] 139; trans. of *Kohelet*. NEchtB [Würzburg: Echter Verlag, 1980]).
28. For the translational problems with בעלי אספות see Seow, *Ecclesiastes*, 387.
29. The Masoretes placed a disjunctive accent under the verb, הזהר, but Martin Shields argues that, based on uses of the imperative + infinitive construct, that הזהר should be part of the clause that includes עשות. He reads the beginning of verse 12 (הזהר בני מהמה ויתר הרבה ספרים עשות) as "And more than these, my son, Be careful to make many books of wisdom . . ." ("Re-Examining the Warning of Eccl XII 12," *VT* 50 [2000]: 125).

30. Some read verses 10–12 as a critique of Qohelet too, pointing out that it states only that Qohelet "sought" (בקש) to find wise sayings and that the warning about reading too many books includes Ecclesiastes itself (so Martin A. Shields, "Ecclesiastes and the End of Wisdom," *TynBul* 50 [1999]: 128). Others see in the epilogue an approval of Qohelet and his message, mainly by emphasizing verses 9–12, which are read as extolling Qohelet as a sage (חכם) whose careful collection and curating of wisdom make recourse to any others books unnecessary. Because these verses praise Qohelet, it is argued that verses 13–14 must be from a different writer (e.g., James L. Crenshaw, *Ecclesiastes*, OTL [Philadelphia: Westminster Press, 1987] 34; William P. Brown, *Ecclesiastes*, IBC [Louisville, KY: John Knox Press, 2000] 118).
31. Lohfink, *Qoheleth*, 144.
32. Equally ideological is James A. Loader's reading of the epilogue, which for him expresses a "repetition" of the "orthodox Jewish conviction" in divine retribution (*Ecclesiastes: A Practical Commentary*, trans. John Vriend, Text and Interpretation [Grand Rapids, MI: Eerdmans, 1986] 135; trans. of *Prediker: Een praktische bijbelverklaring*, Tekst en Toelichting [Kampen: Kok, 1984]). Compare Crenshaw, for whom the epilogue's author was "a detractor who thinks of Qohelet's teachings as inadequate and perhaps perverse" and the epilogue "totally alien to Qohelet's thinking" (*Ecclesiastes*, 190–2); R. Norman Whybray: "The epiloguist [sic] is deliberately interpreting Qoheleth's teaching in terms of the keeping of the Law and thus attempting to represent him as an 'orthodox' wisdom teacher like Ben Sira" (*Ecclesiastes*, NCB [Grand Rapids MI: Eerdmans, 1989] 173); and Schoors: "An addition from somebody who felt uneasy about the book. The epilogist deemed the book to be dangerous" (*Ecclesiastes*, HCOT [Leuven: Peeters, 2013] 852).
33. Nili Samet, "Religious Redaction in Qohelet in Light of Mesopotamian Vanity Literature," *VT* 65 (2015): 1–16. Quotations taken from pages 1–4, 16.
34. Loader, *Ecclesiastes*, 135; see also Schoors: "These verses are best understood as an orthodox epilogue, which in all probability saved the book for the biblical canon" (*Ecclesiastes*, 851–2).
35. PL 23:116a. Compare the English translation of Richard J. Goodrich and David J. D. Miller, *Jerome: Commentary on Ecclesiastes*, ACW (Mahwah, NJ: Paulist Press, 2012) 133–4.
36. Jerome's commentary on Eccl 12 appears to be influenced by several rabbinic traditions; see Matthew Kraus, "Christians, Jews, and Pagans in Dialogue: Jerome on Ecclesiastes 12:1–7," *HUCA* 70–71 (1999–2000): 183–231.
37. So too Christianson: "Despite its obvious conservatism, there is no conclusive evidence that the epilogue contributed to Ecclesiastes' acceptance into the canon, and it is impossible to say what the book's reading history would look like without it" (*Ecceleisastes through the Centuries*, Blackwell Bible Commentaries [Malden, MA: Blackwell, 2007] 254). For more discussion of rabbinic debates over Ecclesiastes, see Michael J. Broyde, "Defilement of the Hands, Canonization of the Bible, and the Special Status of Esther, Ecclesiastes, and Song of Songs," *Judaism* 44 (1995): 65–79.
38. Shields, "Ecclesiastes and the End of Wisdom," 138–9.
39. Martin A. Shields, *The End of Wisdom: A Reappraisal of the Historical and Canonical and Function of Ecclesiastes* (Winona Lake, IN: Eisenbrauns, 2006) 47.
40. See also Sharp, "Ironic Representation," 37–68.
41. On the peculiar characteristics of LXX Ecclesiastes as a translation see the discussion in Françoise Vinel, *L'Ecclésiaste*, L'Bible d'Alexandrie 18 (Paris: Editions du Cerf, 2002). Jerome cites the LXX in his commentary on 2:15 and states that, although the added phrase of repentance is not in the Hebrew, the Greek nevertheless best captures the sense of the Hebrew, because Solomon would repent of a foolish remark: "Apertius in hoc loco sensum Hebraicum Septuaginta interpretes transtulerunt, licet verborum ordinem non sint secuti. . . . Quod videlicet priorem opinationem suam stultam esse

convincens, insipienter se locutum esse testatus sit, et errasse, quia ante sic senserit" ("The Septuagint translators rendered here the sense of the Hebrew clearly, although they did not follow the wording . . . Clearly he is convinced that his prior opinion was foolish, admitting that he spoke foolishly, and that he erred to think that way" [PL 23:1031a-1031b]). See the discussion in Svend Holm-Nielsen, "On the Interpretation of Qoheleth in Early Christianity," *VT* 24 (1974): 175–6.

42. PL 23:1043c.
43. Hugo Grotius, *Annotationes in Vetus Testamentum* in *Hugonis Grotii Opera omnia theologica, in tres tomos divisa, ante quidem per partes, nunc autem conjunctim et accuratius edita, curis Petri Grotii*, 4 vols. (London: Moses Pitt, 1679) 1.258, most likely drawing on Jerome: "Aiunt Hebraei hunc librum Solomonis esse, poenitentiam agentis" (PL 23:1021a)
44. Michael V. Fox, "Frame-Narrative and Composition in the Book of Qohelet," *HUCA* 48 (1977): 83.
45. "Frame Narrative," 91. See also *Qohelet and His Contradictions*, JSOTSup 71 (Sheffield: Almond Press, 1989), revised as *A Time to Tear Down and a Time to Build Up: A Rereading of Ecclesiastes* (Grand Rapids, MI: Eerdmans, 1999).
46. Samuel Beckett, *Krapp's Last Tape and Other Dramatic Pieces* (New York: Grove Press, 1960). In a piece written on the play not long after its composition, drama critic Robert Hatch quotes a line from a Robert Lowell translation of Heinrich Heine: "Sleep is lovely, death is better still/not to have been born is of course/the miracle" (Robert Hatch, "Laughter at Your Own Risk," *Horizon: A Magazine of the Arts* 3 [January 1960]: 112). The line bears a striking resemblance to Eccl 4:2–3.
47. For example, in the commentaries of Krüger, Schoors, and Seow.
48. Fox, "Frame Narrative," 100–4.
49. For example, Tremper Longman III, *The Book of Ecclesiastes*, NICOT (Grand Rapids, MI: Eerdmans, 1998) 38. It is not necessary to have the same theological commitment as Longman to read the epilogue in this way. In a non-confessional analysis, Jacqueline Vayntrub notes that in the epilogue "the voice of Qohelet can be described as the ramblings of a self-proclaimed former king." ("Proverbs and the Limits of Poetry," [PhD diss., University of Chicago, 2015] 321).
50. Craig Bartholomew critiques both Fox and Longman in this regard. For Bartholomew, there is no contradiction between the epilogue's command to fear God and obey the commandments and Qohelet's thought (*Reading Ecclesiastes: Old Testament Exegesis and Hermeneutical Theory*, AnBib 139 [Rome: Pontifical Biblical Institute, 1993] 158–70).
51. Mariano Gómez-Aranda, "Ibn Ezra and Rashbam on Qohelet: Two Perspectives in Contrast," *HS* 46 (2005): 257.
52. *Dialogue* 4.4 (PL 77:324) translated in J. Robert Wright, ed., *Proverbs, Ecclesiastes, Song of Solomon*, ACCS, Old Testament IX (Downers Grove, IL: Inter Varsity, 2005) 277.
53. *Dialogue* 4.4 (PL 77:321–4) translation in Wright, *Ecclesiastes*, 284.
54. PG 93.480.
55. PL 23:1082d-1083a. Marc Hirshman notes that in early Christian works Qohelet is "seen as a master of role-playing" ("The Greek Fathers and the Aggada on Ecclesiastes: Formats of Exegesis in Late Antiquity," *HUCA* 59 [1988]: 139–40).
56. *Homilies in Ecclesiastes*, 5.5; Greek text in Françoise Vinel, *Grégoire de Nysse: Homélies sur l'Ecclésiaste*, SC 416 (Paris: Éditions du Cerf, 1996) 278.
57. Vinel notes that ἀντιθέσις, along with ἀνθυποφορά "are used to mark the limits of each response in a fictional dialogue" (*Grégoire de Nysse*, 278, note 1; my translation from the French).
58. R. Norman Whybray, "The Identification and Use of Quotations in Ecclesiastes," in *Congress Volume Vienna 1980*, ed. John A. Emerton, Vetus Testamentum Supplements 32

(Leiden: Brill, 1981) 435–51 and *Ecclesiastes*, 19: "If [the author] sometimes oscillates between what appear to be irreconcilable poles, he is merely expressing the tension within his own mind."

59. "The author employs the figure of Qohelet in a sort of thought experiment: Let us posit a man" (*A Time to Tear Down*, 373).
60. Theodore A. Perry, *Dialogues with Kohelet: The Book of Ecclesiastes* (College Park, PA: Penn State University Press, 1993) 33–48.
61. Michael Payne, "The Voices of Ecclesiastes," *College Literature* 15 (1988): 262–8. "Koheleth's thought exfoliates: first the dark blossom of Vanity, then the multi-colored petals of Vitality, and finally the delicate center of Piety. By this means Ecclesiastes reconciles the two manifestations of wisdom and provides a new foundation for the old teachings of the Law and the Prophets" (267).
62. Kyle Greenwood, "Debating Wisdom: The Role of Voice in Ecclesiastes," *CBQ* 73 (2012): 476–91.
63. Perry, *Dialogues with Kohelet*, 190; Whybray, "The Identification and Use of Quotations," 437; Greenwood, "Debating Wisdom," 479.
64. Jaroslav Pelikan and Hilton C. Oswald, *Notes on Ecclesiastes, Lectures on the Song of Solomon, Treatise on the Last Words of David*, Luther's Works 15 (St. Louis: Concordia Press, 1972) 95.
65. Pelikan and Oswald, *Notes on Ecclesiastes*, 12. Similarly, in his 1524 Preface to Ecclesiastes, Luther notes that the epilogue was added by those who took notes of Solomon's discourses. In particular, Luther reads the fixed goads and nails in 12:11 to refer to those scribes who fixed and arranged the words of Solomon, who is the one shepherd in the verse (Theodore E. Bachmann, *Word and Sacrament I*, Luther's Works 35 [Philadelphia: Fortress Press, 1960] 263).
66. The text is based on notes taken by a student named Georg Rörer during the series of 24 lectures Luther gave on the book in the second half of 1526 (see Jaroslav Pelikan's introduction to *Luther's Works* 15).
67. William P. Brown, *Ecclesiastes*, IBC (Louisville, KY: John Knox Press, 2000) 17. See also Kurt Galling, "Koheleth-Studien," *ZAW* 50 (1932): 276–99. Walter Zimmerli struggles with this question. He sees the book as an example of the traditional wisdom collection (Spruchweisheit). "The book of Ecclesiastes is not a treatise with a clearly recognizable outline and single, indentifiable theme. But it is also more than a loose collection of statements, although its structure as a collection in individual places cannot be ignored" ("Das Buch Kohelet—Traktat Oder Sentenzensammlung?" *VT* 24 [1974]: 221–30, repr., *VT* IOSOT [2013]: 85; "Das Buch Kohelet ist kein Traktat mit klar erkennbarem Aufriss und einem einzigen, bestimmbaren Thema. Es ist aber zugleich mehr als eine lose Sentenzensammlung, obwohl der Sammlungscharakter an einzelnen Stellen nicht zu übersehen ist.").
68. Loader, *Polar Structures*, quotation on page 1.
69. Mark Sneed, "(Dis)closure in Qohelet: Qohelet Deconstructed," *JSOT* 27 (2002): 120.
70. Sneed, "(Dis)closure in Qohelet," 121.
71. John Jarick, "The Hebrew Book of Changes: Reflections on *Hakkol Hebel* and *Lakkol Zeman* in Ecclesiastes," *JSOT* 90 (2000): 79–99.

4 Qohelet, Saint and Sinner

An important element of Foucault's author function that I have deferred discussing until now involves the roles of institutions in the creation and maintenance of normative authors and texts. Foucault speaks of government and legal institutions, but we can also add religious and scholarly communities to the list. Both religious groups and academic guilds are institutions that shape and limit discourse, marking off what is acceptable from what is considered heretical or unorthodox. The author function plays an important role in this.

> The "author-function" is tied to the legal and institutional systems that circumscribe, determine, and articulate the realm of the discourses; it does not operate in a uniform manner in all discourses, at all times, and in any given culture; it is not defined by the spontaneous attribution of a text to its creator, but through a series of precise and complex procedures; it does not refer, purely and simply, to an actual individual insofar as it simultaneously gives rise to a variety of egos and to a series of subject positions that individuals of a class may come to occupy.[1]

At the end of the last chapter, I highlighted how reception history can decenter scholarly readings by showing how they are part of non-academic—or better, pre-academic—interpretive traditions that are otherwise invisible. This invisibility lends to scholarly readings an illusory quality of objectivity or neutrality. Nowhere might this be clearer than in readers' theological evaluations of Qohelet. I noted in my discussion of Solomonic authorship of Qohelet in chapter two that philology led the way in challenging religious traditions about the authorship of Ecclesiastes. Drawing on the work of James Turner, I also pointed out how in the 19th century biblical philology retreated into religiously affiliated institutions, with the result that most of the critical biblical scholarship of the 20th century was produced by scholars at seminaries, theological schools, or religious institutions.[2] There is nothing inherently wrong with this, by the way. I teach at a religiously affiliated institution. But it is problematic when biblical scholars who attempt historical critical biblical study are unaware of their own place in the ideological landscape, or mistake their limited horizon for an Archimedean point of view from which they mistakenly believe they can see everything. At work here are the explicit and implicit roles that theology plays in biblical scholarship. Among theology's explicit roles in biblical studies, there is descriptive biblical theology that seeks to describe the religious and theological ideas of the biblical authors. This is distinct from another explicit role, creative biblical theology, a mainly Christian undertaking that uses the Bible to construct a theology relevant for the theologian's time and place.[3] One problem at work in the field for a long time is that creative biblical theology masquerades as its descriptive counterpart in a way that the interpreter may not see. Or creative biblical theology implicitly undergirds an attempt at historical reconstruction or philological analysis of biblical texts, again in a way not immediately apparent to the interpreter. Scholars are beginning to interrogate and expose these blind spots. Brent Nongbri has shown that the concept of "religion" as used by scholars of antiquity is itself an anachronism that is part of the Enlightenment's legacy on modern scholarship. More specific to biblical studies, David Lambert describes how much of the scholarship on repentance in ancient Israel is informed by ideas of inner subjectivity and ideas of the self that were foreign to the biblical authors.[4] It is one thing to talk about how an ancient Jewish or Christian reader struggled with theologically problematic statements in a text believed to have been written by Solomon. My inclusion of historical-critical readings alongside these older ones demonstrates that they too are conditioned by biases and assumptions about what is valid or orthodox religion in ancient Israel, and that these biases rely in part on those at work in the older readings.

Qohelet the Saint

For many readers Ecclesiastes is a normative religious text, and Qohelet—whether believed to be Solomon or not—is a sacred author. It is therefore incumbent on the interpreter that the book not be seen as teaching anything contrary to the reader's religious beliefs. The problem of reconciling normative texts with the values of their readers is older than the Bible. The origins of Greek philosophy lay in part with intellectuals' critique of the morality of the Homeric gods. In contrast to Plato's plan to censor Homer, allegorical reading was honed into a sharp hermeneutical tool used to uncover non-obvious and morally acceptable meanings in the Homeric poems. The rationale of allegorical reading is that the text does not say—or does not only say—what its surface meaning suggests. The text is a cipher, and only a reader with the right key can correctly interpret it. Deeper, truer, more mystical meanings lie inside the text, to be found by the diligent and the wise. The practical interpretive benefit to allegorical reading is that, because the text cannot only mean what it appears to say, it can mean things that it does not seem to say at first. In the hands of a clever reader, it can express a variety of meanings. Allegory overlaps with Breed's understanding of texts as containing potential meanings that are actualized by readers. As Breed makes clear, though, this does not mean that a reader can make a text say whatever they want.

Both Jews and Christians read Ecclesiastes allegorically. Readers for whom Qohelet's repeated calls for sensuous enjoyment, or his attacks on divine justice, did not square with the picture of what a righteous king Solomon or a biblical author would teach had recourse to allegorical readings of these problematic statements in Ecclesiastes.[5] Allegory is not the only reading strategy employed in the nodes I discuss here, nor am I able to fully discuss the different allegorical readings of Ecclesiastes. But it is prevalent in the reception history of the book.[6]

Airbrushing the perceived flaws of biblical figures is not uncommon, and there is evidence for it as far back as the 3rd century BCE. A relevant example is the biography of Solomon in 2 Chronicles. In contrast to the Solomonic biography in 1 Kings discussed in chapter one, 2 Chronicles devotes most of its description of Solomon to his building of the Jerusalem temple. It mentions briefly his great wealth and wisdom, including the dream at Gibeah and the visit of the queen of Sheba. Regarding Solomon's sins of marrying foreign women and worshiping their gods, 1 Chronicles 8 mentions only one wife, Pharaoh's daughter, and says that he built a house for her outside of the temple-palace complex so that she would not profane it.

> את בת פרעה העלה שלמה מעיר דויד לבית אשר בנה לה כי אמר לא תשב אשה לי בבית דויד מלך ישראל כי קדש המה אשר באה אליהם ארון יהוה
>
> Solomon brought Pharaoh's daughter up from the City of David to the house that he had built for her because he said, "My wife will not live in the house of David, King of Israel, because the places where the ark of Yahweh have come are holy."
>
> (2 Chron 8:11)

There are places in the LXX of Ecclesiastes that show evidence of readers' interpreting some statements of Qohelet in a way that neutralizes any potential theological problems. Here are two, with relevant differences noted in bold type.

> כי ברב חכמה רב כעס ויוסיף דעת יוסיף מכאוב
>
> For in much wisdom is much **grief**, and whoever increases their knowledge also increases their suffering.
>
> (Eccl 1:18)
>
> ὅτι ἐν πλήθει σοφίας πλῆθος **γνώσεως**, καὶ ὁ προστιθεὶς γνῶσιν προσθήσει ἄλγημα.
>
> For in much wisdom is much **knowledge**, and whoever augments wisdom also augments pain.

There is no apparent textual reason for the LXX to have read כעס ("grief") as γνῶσις ("knowledge"). It destroys the parallelism of the verse, which aligns wisdom and knowledge alongside grief and suffering. I might surmise that the translator mistakenly read דעת in the second half of the verse for כעס, another three-letter word whose second letter is *ayin*. But that is nothing more than a guess. The editors of *BHQ* mark the phrase as "theologically motivated."

יקר מחכמה מכבוד סכלות מעט

> A little foolishness outweighs wisdom and honor.
>
> (Eccl 10:1b)

> τίμιον ὀλίγον σοφίας ὑπὲρ δόξαν ἀφροσύνης μεγάλης.
>
> A little wisdom is more honorable than the glory of great foolishness.

The Hebrew is in parallelism with the first half of the verse, in which something small and bad (dead flies, foolishness) ruins something large and good (ointment, wisdom and honor). The Greek reads the opposite meaning into the saying: a little of something good (wisdom) is better than a great deal of something bad (foolishness).[7]

Many readings that see Qohelet as free from any theological error can be grouped into two smaller nodes. Each responds to a potential theological problem in Ecclesiastes. The first is Qohelet's repeated claim that all human effort is useless or futile, specifically his use of the terms "toil," and "under the sun." Readers add distinctions to these terms, limiting the universal nature that Qohelet gives them. In Ecclesiastes Rabbah 1:3, Qohelet's statement that there is no profit to any human toil under the sun (מה יתרון לאדם בכל עמלו שיעמל תחת השמש) is clarified so that it refers to all human labor except the labor of studying the Torah.

ואמרו לא אמר בכל עמל אלא בעמלו בעמלו אינו עמל אבל עמל הוא בעמלה של תורה

> They said, "He [Solomon] did not say 'all toil' [עמל] is meaningless but 'all *his* toil' [עמלו]. Truly one should not toil in *his* toil but in the toil of the Torah." [emphasis mine]

Jerome offers a similar limiting interpretation of labor. Commenting on Eccl 2:19 he says that Qohelet does not issue a blanket condemnation of work. Instead, what makes a person's labor futile is its misuse by others.

> Sed mihi altius contemplanti, de labore videtur dicere spirituali, quod diebus ac noctibus vir sapiens in Scripturis laboret, et componat libros, ut memoriam sui posteris derelinquat, et nihilominus in manus stultorum veniant, qui frequenter secundum perversitatem cordis sui, semina inde haereseon capiant, et alienos labores calumnientur.
>
> But when I think on [this verse] more deeply, it seems to speak of spiritual labor, of the wise man who toils in the Scriptures day and night, composing books so that he might leave behind his memory to those who come after. But nevertheless [his writings] come into the hands of fools, who often follow the perversity of their hearts, reap from them the seeds of heresies, and slander the work of another.[8]

Returning to the Midrash, in the same way that "toil" did not mean all toil, so too Qohelet's use of "under the sun" does not refer to everything in human life. In the Midrash, at 1:3, a distinction is made between human life "under the sun" and the afterlife, which the rabbis refer to as "above the sun." Qohelet is technically correct that there is no reward for labor in this life, but there is reward in the next.

עמלו תחת השמש ואוצר לו למעלה מהשמש תחת השמש אין לו למעלה מן השמש יש לו

> A person's toil is "under the sun," but their treasury of profit is above the sun. Under the sun there is no profit for a person, but above the sun there is.
>
> (Ecclesiastes Rabbah 1:3)[9]

For the rabbis, "above the sun," which accords with ancient cosmology, is the heavenly realm for which everyone should strive. Working "under the sun" (i.e., for benefits is this life) is futile. Didymus the Blind also understands Qohelet's use of "under the sun" as reference to only a portion of human existence. Unlike the Midrash, Didymus contrasts life "under the sun" with life "in the sun." In response to the question of the "spiritual interpretation" (τὴν ἀναγωγήν) of Eccl 2:11, in which Qohelet says that there is no profit "under the sun" for all of his works, Didymus distinguishes between life "under the sun" (ὑπὸ τοῦ ἥλιος) and life "in it [the sun]" (ἐν αὐτῷ). Life "in the sun" describes the existence of the faithful Christian, which Dionysus adduces by citation of Matt 13:43: "The righteous will shine like the sun in their Father's kingdom" (οἱ δίκαιοι ἐκλάμψουσιν ὡς ὁ ἥλιος ἐν τῇ βασιλείᾳ τοῦ πατρὸς αὐτῶν). While he does not describe exactly how a Christian lives this life in the sun, Didymus does make clear that its opposite, life under the sun, is without profit because a person thinks about and works for created things (τὰ ἀνθρώπινα πράττῃ καὶ σπουδάζῃ ταῦτα).[10] Rather than understand "in the sun" as a reference to heaven, which Didymus could have done with his citation of Matt 13:43, he instead opts for a understanding of life "in the sun," in "the Father's kingdom" in this world. One lives "in the sun" while living under the sun and not striving for worldly things.

The Midrash also states in several places that when Qohelet claims that all human toil under the sun is vanity, he means everything "except for repentance and good deeds" (חוץ מתשובה ומעשים טובים). Jerome too, in commenting on Qohelet's statement in 3:22 that humans should rejoice in their labor, states that the labor referred to are works of mercy that store up treasure in heaven.

> Nihil est ergo bonum in vita ista, nisi quod laetatur homo in opere suo, faciens eleemosynam et futuros sibi thesaurus in regno coelorum preparans.
>
> Therefore, there is nothing good in this life except for a person to rejoice in his works, giving alms and preparing a future treasure for himself in the kingdom of heaven.[11]

The LXX also tempers Qohelet's condemnation of human effort.

וסבותי אני ליאש את לבי על כל העמל שעמלתי תחת השמש

> I turned and my heart **despaired** over all of the toil at which I had toiled under the sun.
>
> (Eccl 2:20)

> καὶ ἐπέστρεψα ἐγὼ τοῦ **ἀποτάξασθαι** τῇ καρδίᾳ μου ἐπὶ παντὶ τῷ μόχθῳ, ᾧ ἐμόχθησα ὑπὸ τὸν ἥλιον
>
> And I turned and **renounced** in my heart all the toil that I had toiled under the sun.[12]

Jerome follows the LXX here, rendering 2:20, "Et conversus sum ego ut renuntiarem cordi meo in omni labore meo quo laboravi sub sole."[13] Renunciation of but not despair over one's worldly life fits nicely with Jerome's reading of Ecclesiastes as a book that teaches asceticism.

Another number of readings can be grouped around responses to Qohelet's repeated advice to enjoy sensual pleasures. Many of these readings recast Qohelet's claim that nothing is better than eating and drinking to refer to something other than eating and drinking. Philological ambiguities in the text provide opportunities for creative readers. The exact meaning of Qohelet's boast in 2:8 that he possessed תענגות בני האדם שדה ושדות has long puzzled readers and offers a good example of modern exegetes following ancient readings. The LXX read שדה ושדות as "male and female cupbearers" (οἰνοχόον καὶ οἰνοχόας).[14] Ibn Ezra read "women" (i.e., "concubines").[15] Others, following the meaning of שִׁדָּה in the Mishnah as "chest," understand the phrase to refer to coffers of treasures.[16] Ecclesiastes Rabbah read the phrase "the delights of humankind" (ותענוגת בני אדם) as reference to public baths and lavatories in Jerusalem and the שדה ושדות as demonesses (from שד) whom Solomon used to heat the water.[17]

The Midrash states that "everything that is said in this scroll about eating and drinking is intended to refer to Torah and good works" (כל אכילה ושתיה שנאמר במגילה הזאת בתורה ובמעשים טובים הכתוב מדבר, Ecclesiastes Rabbah 2:24). The Targum translates Eccl 3:12 and clarifies that happiness and joy consist in Torah study.

ידעתי כי אין טוב בם כי אם לשמוח ולעשות טוב בחייו

> I know that there is nothing better for them than to rejoice and enjoy themselves[18] in their life.

אמר שלמה מלכא ידעית ברוח נבואה ארום לית טב בהום בבני נשא ארום אילהין למחדי בחדות אוריתא למעבד טב ביומי חייוי

> Solomon the king said, "I know by a prophetic spirit that there is nothing good for a person except to rejoice in the joy of the Torah and to do good deeds in their lifetime.

So too Jerome, commenting on Eccl 2:24, notes that, "consequently it is good for us to take up the true food and true drink of the flesh and blood of the lamb whom we find in the sacred books" ("Bonum est itaque veros cibos et veram sumere potionem, quos de agni carne et sanguine in divinis voluminibus invenimus").[19] Not content with denying that Ecclesiastes advocates a hedonistic lifestyle, Jerome will argue that the entire point of the book is to teach the reader asceticism.

> Male igitur quidam opinantur, nos ex hoc libro ad voluptatem et luxuriam provocari: cum e contrario omnia, quae in mundo cernimus, vana doceantur.[20]
>
> Those who think the book provokes us to pleasure and comfort are wrong. On the contrary, it teaches that everything we see in the world is empty.

William P. Brown, in a commentary designed to make biblical books relevant for modern Christian faith, connects Qohelet's praise of food and drink with the "table fellowship" of Jesus. This allows Brown to speak of Jesus's "inclusiveness" at table and highlight the similarities between Qohelet's joy in eating and drinking and the selflessness and communion between Christians at table described in the New Testament.[21] Like Jerome, Brown draws a line from Qohelet's enjoyment of food to the Christian Eucharist, but without Jerome's embrace of asceticism.

Luther, for whom eating and drinking were legitimate pleasures, expends no little rhetorical energy attacking Jerome's reading. At the outset of his lectures on Ecclesiastes, Luther takes Jerome to task.

> Some foolish men have not understood this and have therefore taught absurd ideas about contempt for the world and flight from it, and they themselves have done many absurd things . . . The proper contempt of the world is not that of the man who lives in solitude away from human society, nor is the proper contempt of gold that of the man who throws it away or who abstains from money, as the Franciscans do, but that of the man who lives his life in the midst of these things and yet is not carried away by his affection for them.[22]

Luther reads Eccl 2:24, which for the rabbis meant Torah study and for Jerome the Eucharist, as "the point of the whole book," because it teaches that "those pleasures and labors which God gives are good and they are to be used for the present without anxiety."[23] Commenting on 2:10, where Qohelet says that he held himself from no available pleasure, Luther states that Solomon was not a hedonist.

> I extended myself even further and *wanted* to enjoy all these good things that I had prepared, but it was not allowed. I *wanted* this to be my portion in life, but God does not permit me to decide these pleasures by my own counsel . . . When I *wanted* to enjoy my pleasures and my gardens, the business of the realm called me away; there were judicial decisions to be handed down, conflicts to be adjudicated and settled, etc. [emphasis mine][24]

Here, despite his antipathy to Jerome's ascetic reading, Luther uses a strategy of Jerome's, who also read Eccl 2:3 this way, explaining that Solomon did not really drink too much, but merely that he thought about it. "I *wanted* to give my life over to delights and to free my flesh from every care" ("*Volui* vitam tradere deliciis, et carnem meam ab omnibus curis liberare" [emphasis mine]).[25]

Luther's reading of Qohelet is informed by his aversion to asceticism. He viewed food, drink, music, and companionship as divine gifts, unmerited goods whose proper enjoyment is expressed by a person's grateful acceptance of them. This persistence of this belief in Christian theology has led to a number of modern readings of Ecclesiastes that follow in Luther's footsteps, and see nothing sinful in Qohelet's call to pleasure, albeit within limits. Norbert Lohfink argues that ענה in Eccl 5:19 (כי האלהים מענה בשמחת לבו) should not be read as ענה IV ("be troubled with") but as ענה I ("answer"). Qohelet is therefore not saying that God has given human beings joy "to be busied with," but that God has given joy to human beings as "a response" to their toil. Lohfink is clear about the theological implications of his reading; he ends his article with the observation that "if the interpretation of Qoh 5:19 proposed here is correct, it will not be possible to say that Qoheleth is opposed to all the other books of the Bible."[26] For Graham Ogden, Qohelet's awareness of the inevitability of death and the need for one to enjoy life with that in mind means that Qohelet "is not a simple hedonist, but one, who from a standpoint of faith wishes to confront directly the reality of human existence."[27] Eunny Lee's book-length treatment of the question seeks to situate Qohelet's call to enjoyment in the theology of Ecclesiastes. She relates enjoyment with Qohelet's advice to fear God. For Lee, the proper fear of God lies in human enjoyment. Enjoyment, then, is a moral imperative, but only when engaged with others. Qohelet's "ethic of joy" therefore embraces "social responsibility."[28] Theodore Perry chides modern scholars for reading too much negativity in Qohelet, and argues that the term הבל is to be understood as "life breath," and read positively. Ecclesiastes is thus a guide book for how to live a joyous life.[29]

Some readings address other theological implications of Ecclesiastes directly and argue that Qohelet is not so much a heterodox thinker as an orthodox believer ahead of his time, or a creative pastoral mind making old theology relevant for his own time. For Stephen Curkpatrick, Qohelet's thought fits more with modern life than other biblical texts, specifically in the focus on God's transcendence, the totality of the present moment, and our own transience, all done in the rough and tumble of ordinary life.[30] Stephan de Jong sees many commonalities between the Hebrew Bible as a whole and Qohelet's statements about divine transcendence and power and corresponding human limitations. This is a reading I have given too.[31] Qohelet's statements about divine transcendence make easy bridges with Christian theology, especially in Reformation and Barthian articulations. John McKenna does just that in a study of Qohelet's use of הבל.

> Qohelet desires the community of faith to stand in all of its vanity and nothingness before its Creator with a trust that will take her quite beyond the word of death and ultimate nihilation to God himself.[32]

Alternatively, Qohelet is seen as a practical religious thinker who seeks to make Judaism relevant to the coreligionists of his own time. This makes him not only a theologian but an apologist of Judaism for R. Norman Whybray,

> Since [Qohelet] was concerned to present the Jewish faith to his readers in a realistic way that would be acceptable to his contemporaries, who were living in a world in which many of the old traditional certainties seemed to have become untenable. He should thus be seen not as a destroyer but as a would-be defender of the Jewish faith.[33]

Notice how a reception history that groups readings into interpretive nodes allows us to see the common thread between readings that ordinarily would be separated between Jewish and Christian, or ancient and modern. The readings of Luther, Ogden, Lohfink, Lee, Curkpatrick, and Whybray all seek to preserve Qohelet's theological orthodoxy with the claim that he is adapting his teaching for a constructed historical context—ancient, contemporary, or both. This is one of the basic aims of pastoral theology, and so these readings all view interpreting his thoughts as a ministerial exercise. Elsa Tamez brilliantly combines Qohelet's ancient socio-economic context (which she places in an exploitative Ptolemaic empire) with the equally exploitative modern globalized economy and reads Ecclesiastes as a biblical voice of advice and comfort for the economically marginalized of Qohelet's time and today. For Tamez, Ecclesiastes is a book of hope and not despair.[34]

In some Greek Christian readings, the sanctity of Solomon/Qohelet was essential because he was read as an Old Testament type of Christ. Origen uses a Hebrew etymology of Solomon to argue that Christ is the true king of peace and a Greek etymology of the LXX translation of Qohelet as ὁ Ἐκκλησιαστής to say that Christ is the true "assembler of the church."

> The true "Ecclesiastes" is the one who, though he was in the form of God, emptied himself, taking the form of a servant (Phil 2:6–7) in order to assemble the Church. For "Ecclesiastes" is derived from "to assemble the Church."[35]

Gregory of Nyssa also sees Solomon/Qohelet as a type of Christ.

> ὁ γὰρ ἀληθινὸς ἐκκλησιαστὴς ὁ τὰ ἐσκορπισμένα συνάγων εἰς ἓν πλήρωμα καὶ τοὺς πολλαχῇ κατὰ τὰς ποικίλας ἀπάτας πεπλανημένους εἰς ἕνα σύλλογον ἐκκλησιάζων τίς ἂν ἄλλος εἴη εἰ μὴ ὁ ἀληθινὸς βασιλεὺς τοῦ Ἰσραήλ, ὁ υἱὸς τοῦ θεοῦ . . . ἄρα ὁ αὐτὸς καὶ ἐκκλησιαστὴς ὀνομάζεται.
>
> The true Ecclesiastes is the one who reunites the lost into a single fullness and who brings together into one assembly those who have gone astray in various errors. Who else might this be other than the true king of Israel, the son of God? . . . It is the same one who is called "Ecclesiastes."[36]

Gregory's christological interpretation of Solomon/Qohelet prohibits his acknowledging any kind of moral failing in Ecclesiastes. He rises to this challenge by use of the allegorical and philosophical tradition available to him as a Greek-speaking elite in Late Antiquity. For Gregory, Qohelet's test of pleasure outlined in Eccl 1–2 is an allegorical reference to the Incarnation, where God descends into the human world, to live in it but not of it.

> Ταῦτα οὖν ὁ ἀληθινὸς ἐκκλησιαστὴς διεξέρχεται διδάσκων, οἶμαι, τὸ μέγα τῆς σωτηρίας μυστήριον, ὅτου χάριν ὁ θεὸς ἐν σαρκὶ ἐφανερώθη. Ἔδωκα γάρ, φησί, τὴν καρδίαν μου τοῦ ἐκζητῆσαι καὶ τοῦ κατασκέψασθαι ἐν τῇ σοφίᾳ περὶ πάντων τῶν γενομένων ὑπὸ τὸν οὐρανόν. αὕτη ἡ αἰτία τοῦ ἐπιδημῆσαι διὰ σαρκὸς τοῖς ἀνθρώποις τὸν κύριον.
>
> The true Ecclesiastes continues to teach, it seems to me, the great mystery of salvation which by grace, God is revealed in the flesh. "I gave," he says, "my heart over to search and to examine with wisdom everything that is done under the heaven" [Eccl 1:13]. This is the reason why the Lord dwelled among human beings in the flesh.[37]

Because Gregory will not to attribute sinfulness to Solomon, he sees the king as a selfless shepherd, willingly exposing himself to the base temptations of the world—knowing that he can withstand them—in order to impart to weak and foolish readers the necessity of avoiding the world's empty pleasures. Gregory compares Qohelet's sensual indulgence to how a pearl diver plunges into the depths without enjoying the experience.[38] This leads him to some extreme ascetic positions, such as his interpretation of Qohelet's statement in Eccl 2:2 that laughter is mad.

> ἐπεὶ τό γε κατ' ἀρχὰς ἐχθρὸν ἑαυτοῦ ποιεῖται τὸν γέλωτα καὶ περιφορὰν ὀνομάζει τὸ πάθος, ὅπερ ἴσον ἐστὶ κατὰ διάνοιαν τῇ παραφορᾷ τε καὶ παρανοίᾳ· ἢ τί γὰρ ἂν ἄλλο τις ὀνομάσειε κυρίως τὸν γέλωτα, ὃς μήτε λόγος ἐστὶ μήτε ἔργον ἐπί τινι σκοπῷ κατορθούμενον, διάχυσις δὲ σώματος ἀπρεπὴς καὶ πνεύματος κλόνος καὶ βρασμὸς ὅλου τοῦ σώματος καὶ διαστολὴ παρειῶν καὶ γύμνωσις ὀδόντων τε καὶ οὔλων καὶ ὑπερῴας αὐχένος τε λυγισμὸς καὶ φωνῆς παράλογος θρύψις συνεπικοπτομένης τῇ κλάσει τοῦ πνεύματος· τί ἂν ἄλλο εἴη τοῦτο, φησί, καὶ οὐ παράνοια; διό φησι τῷ γέλωτι εἶπον περιφοράν, ὡς ἂν εἰ ἔλεγε τῷ γέλωτι, ὅτι· μαίνῃ καὶ παρεξέστηκας καὶ οὐκ ἐντὸς τοῦ καθεστῶτος μένεις, ἑκουσίως ἀσχημονῶν καὶ διαστρέφων ἐν τῷ πάθει τὸ εἶδος, ἐπ' οὐδενὶ χρησίμῳ τὴν διαστροφὴν ἐργαζόμενος. εἶπον δὲ καὶ τῇ εὐφροσύνῃ, τί τοῦτο ποιεῖς; ὅπερ ἴσον ἐστὶ τῷ λέγειν, ὅτι· πρὸς τὴν ἡδονὴν ἀντιστατικῶς ἔσχον ὑποπτεύων αὐτῆς τὸν προσεγγισμόν.
>
> From the beginning [Solomon] makes laughter into an enemy and calls passion "madness," equal to confusion and insanity. How could a person say anything else about laughter, which has neither any rational nor practical purpose? It is an unseemly relaxation of the body, an agitation of the spirit, a shaking of the entire body. The cheeks puff out. Teeth, gums and palate are exposed. The neck swells and twists. The voice cracks because the breath comes in bursts. What else can it be, he says, but madness? This is why he says, "I said

> of laughter that it is madness" [Eccl 2:2] It is as if he were to say to laughter: "You are crazy. Out of your mind. Not in your right mind. You willingly make yourself disgraceful by distorting your appearance with passion, creating an effect that has no useful purpose." And when he says, "Concerning joy. What use is it?" [Eccl 2:2] it is as if he were to say, "I am against pleasure. I am suspicious of its approach."[39]

Nyssa's description seems more apt for Brother Jorge de Burgos, the moralistic, murderous monk in Umberto Eco's *The Name of the Rose*,[40] than it does for Qohelet. By way of contrast, the Talmud (b.Šabb 30b) interprets Eccl 2:2 to read that laughter is praiseworthy, deriving the root of מהלל ("madness") from הלל I ("praise") instead of הלל III ("boast"). This praiseworthy laughter is that of the righteous in the world to come.

Seeing Qohelet as a type of Christ allows me to examine another group of readings in the node of Qohelet as saint. Saints, of course, are role models, and believers are encouraged to imitate them. It is no surprise, then, that there are readings of Qohelet as a saint into which readers have read themselves. In chapter three I showed how Luther did this in imagining Ecclesiastes as a Solomonic *Tischreden*. Jerome, commenting on Eccl 9:11, applies the verse toward ecclesiastical matters. Regarding the words, "there is no bread for the wise," he observes "Everyday this example is proven by many who are very wise but lack basic needs" ("Multorum quotidie probatur exemplo qui cum sapientissimi sint necessariis indigent"). Then he continues

> "Non est scientibus gratia" videas enim in Ecclesia imperitissimos quosque florere . . . et. e contrario eruditum virum latere in obscure persecutiones pati et non solum in populo gratiam non habere sed inopia et egestate tabescere. Haec autem fiunt quia incerto statu feruntur omnia et non est in praesenti retribution meritorum sed in future.
>
> "The learned have no favor" [Eccl 9:11]. You see this in the Church where the most ignorant people thrive . . . While on the other hand a learned person slaves away overlooked and in obscurity, suffering persecution and not only in popularity but wasting away in poverty and extreme need. These things are so because everything happens in an uncertain manner and the reward for one's merits is not in the present but in the future.[41]

At the time he wrote his Ecclesiastes commentary, Jerome was already very familiar with ecclesiastical politics. He had been banished from Rome by the city's clergy after the death of his protector, Pope Damasus, because of his undue influence as spiritual director of wealthy Roman women.[42] He went to Bethlehem, where he spent the rest of his life writing commentaries, translating, and engaging in strident polemics with theological opponents. His Ecclesiastes commentary was written not long after he arrived in Bethlehem. It is addressed to two aristocratic Roman women, Paula and her daughter Eustochium, and mentions a third, Blesilla, another daughter of Paula's whose death precipitated Jerome's banishment from Rome. Jerome's remarks about scholars who live in penury and are persecuted ("persecutiones pati") by those less intelligent, but who are also are successful in the church ("in Ecclesia") is a not-so-subtle reference to his own situation in Bethlehem, far away from the centers of ecclesiastical power and a place he describes in the commentary as constricting.[43]

A more recent example of writing oneself into Ecclesiastes is Morris Jastrow's 1919 book, tellingly entitled *A Gentle Cynic*.[44] Much like the readings of Paul Haupt and George Barton (to whom *A Gentle Cynic* is dedicated) that I discussed in the previous chapter, Jastrow was a proponent of historical-critical exegesis as an antidote to what he saw as simplistic religious biblical interpretation. Jastrow himself is one of the more interesting figures in American Judaism. The son of the prominent rabbi and scholar, Marcus Jastrow, Morris was trained in Europe and ordained. One Sabbath morning he announced from the pulpit his resignation and took up an academic position at the University of Pennsylvania.[45] Throughout *A Gentle Cynic*, Jastrow operates with a template of binary opposites: primitive/modern, naïve/scholarly, somber/playful, orthodox/realistic, bad/good.[46] This leads him to remark on the "naiveté characteristic of an entirely uncritical age"[47] that ascribed wisdom texts to Solomon, or of the scribes who inserted material into the book to neutralize its heterodox content, as well as the rabbis who debated the book's canonical status.[48] Jastrow does not conceal his disdain for the editorial practices of ancient biblical scribes, whom he repeatedly describes as "uncritical."

> So close was the association between Solomon and the inditing of maxims, especially such as illustrated wisdom from various angles, that it not only seemed perfectly natural to add maxims to a book ascribed to the wise king, but such additions furnished to a later but still uncritical age a further proof of the Solomonic authorship of the book into which they were inserted. The "vicious circle" which is part and parcel of an uncritical age is made complete.[49]

Jastrow is unwittingly describing how the author function is present in the wisdom literature in general and Ecclesiastes in particular.

Jastrow's book was not written only for scholars. It was also intended "to place before a general public, and in popular form, the results of the critical study of the Old Testament."[50] This is a theological aim, seeking to convert readers to the validity of historical critical study of religious texts. To that end, *A Gentle Cynic* deals with things such as the Mosaic authorship of the Pentateuch (which Jastrow denies, saying that "the greatest figures in history, the world's greatest teachers such as Moses, Buddha, Jesus and Mohammed did not write").[51] Elsewhere he talks about the Solomonic attribution of Song of Songs that "led . . . to an allegorical interpretation so as to disguise the secular and indeed sensual character of these charming love ditties."[52] Traditional, religious readings are, for Jastrow, misinterpretations driven by primitive views of God and the world.

The "gentle cynic" of Jastrow's title is, of course, Qohelet, whom Jastrow also calls "the Omar Khayyam of the Bible." Here is his description of Qohelet:

> In reading Koheleth, we should picture him to ourselves as an amiable man who has grown old gracefully, who looks back upon his own career with a realization of the vanity of most things that he once coveted. The storm-and-stress period of life is over. He has grown mellow and the evening calm has set in. He may have his regrets but he prefers to smile. Life appears to him to be a big game of "chasing after wind," and he does not hesitate to say so and to try to prove his thesis in a series of charming and witty talks. He does not want to be taken too seriously and would smile at the thought of being regarded as the exponent of any system of philosophy. He is a dilettante in philosophy and a free lance in religion. He has no especial interest in Judaism, except as the religion which he sees around him.[53]

Jastrow's Qohelet is, unsurprisingly, much like Jastrow. Both are scholars who are not particularly religious and who are often misunderstood by pious, "uncritical" religious practitioners. Here are all the elements of Foucault's author function: the "biography" of the author, the consistency of this thought, and ultimately, his presence as a validation of a particular kind of interpretation.

Both Jastrow and Jerome read themselves into Qohelet, but from opposite ideological perspectives. Sanctity is in the eye of the beholder. Jerome was cast out of Rome by the city's clergy when a Roman noblewoman died not long after adopting ascetic practices under his tutelage. His Qohelet espouses the self-denial of physical pleasures and acknowledges the injustice of a world where the unqualified persecute their intellectual superiors who toil in obscurity and want. Jastrow's Qohelet is the embodiment of Jastrow himself: an older intellectual, comfortable with this past and himself, with no religious commitments, and only interested in Judaism from a critical, objective distance.

Qohelet the Sinner

The biography of Solomon in 1 Kings makes clear that he was wise *but* sinful. In other words, his sinfulness was not a result of his wisdom. In contrast, Ecclesiastes Rabbah 2:2 connects Solomon's sinfulness specifically with the description of his rule in 1 Kings to show that the king violated Mosaic law.

> כתיב ולא ירבה לו נשים וכתיב ויהי לשלמה שבע מאות שרות ושלש מאות פלגשים. כתיב לא ירבה לו סוסים וכתיב ויהי לשלמה ארבעים אלף ארות סוסים. כתיב וכסף וזהב לא ירבה לו מאד וכתיב ויתן המלך את הכסף ואת הזהב בירושלם כאבנים . . . אמר הקדוש ברוך הוא ולשמח מה זה עושה מה עטרה זו עושה בידך רד מכסאי. באותה שעה ירד מלאך בדמותו של שלמה וישב על כסאו
>
> It is written, "He shall not have many wives" [Dtr 17:17] but it is also written, "Solomon had seven hundred wives and three hundred concubines" [1 Kgs

> 11:3]. It is written, "He shall not have many horses" [Dtr 17:16] but it is also written, "Solomon had four thousand stalls for horses" [1 Kgs 5:6]. It is written, "he shall not amass silver and gold for himself" [Dtr 17:17] but it is also written, "The king made silver and gold like rocks in Jerusalem" [1 Kgs 10:27] . . . The Holy One, blessed be he, said to Solomon, "What good is pleasure? [Eccl 2:2] What have you done with this crown that you have? Come down from my throne!" Then an angel in the likeness of Solomon came down and sat on his throne.

Other rabbinic texts tackle contradictions between Ecclesiastes and the Pentateuch, as I discuss in chapters one and three. Here the implicit contradiction in the positive description of Solomon in 1 Kings is given a negative interpretation when brought into the orbit of Deuteronomy's laws for the king. This allows the Midrash to criticize Qohelet's praise of pleasure in Ecclesiastes.

The question of how Solomon's wisdom related to his sinfulness persists for readers. Was he wise, *but* sinful as 1 Kings describes? Or was he sinful *because* wise, in that his wisdom played a role in his sinfulness? Wisdom is equated with cunning in many cultures, ancient and modern. Gods of wisdom are often also trickster figures.[54] The moral dimension of wisdom in the Hebrew Bible includes not only the need to be wise, but also the recognition that some wisdom is either beyond the human capacity to know or off limits to human beings. Psalms 131 and 139 speak of a knowledge that is "too wonderful" (נפלאיה ממני,נפלאות ממני) for the speaker, and the tree of knowledge is forbidden to the man and woman in Genesis 2–3. As I discuss in chapter one, the description of Solomon's wisdom in later Jewish, Christian, and Muslim traditions saw the king's sapiential powers expand to include pharmaceutical knowledge, culinary skill, control of nature, and power over demons. For some readers, Solomon's expanding wisdom encompassed also wisdom's dark side. The king became proud and was subject to a deserved divine punishment. The Talmud (*b. Roš Haš.* 21b) has an important reading in this node.

> רב ושמואל חד אמר נ׳ שערי בינה נבראו בעולם וכולן ניתנו למשה חסר אחד שנאמר ותחסרהו מעט מאלהים בקש קהלת למצוא דברי חפץ בקש קהלת להיות כמשה יצתה בת קול ואמרה לו וכתוב יושר דברי אמת ולא קם נביא עוד בישראל כמשה וחד אמר בנביאים לא קם במלכים קם אלא מה אני מקיים בקש קהלת למצוא דברי חפץ בקש קהלת לדון דינין שבלב שלא בעדים ושלא בהתראה יצתה בת קול ואמרה לו וכתוב יושר דברי אמת על פי שנים עדים
>
> Rab and Samuel, one said: "Fifty gates of understanding were created in the world and all of them were given to Moses except for one, for which it says, "You have made him just a little less than God" [Ps 8:5]. "Qohelet sought to find pleasant words" [Eccl 12:10a]. Qohelet sought to be like Moses but a heavenly voice went forth and said to him, "The words of truth are written clearly" [Eccl 12:10b]: "There never again arose a prophet in Israel like Moses" [Deut 34:10]. The other said, "There never arose one among the prophets but one arose among the kings." How do I interpret "Qohelet

> sought to find pleasant words" [Eccl 12:10a]? Qohelet sought to make judgments using only his intellect and not by means of witnesses or prior legal warning. A heavenly voice went forth and said to him "The words of truth are written clearly" [Eccl 12:10b]: "By the word of two witnesses" [Deut 19:15].

There are several important parts of this particularly rich reading. First is the rivalry between Moses and Solomon/Qohelet, something I discuss in chapter one in a reading from Ecclesiastes Rabbah 11:9. The problem made explicit in that reading is implicit here, namely that Solomon/Qohelet teaches things in Ecclesiastes that contradict the Torah. Here Moses is compared favorably with Solomon as one who is both the most exalted human being but also humble. Moses was content to be "a little less than God" and did not seek to access the fiftieth gate of understanding. In contrast, Solomon wrongly sought equality with Moses and had to be stopped by a heavenly voice. Similarly, the king's pride in his intellect led him to violate Mosaic law in regard to legal decisions, and the king required a second divine warning.

Jerome also thinks that Solomon/Qohelet sinned in applying his mind "to know all that is done under heaven" (Eccl 1:13).

> Dedit ergo Ecclesiastes primo omnium mentem suam ad sapientam requirendam, et ultra licitum se extendens voluit causas rationesque cognoscere: quare parvuli corriperentur a daemone, cur naufragia et justos et impios partiter absorberent. Utrum haec et his similia casu evenirent an judicio Dei. Et si casu, ubi providentia? Si judicio, ubi justitia Dei?
>
> Ecclesiastes, then, dedicated his mind foremost to the pursuit of wisdom, but he went beyond what is allowed because he wanted to know the causes and reasons for things, such as why babies are possessed by demons or why shipwrecks drown the just and impious alike, whether these and similar examples happen out of chance or because of God's judgment. If by chance, then what about divine Providence? If by God's judgment, there how is it just?[55]

This kind of knowledge is sinful for Jerome because it leads to questions about divine justice and care. It is significant that the issues of divine providence and justice Jerome mentions are exactly where the influential philosophical schools of Stoicism and Epicureanism disagree. As the recipient of the finest secular education of his day, Jerome most likely chose these with that philosophical background in mind. Dionysius of Alexandria, in his commentary on Ecclesiastes, also sees Solomon's wisdom as sinful, but uses both biblical and philosophical backgrounds to describe it. Commenting on Eccl 1:18 (καὶ ὁ προστιθεὶς γνῶσιν προσθήσει ἄλγημα ["Whoever adds to knowledge adds to sorrow"]) he explains this saying as applying to forbidden or inferior wisdom.

> Ἐφυσιώθην μάτην καὶ προσέθηκα σοφίαν, οὖκ ἥν ἔδωκεν ὁ θεὸς, ἀλλὰ περὶ ἧς φησιν ὁ Παῦλος. ἡ σοφία τοῦ κόσμου τούτου μωρία παρὰ τῷ θεῷ ἐστι. Σολομὼν γὰρ καὶ ταύτην ἐπεπαιδεύετο ὑπὲρ τὴν φρόνησιν ὑπὲρ πάντων τῶν

> ἀρχαίων. δείκνυσιν οὖν ταύτης τὸ μάταιον, ὡς δηλοῖ καὶ τὰ ἑξῆς . . . Σοφίαν δὲ καὶ γνῶσιν οὐ τὴν ἀληθὴ ἀλλ' ἥ τισ κατὰ Παῦλον φυσιοῖ. Εἶπε δὲ καθὰ γέγραπται τρισχιλίας παραβολάς, ἀλλ' οὐ τὰς ἐν πνεύματι . . . πλῆθος δὲ γνώσεως οὐ τοῦ ἁγίου πνεύματος ἀλλ' ὅπερ ὁ ἄρχων ἐνεργεῖ τούτου τοῦ κόσμου καὶ ἐπιπέμπει σκελίζεσθαι τὰς ψύχας, πολυπραγμονῶν οὐρανοῦ μέτρα, γης θέσιν, θαλάσσης πέρατα.
>
> "I was full of myself,[56] and increased wisdom." This is not the wisdom that God gives but the kind that Paul calls, "The wisdom of the world, which is foolishness to God" [1 Cor 3:19]. Solomon was learned in this kind of wisdom, surpassing the knowledge of all the ancients. Thus he shows its emptiness . . . This is not the true wisdom or knowledge but that which, according to Paul, "puffs up" [1 Cor 8:1]. It is written, "He spoke three thousand proverbs [1 Kgs 5:12] but these were not in the Spirit . . . Full of knowledge, [the proverbs] were not from the Holy Spirit but instead those which the prince of this world enacts and sends to disturb their souls with busybody questions such as the size of the sky, the placement of the earth and the limits of the sea.[57]

Similar to the rabbis bringing Solomon's wisdom into dialogue with texts from the Torah, and finding Solomon wanting, Dionysius of Alexandria sets Solomon's wisdom in Ecclesiastes alongside a text from Paul and arrives at the same result. Dionysius pulls no punches, equating Solomon's three thousand proverbs with useless (dare I say, academic?) wisdom that is nothing less than diabolical.

Here is yet another example where reception history that looks at the similarity of readings, instead of the similarity of readers, reveals things that otherwise go unseen. At first glance these readings of the rabbis, Jerome, and Dionysius of Alexandria seem far removed from modern biblical scholarship. But they are, in fact, part of a node in which much modern scholarship on Ecclesiastes also belongs. For most of the 20th century and continuing today, the default position of biblical scholarship has been to view biblical wisdom literature in general, and Ecclesiastes in particular, as an outlier to a "normative" biblical theology, which is constructed from other texts in the Hebrew Bible. A clear example of this is Walther Zimmerli's argument that, because the normative faith of Israel was covenantal and historical, wisdom texts can be at best only partial expressions of that faith.[58] Zimmerli, along with many others, negatively contrasts wisdom literature's focus on creation with the historical focus of the rest of the Hebrew Bible. This is Dionysius's critique of "worldly" wisdom concerned about the sky, earth, and sea in modern academic dress. Zimmerli goes further, implicitly equating wisdom literature's emphasis on how to live with a Lutheran works righteousness, and contrasting it with the grace righteousness of his constructed covenantal theology, which for him is the orthodox faith of ancient Israel.[59] Other examples of wisdom's marginalization in the theological descriptions of the Hebrew Bible by modern scholars abound, and I include only a few here. Frank-Lothar Hossfeld, while not explicitly critiquing Qohelet, notes how scholars distinguish Ecclesiastes from a "biblical" theology that is "focused on revelation."[60] The contrast is no more stark than in Jack T. Sander's descriptions of two different religious worldviews—the Mosaic Torah and the wisdom tradition—colliding, with each side seeking to accommodate or neutralize the other.[61] Ecclesiastes in particular has been marginalized by modern biblical scholars. That is the exact image used by Walter Brueggemann.

> The shrill and incessant voicing of negativity about Yahweh takes its toll . . . confidence in Israel's core testimony seems to erode . . . *At the very edge of the Old Testament*, culturally and epistemologically, the Book of Ecclesiastes gives us the residue and outcome of that shrill and incessant voicing of negativity [emphasis mine].[62]

While Brueggemann places Ecclesiastes "at the very edge" of the Bible, he frames his discussion of it between two occurrences of the phrase, "shrill and incessant voicing of negativity." This characterization of Ecclesiastes makes it distinct from "Israel's core testimony." At the edge are shrillness and negativity, contrasted to the core which commands "confidence." This is not something unique to Brueggemann. Writing almost thirty years earlier, Gerhard von Rad can confidently say that he is "justified" in seeing Qohelet "as an outsider completely free of tradition."[63] Tremper Longman, whose reading I discussed in chapter three with others that see multiple voices in Ecclesiastes,[64] not only argues that Qohelet and the frame narrator are two distinct people, he also asserts that narrator's theology in the epilogue is to be read as "the normative theology of the book as a whole."[65] All the words of Qohelet exist only to serve as "a foil, a teaching device . . . concerning the dangers of speculative, doubting wisdom in Israel."[66] Longman in particular contrasts Qohelet's view of God with what he considers to be normative biblical thought. He interprets the absence of the Tetragrammaton in Ecclesiastes as evidence that Qohelet sees God as cold and distant. In contrast use of the name "Yahweh" would "after all . . . invoke warm covenantal feelings and memories."[67] The idea that the name "Yahweh" would immediately cause an ancient Israelite reader to think warmly of the covenant is not only impossible to prove, but also flies in the face of numerous biblical texts where the god Yahweh does decidedly not comforting or edifying things. Longman here is reading a theology of ancient Israel—his theology—into the text and after drawing that circle, making the observation that Ecclesiastes is outside of it. The opening line of James Limburg's recent popular book on Ecclesiastes is straightforward: "Ecclesiastes is not for everyone." For Limburg, the book is best suited for the believer who is fed up with pieties or platitudes, or "an honest seeker," not content with pat theological answers. Ecclesiastes is the outsider inside the Bible, and thus offers a way in for those who might otherwise not enter.[68] The whole idea that the Hebrew Bible presents us with the "faith" (only one?) of ancient Israel is historically problematic and theologically fraught.

One final node in this reading of Qohelet as a sinner deals with his repentance. Despite being a sinner, Qohelet is also the author of a biblical book, and many readings mention his repentance. Here the relationship between his wisdom and sinfulness can be seen as either he repented *because* he was wise or that his repentance was how he came to be wise. This puts Qohelet in the position of being a role model for readers, as he is in the readings that see him as a saint. This illustrates Oscar Wilde's maxim that, "the only difference between the saint and the sinner is that every saint has a past and every sinner has a future."[69] In chapter three I discussed the LXX of Eccl 2:15, which explicitly contains a repudiation by Qohelet of one of his statements,[70] along with other readings of Ecclesiastes that made sense of the multiple voices by reading them as a repentant Solomon quoting his sinful, younger self. The passage from Ecclesiastes Rabbah discussed above mentions that Solomon is deposed by God and replaced by an angelic double in punishment for his decadent lifestyle in violation of the Torah. Variations of Solomon's being deposed occur elsewhere in rabbinic literature.[71] Here is a representative example from the Targum of Eccl 1:12.

> כד הוה שלמה מלכא יתיב על כורסי מלכותא איתגס ליביה לחדא על עותריה ועבר על גזירת מימרא דייי וכנש סוסוון ורתיכין ופרשין סגיאין וצבר כספא ודהבא לחדא ואיתחתן בעממין נוכראין מן יד תקיף רוגזא דייי עילווי ושדר לותיה אשמדאי מלכא דשידי וטרד יתיה מן כורסי מלכותיה ונטל גושפנקיה מן ידיה בגין דיהך מטלטל וגלי בעלמא לאוכחותיה יהיה מחזר בכל פילכי וכרכי ארעא דישראל בכי ופגן וכן אמר אנא קהלת דהיה שמי מתקרי שלמה מן קדמת דנא הויתי מלכא על ישראל בירושלם.
>
> When Solomon was king and sat on his royal throne, he was arrogant about his wisdom and great wealth. He transgressed the decree of Yahweh and amassed horses and chariots, and much cavalry. He piled up much silver and gold and married foreign, Gentile women. Immediately there was great punishment from Yahweh who sent Asmodeus, the king of the demons against Solomon to expel him from his royal throne. And he carried a signet ring on his hand but was disguised as a homeless beggar exiled in the world. And he went through all the districts and towns of Israel weeping and crying out, "I am Qohelet, but I was called Solomon and was once king over Israel in Jerusalem."

Doomed thus to wander and beg, Solomon reflects on his own sinfulness. The Targum notes that after this when he experiences the theophany at Gibeon, asking for the wisdom "to know good and evil" (למידע בין טב לביש). This reading creates an interesting chronological scenario for Solomon. He appears to already be wealthy and sinful and is only given wisdom in his asking God for it at Gibeon. This inverts the narrative in 1 Kings 3 where Solomon asks for wisdom at Gibeon and is given wealth as a reward for his request.

Conclusion

I discussed in chapter one that the biography of Solomon from 1 Kings says that he was wise, wealthy, and sinful. In his self-description, Qohelet emphasizes that he was wise and wealthy, but nowhere does he mention that he was sinful. This is important because it demands that readers who see Qohelet as a sinner, reformed or otherwise, must bring his sinfulness to Ecclesiastes from an ethic external to the book. Added to this is the complication that, for many of these readers, Ecclesiastes is a sacred text, attributed to a figure renowned for wisdom, but rife with heterodox statements about divine justice and human destiny. But even for readers who do not subscribe to Solomonic authorship, the theological thorns of Ecclesiastes demand pruning, and ancient readings persist into the 21st century. The complexity of the readings in this chapter mirror the complexity of the text.

Notes

1. Michel Foucault, "What Is an Author?" in *Professing the New Rhetorics: A Sourcebook*, trans. Donald Bouchard and Sherry Simon, eds. Theresa Enos and Stuart C. Brown (Englewood Cliffs, NJ: Prentice Hall, 1994) 188; trans. of "Qu'est ce qu'un auteur?" *Bulletin de la société française de philosophie* 63 (1969): 73–104.
2. James Turner, *Philology: The Forgotten Origins of the Modern Humanities* (Princeton, NJ: Princeton University Press, 2014).
3. For background, see John H. Hayes and Frederick Prussner, *Old Testament Theology: Its History and Development* (Atlanta, GA: John Knox Press, 1985). For critique of creative biblical theology as a project, see James Barr, *The Concept of Biblical Theology* (Minneapolis, MN: Fortress Press, 1999).
4. Brent Nongbri, *Before Religion: The History of a Modern Concept* (New Haven, CT: Yale University Press, 2013); David A. Lambert, *How Repentance Became Biblical: Judaism, Christianity, and the Interpretation of Scripture* (New York: Oxford University Press, 2016).
5. For the idea of allegory as a way to read a text and not simply a genre see Sayre N. Greenfield, *The Ends of Allegory* (Newark, DE: University of Delaware Press, 1998).
6. Discussion in Eric Christianson, *Ecclesiastes through the Centuries*, Blackwell Bible Commentaries (Malden, MA: Wiley-Blackwell, 2007) 227–32.
7. The editor of *BHQ* surmises a translator's error. "In the source text of G, the word רב was read at the end of the verse (dittography for לב?) and מעת moved to determine חכמה" (Yohanan A. P. Goldman, "Qoheleth," in *Megilloth*, *BHQ* 18 (Stuttgart: Deutsche Bibelgesellschaft, 2004) 106*.
8. PL 23:1031d–1032a.
9. See my discussion in chapter three of the passage from b. Šabb. 30b that distinguishes "under the sun" from "before the sun" (קודם שמש).
10. *Commentary on Ecclesiastes*, 46.6–10 in Gerhard Binder and Leo Liesenborghs, *Didymos der Blinde: Kommentar zum Ecclesiastes (Tura-Papyrus) Teil I.1* (Bonn: Rudolf Habelt Verlag, 1979) 224.
11. PL 23:1043b.
12. Here following Françoise Vinel's translation of ἀποτάξασθαι: "Et j'en suis venu, moi, à renoncer dans mon cœur à tout le tourment don je fus tourmenyé sous le soleil" (*L'Ecclésiaste*, La Bible d'Alexandrie 18 [Paris: Editions du Cerf, 2002] 116. Compare NETS:" And I turned to bid farewell with my heart to all the toil at which I toiled under the sun."
13. PG 23:1032a.
14. So also Anton Schoors, *Ecclesiastes*, HCOT [Leuven: Peeters, 2013] 165.
15. So also Thomas Krüger, *Qoheleth*, Hermeneia [Minneapolis: Fortress, 2004] 56–8; NRSV; and me in chapter one.
16. Seow, *Ecclesiastes*, 131–2; NJPS.
17. In the *Qur'an*, Solomon also has demons and jinns at his service: 2.81–82, 34.12–13, 38.30.

18. "The parallelism with *liśmoaḥ* 'to enjoy' suggests that *la'ăśôt ṭôb* does not have the moral connotations it has elsewhere in the Bible. Here it must mean something like *lir'ôt ṭôb* 'to see good' = 'to enjoy,' as the next verse makes clear" (Choon-Leong Seow, *Ecclesiastes*, AB [New York: Doubleday, 1997] 164).
19. PL 23:1033b. Jerome will reiterate that for Ecclesiastes, the true food and drink are the Eucharist at 3:12–13, 8:14, and 9:7–8.
20. PL 23:1014a.
21. William P. Brown, *Ecclesiastes*, IBC (Louisville, KY: John Knox Press, 2000) 128–9. For a substantive critique of the implicit Christian bias at work in seeing the practice of Jesus as inclusive compared to his Jewish contemporaries, see Amy-Jill Levine, *Short Stories By Jesus* (New York: HarperOne, 2014).
22. Jaroslav Pelikan and Hilton C. Oswald, *Notes on Ecclesiastes, Lectures on the Song of Solomon, Treatise on the Last Words of David*, Luther's Works 15 (St. Louis: Concordia Press, 1972) 9.
23. Pelikan and Oswald, *Notes on Ecclesiastes*, 46–7.
24. Pelikan and Oswald, *Notes on Ecclesiastes*, 37.
25. PL 23:1024d.
26. Norbert Lohfink, "Qoheleth 5:17–19: Revelation by Joy," *CBQ* 52 (1990): 625–35, 635.
27. Graham S. Ogden, "Qoheleth xi 7-xii 8: Qoheleth's Summons to Enjoyment and Reflection," *VT* 34 (1984): 27–38, 38.
28. Eunny P. Lee, *The Vitality of Enjoyment in Qohelet's Theological Rhetoric*, BZAW 353 (Berlin: De Gruyter, 2005) 125–35. William H. U. Anderson argues that Ecclesiastes is "pessimistic literature," and that the only way to see it as advocating joy is by means of a "counter-reading to the traditional understanding of the essential ethos of Qoheleth" ("Philosophical Considerations in a Genre Analysis of Qoheleth," *VT* 48 [1998]: 295).
29. Theodore Perry, *The Book of Ecclesiastes (Qohelet) and the Path to Joyous Living* (New York: Cambridge University Press, 2015).
30. Stephen Curkpatrick, "A Disciple for Our Time: A Conversation," *Int* 55 (2001): 285–91.
31. Stephan de Jong, "God in the Book of Qohelet: A Reappraisal of Qohelet's Place in Old Testament Theology," *VT* 47 (1997): 154–67 and Thomas M. Bolin, "Rivalry and Resignation: Girard on Qoheleth and the Divine-Human Relationship," *Bib* 86 (2005): 245–59.
32. John McKenna, "The Concept of *Hebel* in the Book of Ecclesiastes," *SJT* 45 (1992): 24.
33. R. Norman Whybray, "Qoheleth as a Theologian," in *Qohelet in the Context of Wisdom*, ed. Anton Schoors (Leuven: Leuven University Press, 1998) 239.
34. Elsa Tamez, *When the Horizons Close: Rereading Ecclesiastes* (Maryknoll, NY: Orbis, 2000) and also in her "Ecclesiastes: Reading from the Periphery," *Int* 55 (2001): 250–9. Discussion of Tamez in the reception history of Ecclesiastes is also in Katharine J. Dell *Interpreting Ecclesiastes: Readers Old and New*, Critical Studies in the Hebrew Bible 3 (Winona Lake, IN: Eisenbrauns, 2013) 76–83. For the idea that Qohelet's seeming pessimism is a response to a larger cultural crisis, be it social, economic, or both, is widespread in biblical scholarship, see the programmatic statement in Hartmut Gese, "The Crisis of Wisdom in Koheleth," trans. Lester Grabbe, in *Theodicy in the Old Testament*, ed. James Crenshaw, IRT 4 (Philadelphia, PA: Fortress, 1983) 141–53; trans. of "Die Krisis der Wiesheit bei Koheleth," in *Le sagesses du Proche-Orient ancien* (Paris: Presses Universitaires de France, 1963) 139–51.
35. *Prologue to the Commentary on the Song of Songs*, in Rowan A. Greer, *Origen: An Exhortation to Martyrdom, Prayer, and Selected Works*, CWS (New York: Paulist, 1979) 240.
36. *Homilies on Ecclesiastes*, 1.2; Greek text in Françoise Vinel, *Grégoire de Nysse: Homélies sur l'Ecclésiaste*, SC 416 (Paris: Éditions du Cerf, 1996) 112.

37. *Homilies on Ecclesiastes*, 2.2 in Vinel, *Grégoire de Nysse*, 152–5. Gregory's homilies on Ecclesiastes deserve much more attention than I can give them here. See also the discussion in Stuart George Hall, ed., *Gregory of Nyssa: Homilies on Ecclesiastes* (Berlin: De Gruyter, 1993); Vinel, *Grégoire de Nysse*, 7–90; and Christianson, *Ecclesiastes through the Centuries*, 157–9.
38. Gregory is deliberately ambiguous in his description of Qohelet's indulgence in Eccl 2. On the one hand, he states that it is up to the reader to decide whether Qohelet really experienced these things, but on the other, he makes clear that he believes that Qohelet did not experience pleasure from them: εἰ δέ τις λέγοι τῷ ὄντι γεγενῆσθαι αὐτὸν ἐν τῇ τῶν ἡδέων πείρᾳ, οὕτως ὑπολαμβάνομεν ("If someone were to say that he [Solomon] experienced pleasure, this is how we interpret it" (*Homilies in Ecclesiastes* 3.3 in Vinel, *Grégoire de Nysse*, 192). I disagree with Christianson, who thinks that Gregory of Nyssa is "acutely aware of what has now become a fine and controversial epistemological distinction between historical and fictional truth, the world of real and implied authors" (*Ecclesiastes through the Centuries*, 158).
39. *Homilies on Ecclesiastes*, 2.7 in Vinel, *Grégoire de Nysse*, 177.
40. Spoiler alert: Brother Jorge de Burgos is the murderer in Eco's novel. His motive for murder is to keep suppressed a manuscript containing a lost work of Aristotle praising laughter. At the novel's climax, Brother Jorge is confronted by Eco's sleuth, the Franciscan William of Baskerville. When questioned as to why he wants no one to know about Aristotle's praise of laughter, Brother Jorge says: "But laughter is weakness, corruption, the foolishness of our flesh . . . That laughter is proper to man is a sign of our limitation, sinners that we are" (Umberto Eco, *The Name of the Rose*, trans. William Weaver [New York: Harvest, 1983] 474; translation of *Il nome della rosa* [Milan: Fabbri-Bompiani, 1980]). Brother Jorge was played to eerie perfection by the late Feodor Fedorovich Chaliapin Jr. in Jean-Jacques Annaud's 1986 film adaption of the novel.
41. PL 23: 1087a-b. The only response to Jerome is his own rendering of Eccl 1:9: "Nihil sub sole novum."
42. See biographical sketch in Richard J. Goodrich and David J. D. Miller, *Jerome: Commentary on Ecclesiastes*, ACW (Mahwah, NJ: Paulist Press, 2012) 1–4; Gérard Fry, *Jérome Lit l'Ecclesiaste*, Les pères dans la Foi 79–80 (Paris: Migne, 2001) 11–16 and, above all, J.N.D. Kelly, *Jerome: His Life, Writings, and Controversies* (New York: Harper and Row, 1975).
43. Goodrich and Miller note (*Jerome*, 136) that, while the oldest manuscript of the commentary reads: "Nunc in Bethleem positus **augustori** videlicet civitate" ("Now here in Bethlehem, that **most majestic** city") later copies read "Nunc in Bethleem positus **angustiore** videlicet civitate" ("Now here in Bethlehem, that **more constricting** city").
44. *A Gentle Cynic: Being a Translation of the Book of Koheleth Commonly Known as Ecclesiastes, Its Origin, Growth and Interpretation* (Philadelphia, PA: Lippincott, 1919; repr., New York: Oriole, 1972).
45. For biography, see Harold S. Wechsler, "Pulpit or Professoriate: The Case of Morris Jastrow," *American Jewish History* 74 (1985): 338–55. Jastrow was one of the signatories of a letter to President Woodrow Wilson arguing against political Zionism. See Jastrow's *Zionism and the Future of Palestine* (New York: Macmillan, 1919).
46. Paradoxically, Jastrow, like most biblical scholars of his day, placed more worth on the *earlier* (i.e., unredacted) forms of biblical texts. Although it should be noted that he mentions early in the book that "Koheleth is modern" (*Gentle Cynic*, 8).
47. Jastrow, *Gentle Cynic*, 77.
48. See especially Jastrow, *Gentle Cynic,* 52–5.
49. Jastrow, *Gentle Cynic*, 78.
50. Jastrow, *Gentle Cynic*, 7.

51. Jastrow, *Gentle Cynic*, 41.
52. Jastrow, *Gentle Cynic*, 71.
53. Jastrow, *Gentle Cynic*, 194.
54. See the discussion in Lewis Hyde, *Trickster Makes This World: Mischief, Myth, and Art* (New York: Farrar, Strauss, and Giroux, 1998).
55. PL 23: 1021b.
56. My attempt to capture the sense of ἐφυσιώθην μάτην.
57. PG 10:1577c.
58. Walther Zimmerli, "The Place and Limit of the [sic] Wisdom in the Framework of the [sic] Old Testament Theology," *SJT* 17 (1964):146–58, translation of "Ort und Grenze der Weisheit im Rahmen der alttestamentlichen Theologie," in *Gottes Offenbarung: Gesammelte Aufsätze zum Alten Testament* (München: Kaiser, 1963) 300–15.
59. Zimmerli, "The Place and Limit of Wisdom," see extended critique in Thomas M. Bolin, "Qohelet and the Covenant: Some Preliminary Observations," in *Covenant in the Persian Period: From Genesis to Chronicles*, eds. Richard J. Bautch and Gary N. Knoppers (Winona Lake, IN: Eisenbrauns, 2015) 357–67.
60. Hossfeld describes Ludger Schwienhorst-Schönberger's reading of Ecclesiastes as a "Korrektiv gegenüber einer einseitig offenbarungspositivistisch orientierten (biblischen) Theologie" ("a corrective to a one-sided revelation oriented (biblical) theology." "Die Theologische Relevanz des Buches Kohelet," in *Das Buch Kohelet: Studien zur Struktur, Geschichte, Rezeption, und Theologie*, ed. Ludger Schweinhorst-Schönberger, BZAW 254 [Berlin: De Gruyter, 1997] 269). Hossfeld himself characterizes Qohelet's god as "der monotheistisch-eine und einzige Gott ohne Offenbarungsgeschichte" ("the monotheistic, one and only God without a revelation history") but will maintain that, "insgesamt verkündet Kohelet eine philosophische Position im Horizont des biblischen Gottesglaubens" ("Overall Ecclesiastes proclaimed a philosophical position in the horizon of the biblical faith," ["Die Theologische Relevanz," 387]).
61. Jack T. Sanders, "When Sacred Canopies Collide: The Reception of the Torah of Moses in the Wisdom Literature of the Second Temple Period," *JSJ* 32 (2001): 121–36.
62. Walter Brueggemann, *Theology of the Old Testament: Testimony, Dispute, Advocacy* (Minneapolis: Fortress Press, 1997) 393.
63. Gerhard von Rad, *Wisdom in Israel*, trans. James Martin (London: SCM Press, 1972) 235, translation of *Weisheit in Israel* (Neukirchen-Vluyn: Neukirchener Verlag, 1970). One of the strongest readings in this node is Hans-Peter Müller ("Wie Sprach Qohälät von Gott?" *VT* 18 [1968]: 507–21), who compares Qohelet's thought to the attempt in France after the revolution to replace the Catholic Church with the cult of reason. Qohelet too, failed.
64. Tremper Longman III, *The Book of Ecclesiastes*, NICOT (Grand Rapids, MI: Eerdmans, 1998).
65. Longman, *Ecclesiastes*, 32.
66. Longman, *Ecclesiastes*, 38; cf. the analysis of Carolyn Sharp: "Longman suggests that Qohelet may have been a real person rather than a literary persona, although he gives a nod to the latter possibility. Of interest in Longman's analysis is the suggestion that the frame narrator is quoting the speech of 'Qohelet' for didactic purposes, to warn against skepticism. This nuanced hermeneutical move on Longman's part manages to safeguard some of the heuristic distance of a 'persona' while not abandoning the evangelical affirmation of the literal sense of the text" ("Ironic Representation, Authorial Voice, and Meaning in Qohelet," *Biblical Interpretation* 12 [2004]: 50).
67. Longman, *Ecclesiastes*, 35. Cf. the similar conclusion of Anton Schoors, "God in Qoheleth," in *Schöpfungsplan und Heilsgeschichte: Festschrift für Ernst Haag zum 70. Geburtstag*, ed. R. Broshdscheidt (Trier: Paulinus, 2002) 251–70).

68. James Limburg, *Encountering Ecclesiastes: A Book for Our Time* (Grand Rapids, MI: Eerdmans, 2006) 2–3.
69. Spoken by Lord Illington in Act III of *A Woman of No Importance*.
70. καὶ εἶπα ἐγὼ ἐν καρδίᾳ μου, Ὡς συνάντημα τοῦ ἄφρονος καί γε ἐμοὶ συναντήσεταί μοι, καὶ ἵνα τί ἐσοφισάμην; **ἐγὼ τότε περισσὸν ἐλάλησα ἐν καρδίᾳ μου, διότι ἄφρων ἐκ περισσεύματος λαλεῖ**. ὅτι καί γε τοῦτο ματαιότης ("And I said in my heart, 'What happens to the fool will also happen to me. Why was I so wise?' **Then had I spoken rashly in my heart, because a fool speaks with exaggeration**, so that this too is vanity"). The bold text is not in the Hebrew.
71. Variants in b. Git. 68a and y. Sanh. 20c. Summary in Louis Ginzberg, *Legends of the Bible* (Philadelphia, PA: Jewish Publication Society, 1956) 573–5.

5 Qohelet the Philosopher

In the previous chapter, I discussed some theological readings of Ecclesiastes that negatively contrasted philosophy with religious knowledge. This chapter examines the many readings of Ecclesiastes in its reception history that see it as a kind of philosophy.[1] If any part of the biblical corpus has been understood by readers as philosophical, it is Ecclesiastes. One well-known modern English biblical translation renders "Qohelet" as "philosopher," despite the fact that there is absolutely no lexical warrant for such a choice.[2] Readings of Ecclesiastes as philosophy, and of Qohelet as a philosopher, bear on important methodological issues in modern biblical scholarship that need attention at the outset of this chapter.

Philosophy and Ancient Israel

It was long an unexamined assumption that the Bible is different from philosophical thought. This is in part due to the problematic assumption that philosophy is exclusively Greek. The contrast between biblical thought and Greek thought is also explicitly or implicitly influenced by the anti-Hellenistic rhetoric of 1–2 Maccabees, despite the fact that the problem the author of 1–2 Maccabees has with the Greeks has not so much to do with their philosophy as with their religion. The intellectual histories of Judaism and Christianity (and Islam too, let us remember) demonstrate the tension inherent between their respective (and various) theologies and a number of different philosophical positions. For every Philo, Augustine, Saadia Gaon, or medieval scholastic who has used the Bible in tandem with philosophical concepts, one can find the dissenting voice of a Tertullian scornfully asking what Athens has to do with Jerusalem, or of a Pascal, longing for the biblical God in contrast to "the god of the philosophers."[3]

Recently scholars have begun to expand the rather narrow understanding of philosophy to re-examine ancient intellectual traditions on their own merits and not on their resemblance, or lack thereof, to Greek thought. Marc Van De Mieroop demonstrates that the ancient Babylonians used a sophisticated epistemology in their economic and religious scholarship that was based on their writing system and simultaneous use of Sumerian and Akkadian. The syllabic nature of cuneiform writing, alongside the bilingualism of the literary tradition, allowed a rich variety in how language expressed both what existed in the world around, but also what was linguistically possible even if not really so. Babylonian philosophy was therefore fundamentally a language project.

> Writing was not imitative of thought and secondary to the presentation of knowledge, it was central to it; it created knowledge by adding unsuspected levels and nuances . . . for writings of high culture and special importance the options could be multiplied, adding new levels of understanding and extra nuances.[4]

If Greek philosophy has been characterized as the search for one out of many, Babylonian philosophy is about creating multiplicity out of singularity. Because Babylonian philosophy as described by Van De Mieroop is based on their language(s) and writing system, it cannot be applied analogously to the Hebrew Bible. Some have tried to make sweeping statements about ancient Israelite epistemology or metaphysics based on features of biblical Hebrew, but these attempts have been rightfully debunked.[5] A different and more promising approach is Yoram Hazony's study of philosophy in the Hebrew Bible.[6] I cannot go into a full discussion of this book; it is a significant contribution to the argument that the Hebrew Bible can be read as philosophy in its own right, and not as a derivative from ancient Greek thought. Hazony discusses biblical understandings of political power, truth, knowledge, law, and revelation in order to show that the ancient Israelites approached these same questions at roughly the same time as the Greeks, but independent of them. The Hebrew Bible's philosophical thought has been long overlooked because the Bible and Greek philosophy were transmitted in the Western tradition through the Christian dichotomy of revelation and reason. This locked the Bible into a role where its identity came to be known in part as "not Greek" and "not reason."[7] Approaching the issue from the standpoint of pedagogy, Philip Davies argues for approaching the Hebrew Bible not only as a work of literature, or a theological text, but as a philosophical collection insofar as it explores various answers to existential and metaphysical questions.[8] This is the beginning of a new scholarly investigation into the Bible as a philosophical text, and time will tell how this project will read Ecclesiastes.[9]

Greece and Ancient Israel

In my office I have a reprint edition of Thomas Street Millington's *The Testimony of the Heathen to the Truths of Holy Writ*.[10] Millington, writing at the height of Victorian imperial rule, and with all the condescension of a colonialist, notes that all peoples "however ignorant, however corrupt and darkened in their natural hearts," have knowledge of a creator both from their experience of the natural world and the revelation of natural law. This gives them "a certain religious and moral instinct" that allows them to make "broad distinctions between right and wrong."[11] This observation leads to Millington's more direct purpose: to defend attacks against the teaching of Greek and Latin in the public schools.[12] This defense is not because of any inherent worth of the Classics, but rather because Millington seeks to "make the study of ancient classical literature . . . subservient" to the making of good Christians.[13] In other words, Millington defends the classical tradition in order to perpetuate its use as an example of inferior religion and morality in comparison to Christianity. He does this by assembling quotations from Greek and Latin authors that are similar to biblical texts to demonstrate that the worth of the Classics lies in its resemblance to the Bible.

I begin this section with Millington because what he has done so crudely in connecting classical texts with the Bible continues now. Most of it is conducted with more sophistication and less bias. In addition to expanding the idea of ancient philosophy beyond its Greek setting that I discussed in the previous section, there are scholars who see points of contact between Greek ideas and the narratives of the Hebrew Bible. Much of this work has focused on comparisons between Genesis–2 Kings and Greek historiography. In these studies one finds detailed analyses of how both Greek and biblical historiographers used sources, adapted oral traditions and motifs, and structured their narratives according to overarching themes.[14] In light of the revisions of ancient Israelite history over the past twenty years, a number of books have been written arguing for direct Greek influence on the majority of the Hebrew Bible.[15] The lack of methodological control in some of these arguments is reminiscent of Millington's work 150 years ago. Indeed, the ideological element at work in many attempts to see Greek influence on Israel is so transparent than Niels Peter Lemche has rightfully pointed out the dangers of denying the indisputable fact that the Hebrew Bible is the product of a culture dependent upon the ancient Near East.[16]

Finding clear evidence of Greek influence in a biblical text is no mean feat, and I want to provide an example of something that passes the test. It starts with a biblical Hebrew word with an impeccable Semitic pedigree, משתה. Formed from the root שתה ("drink"), it is attested in both Akkadian (*maštītu*) and Ugaritic (*mšt*) and can refer to a drink, a goblet, or by extension to a festive meal in which wine is served. Abraham has a משתה to celebrate the weaning of Isaac (Gen 21:8). Samson and the Philistines trade riddles at a משתה (Jdgs 14:12–17). Isaiah envisions a משתה hosted by Yahweh for all peoples on Mount Zion (Isa 25:6) and Job's children had a משתה daily with each other before the roof caved in (Job 1:4). In these and many other occurrences where משתה is used, the context makes clear that this is not like the church picnics my relations in North Texas attend, where nothing stronger than iced tea is served. In the Bible these are meals with wine. This makes the occurrence in biblical Hebrew of the phrase, משתה היין, "banquet of wine," oddly redundant, because משתה already refers to a meal where wine is served. משתה היין does not occur in Akkadian or Ugaritic. In the Hebrew Bible, it is found in Esther (5:6, 7:7), and in other early Jewish literature in Hebrew it is also in Sirach (31:31, 32:5). If משתה already describes a festive meal where alcohol is served (and it does), then what is distinctive about a משתה היין? The two terms cannot be synonymous; both occur in Esther (משתה several times). The context in Sirach answers this question. In chapters 31–32, Sirach is offering advice to a young man about how to behave at a משתה היין, which he describes as not just a banquet, but a festive meal that concludes with drinking and formal entertainment presided over by one of the drinkers. Starting in 31:25, Sirach offers standard wisdom advice about eating and drinking in moderation similar to what is found in Proverbs and in Egyptian texts as old as the second millennium. At Sir 31:31, however, a new section starts that offers advice for how to behave at a משתה היין. Specifically, the young man is given advice on what to do if he is made "master of the feast,"[17] with the hopes that he will acquit his duties competently and in the Greek translation be rewarded with a wreath (καὶ εὐκοσμίας χάριν λάβῃς στέφανον; the Hebrew reads, "you will receive understanding because of your discipline" ועל מוסר תשא שכל).[18] It is obvious that Sirach is describing the Greek symposium (συμπόσιον) and adapting the Israelite wisdom tradition to this new Greek practice among Jewish male elites. Indeed, he goes on to extol the music at a משתה היין by comparing it to jewels and precious metals (32:5). It comes as no surprise then, that συμπόσιον is the word used by Greek translators of Sirach and Esther for משתה היין.[19] To summarize: a Greek practice, the symposium, comes to Jewish elites who then adapt the standard Hebrew term for a feast, משתה, to describe the practice. In the Greek translation of Sirach, this term is then translated back into the language of the cultural practice's origin by means of an existing Hebrew term adapted to the new practice. There is no vocabulary in Qohelet that shows signs of a similar process as משתה היין in Sirach.

The LXX, as a product of Hellenistic Judaism, is a significant early witness to how the biblical texts are related to Greek culture. In places one can see that the LXX not only translates the Hebrew text of the Bible into Greek, but emends it to bring it more in line with Greek philosophical thought. The parade example is Exod 3:14, where the LXX renders the Hebrew text's divine self-revelation of "I am who am" (אהיה אשר אהיה) with the substantive participle, ὁ ὤν, a choice doubtless driven by the metaphysical and ontological traditions of Greek philosophy. The LXX version of Qohelet presents a host of fascinating problems. It is a rigid translation that consistently renders the same Hebrew word with the same Greek word every time, regardless of context. Most notably, it oddly and ungrammatically translates the direct object marker את with σύν, a practice that the NETS editor describes as "absurd."[20] That being said, some have argued that Qohelet is borrowing Greek philosophical ideas on the basis of certain key words in Ecclesiastes. Some readings see in Qohelet's use of the Hebrew חלק evidence of the Greek idea of μοῖρα. Both terms mean "lot," and by extension, "destiny." The LXX of Ecclesiastes casts doubt on this. Every occurrence of חלק in Ecclesiastes (2:10, 2:21, 3:22, 5:17–18, 9:6, 9:9, 11:2) is rendered by the Greek μερίς, which *LSJ* notes never means "fate." This might be chalked up to the Greek translator's idiosyncrasy, except that חלק is never rendered by μοῖρα in the entire LXX, but always by μερίς, even in instances where חלק is used to mean "destiny."[21] Martin Hengel reads Qohelet's use of חלק and the related term, מקרה, as Hebrew analogues to the Greek concepts of τύχη ("fortune") and μοῖρα ("fate").[22] But like μοῖρα, τύχη does not occur in LXX Ecclesiastes and is found only twice in the LXX (Gen 30:11, Isa 65:11). Instead, מקרה is consistently rendered as συνάντημα ("occurrence") in the LXX, Ecclesiastes included.[23] Ludger Schweinhorst-Schönberger argues that Qohelet understands divine gift along the same lines as the Greek concept of divine favor (εὐδαιμονία).[24] Dominic Rudman understands Qohelet's use of חשבון ("reckoning, sum, thought") as a Hebrew articulation of the Greek concept of λόγος, conceptualized both by Heraclitus and Stoic thinkers. In particular, Qohelet's use of חשבון in Eccl 7:25 "has the idea of an 'account' or 'rationale' which defines the nature of existence."[25] In a more thoroughgoing way, Alain Buhlman claims that parts of Ecclesiastes that are syntactically or philologically difficult in Hebrew make more sense when translated into Greek, demonstrating, to paraphrase Buhlman, that Qohelet writes in Hebrew but thinks in Greek.[26]

Qohelet and Greek Philosophy

In chapter one I discussed Origen's claim that the three Solomonic books of the Bible (Proverbs, Ecclesiastes, Song of Songs) corresponded respectively to moral, natural, and contemplative philosophy. Origen went ever further and said that the Greeks received knowledge of philosophy from Solomon.[27] Jerome, Dionysius of Alexandria, and Isaac Ibn Ghayyat all read Ecclesiastes as a book of natural philosophy (although both Jerome and Dionysius viewed such thought as inferior to religious content). Samuel Ibn Tibbon, a medieval Jewish commentator on Ecclesiastes, considered Qohelet to be as much of a philosopher as Aristotle.[28] Many modern readers have continued to read the book as a philosophical text and to try to classify it according to known ancient philosophical schools.

Throughout the 19th and the early part of the 20th centuries, numerous parallels were noted between Qohelet and a battery of ancient Greek authors and used to claim the influence of Greek thought on the biblical book.[29] The only kind of methodological principle apparent in much of this work was that volume equaled proof. To that end, the net was cast far and wide throughout the vast corpus of Greek philosophical and literary texts in search of parallels. But there is no comfortable fit between Ecclesiastes and any Greek philosophical school. Qohelet's god is too remote for the Stoics, but too involved for the Epicureans. Qohelet's call to pleasure puts him out of contention as a Cynic. Even the statement in Eccl 3:19–21 that the life of animals and humans is the same, and that they go to the same place after death, does not necessarily need to be seen as a kind of atomism. It fits comfortably into ancient Near Eastern views of the afterlife that go back centuries.[30]

Before looking at various readings that see Qohelet as a philosopher, I need to note briefly scholars for whom Greek influence on Ecclesiastes is unlikely. The decipherment of cuneiform in the 19th century and the subsequent recovery of the literary traditions of the ancient Near East offered scholars another milieu against which to read the Bible. The parallels between Ecclesiastes and the Old Babylonian recension of the *Epic of Gilgamesh* support those readers who do not see any significant similarities the biblical book might have with Greek thought. Among these readers is George Barton, who could write in 1908 that Qohelet "represents, then, an original development of Hebrew thought . . . quite independent of Greek influences."[31] More recently Oswald Loretz has argued strongly for the absence of any evidence of Greek influence on Qohelet, claiming instead that any influences in the book are due to Semitic/ancient Near Eastern literary traditions.[32] Loretz bases his argument in part on the lack of specific, concrete similarities between

Qohelet and Greek literature, combined with the paucity of historical evidence for contact between Palestine and the Greek world prior to Alexander the Great.[33] Christoph Uehlinger has argued that there is no direct dependence of Qohelet on any known piece of cuneiform literature or Greek texts. In place of the dual horizons of Mesopotamia and Greece, he argues for a "third horizon" in which to read Qohelet, consisting of "ancient Levantine literary history . . . Mesopotamian, Egyptian and Levantine wisdom literature of the Persian and Hellenistic periods in their entire scope[34] and not only ancient Old Testament wisdom and/ or Greek-Hellenistic popular philosophy." This brings into the picture heretofore overlooked late first millennium BCE texts from Palestine and Egypt, especially Demotic texts and the *Sayings of Ahiqar*.[35]

Scholars have continuously read Ecclesiastes alongside Greek philosophy. I can group these readings into two basic approaches. In the first are those who see the influence of specific Greek texts on Ecclesiastes. All of these readings share in common the fact that the range of Greek texts at work in Ecclesiastes is varied in both kind and date. I classify these comparative readings as "eclectic influence."[36]

Harry Ranston bases his reading of Qohelet as philosopher on a remark by Isocrates that Hesiod, Theognis, and Phocylides were the most frequently used writers in the inculcation of morals.[37] Ranston claimed that a total of eleven verses in Qohelet betrayed the influence of Theognis and Hesiod's *Works and Days*.[38] The conclusion reached is that

> Koheleth, in his search for suitable proverbs (ix. 9 f.), moved for a time in circles where the minds of the people were stored with the wisdom-utterances of the early sages mentioned by Isocrates as the outstanding teachers of practical morality, Theognis being the most important.[39]

Because he focused not only on a small number of works for comparison, but also on the criterion of the need for there to be similarly arranged blocks of material in order for a parallel to be present, Ranston's analysis anticipates the more successful attempts in recent years by Walter Burkert and Martin West to show ancient Near Eastern influence on Greek epic.[40] I will return to this point later, but for now the question remains: would Ranston have made the same observations about connections between Qohelet and Hesiod, Theognis and Phocylides *without* the quotation from Isocrates?

Another reading of eclectic influence is Rainer Braun's monograph that places Qohelet in a broadly defined intellectual milieu in which numerous sayings, themes, and motifs would be absorbed from Greek thought.[41] Braun argues for similarities between Qohelet and "popular" Greek philosophy, insofar as both share similar viewpoints regarding the worth of wisdom, the understanding of time, the value of wealth, the relationship between occupation and pleasure, critiques of the power structure, and the view of God and human beings.[42] Braun buttresses his claim with a four-page table of parallels between Qohelet and Greek lyric, drama, epic, and gnomic literature, containing over 200 allusions from thirty different Greek authors.[43] John C. Gammie's reading of multiple philosophical schools' influence on Ecclesiastes illustrates the range of possibilities readers are faced with when looking for philosophical material in the book.

> It may be established that Qoheleth did not remain unaffected by gnomic utterances of the Greeks (especially those of Hesiod and Theognis), by Greek philosophical discussion (especially that of the Skeptics and Cynics) and by Greek attitudes toward nature (especially those of the Stoics).[44]

Another example of an eclectic influence reading, but with more methodological rigor than the previous attempts, is that of Schweinhorst-Schönberger who makes a case for Greek influence on Qohelet "as a whole."[45] Rather than pinpoint any specific gnomic expression, Schweinhorst-Schönberger sees a significant point of contact between Qohelet and Greek philosophy in the fact that both exhibit a common concern with the question of human fate. This distinguishes Qohelet from his biblical antecedents in that, while the fundamental question of traditional Israelite wisdom is, "What must a person do to be happy?" Qohelet asks "What is happiness, and on what is it based?" His response—that happiness is fleeting and utterly a divine gift—serves to critique traditional biblical wisdom's idea that happiness could be gained through one's efforts in following the teachings of the sages.[46] More importantly, Schweinhorst-Schönberger compares Ecclesiastes with Greek philosophy on the level of genre, specifically the diatribe. The presence in Ecclesiastes of first- and second-person narrative voices, of a fictional interlocutor (reading the book as a dialogue; see chapter three), and of numerous similes and examples demonstrate that the book is an example of a Hellenistic Jewish diatribe.[47] Apart from the issues of what constituted a genre in antiquity and how one might determine with a sufficient amount of certainty whether an ancient author was choosing a particular genre,[48] the features Schweinhorst-Schönberger identifies as characteristic of the Hellenistic diatribe are—in the case of the use of similes and examples—too dependent upon the inclinations of the reader or—in the case of the presence in Qohelet of a textually constructed interlocutor—still hotly debated among scholars of the book.

The problem with the eclectic influence reading is readily evident: everything depends on what one classifies as a parallel or mark of dependence. Such subjectivity usually leads to a number of parallels from a number of sources. This in turn leads to the problem of how exactly one could imagine an ancient Jewish writer like Qohelet so fully acquainted with a vast array of literature in Greek that he could deftly cite snippets from numerous works of different genres, dates, and provenances. Scholars try to cover this weakness by referring to this hodgepodge of philosophical ideas and allusions as "popular philosophy," but there are precious few examples of similar philosophical cocktails at work in Greek culture. In his very sharp criticism of this method, Loretz underscores this flaw by citing the Latin maxim, *qui nimis probat nihil probat* ("Whoever has proven much has proven nothing").[49] Robert C Harrison is equally skeptical of this entire approach, describing it as "little more than collecting words, phrases, and ideas from Greek literature which remind the researcher of some passage from the Preacher's book."[50]

The other group of readings that see Greek influence on Qohelet do not rely as much on specific texts as they do on an assumed impact of Greek culture on Jerusalem in the Hellenistic period. Martin Hengel's *Judaism and Hellenism* is a milestone in this approach. In his case for Greek influence on Qohelet, Hengel does not draw on the Greek literary tradition for parallels. Instead he relies on inscriptional evidence and data regarding economic and social developments in Hellenistic Palestine.[51] Hengel explicitly states that he does not intend to look for direct textual parallels between Qohelet and Greek texts but rather "to set the thinking of Koheleth beside the spirit and the atmosphere of early Hellenism" in order to see how Qohelet draws upon "the spirit of the time."[52] So his argument for Greek influence in Ecclesiastes is based not so much on the content of the biblical book, but on its literary style, a criterion much more vague than that of genre used by Schweinhorst-Schönberger discussed above. The important features for Hengel are the mediating presence of the author combined with a detached observation of reality. Hengel also draws parallels between the socio-economic situation described by Qohelet and that which obtained during Ptolemaic rule in Palestine, specifically in the rise of *noveau riche* landowners and the concentration of wealth in this new landed gentry. Hengel describes this group as "the well-to-do stratum of society who lived off their capital in the form of land or other investments," and calls them "the really dominant force of the Hellenistic world." He claims that

> Acquaintance with Greek criticism of religion and Greek or Egyptian belief in fate was presumably communicated by Ptolemaic officials, merchants and soldiers, who were not lacking even in Jerusalem . . . In this way Koheleth encountered not the school opinions of the philosophers, but the popular view of the Greek "bourgeoisie."[53]

Hengel's focus on the cultural milieu of Hellenistic Palestine has significantly shaped subsequent arguments both for and against Greek influence in Qohelet. Other readings build on Hengel and seek to explain features of Qohelet in terms of what can be known about Jerusalem in the Ptolemaic era. While archaeological evidence shows the presence of Greek culture in Palestine from the Assyrian period onward, it is difficult to determine how much influence it would have had on the biblical authors in any period.[54] Norbert Lohfink situates Qohelet in the context of a Hellenized Jerusalem elite exploiting the new economic possibilities of third century BCE Palestine.[55] However, in a decisive move away from Hengel's larger aim of downplaying the dichotomy between "Greek" and "Semitic," Lohfink posits in Ptolemaic Jerusalem the kind of tensions between Hellenism and Judaism that mark the rhetoric of the Maccabean texts. He hypothesizes the presence of a Greek school in third-century Jerusalem that competed with the Hebrew school of the Temple. This competition in education was, Lohfink claims, nothing less than the struggle between two opposing cultures.[56] Into the fray then steps Qohelet, who tries to deftly negotiate between the two competing worldviews, in order "to profit as much as possible from the Greek understanding of the world, without forcing Israel's wisdom to give up its status." Because he assumes the presence of Greek educational methods in Jerusalem, Lohfink posits numerous connections between Qohelet and a wide variety of Greek literature, so his reading can also be part of the eclectic influence group.[57] Criticisms of this approach have centered on a problem incisively expressed by Lester Grabbe:

> Even though there is nothing against [the argument for] a Ptolemaic background [in Qohelet] most such suggestions assume we know more about the society and economy of Ptolemaic Palestine than we actually do.[58]

It can also be said that what is known about Jerusalem in this period can also be used to argue against Greek literary influence on Qohelet, as the unpublished dissertation of Harrison does forcefully. Harrison's work manages to construct a socio-economic context for Qohelet in third-century BCE Jerusalem without any Greek literary influences.[59] Any similarities between Qohelet and Greek literature are due not to influence or borrowing, but to similar social and economic crises that elicited similar responses on the part of the respective culture's intelligentsia.[60]

Although my treatment of these readings has been necessarily selective, it gives a sense of the different ways readers have understood Qohelet as a philosopher. These attempts are plagued by the difficulties in the difficult search for Greek parallels to Ecclesiastes discussed above. The book does not comfortably fit with any ancient philosophical school. Close examination of these readings brings significant methodological points into focus. First, there needs to be more care in the use of terminology. As a label, "Hellenism" is an artificial and, in the final analysis, inaccurate description for a significant cultural movement or historical epoch.[61] In particular it is frustratingly ambiguous. In Jewish literary tradition, it refers to Greek culture as opposed to Judaism. Modern scholarship has shown, on the other hand, that "Hellenism" is only partially equated to Greek culture, being instead a synthesis of Greek and ancient Near Eastern cultures. Too often authors writing on the question of Greek influence in Qohelet use the ancient Jewish literary category, a highly charged and tendentious term, as if it were a modern scholarly designation. The solution to this isn't to find a better term than "Hellenism" to describe Palestine in the 4th to 2nd centuries BCE, but to realize that any term is at best a rough place marker for significant new developments occurring alongside stable continuities in Palestine during this time.

Next, it needs to be acknowledged that the nature of wisdom literature makes any kind of comparative work difficult. Proverbial texts are notoriously peripatetic, easily dismantled and rearranged, recast into new contexts, and given different emphases.[62] In wisdom texts, the only clear example of borrowing is the dependence of Prov 22–24 on the Egyptian *Instruction of Amenenope*, but this exception proves the rule, because the parallels there are extensive in both length and ordering. This also makes comparative investigations with Qohelet different from and more difficult than the work done by Burkert and West mentioned above, which compares *Enuma Elish* or *Gilgamesh* to the writings of Homer and Hesiod, because epic texts are narratives and as such offer for comparison elements such as plotlines, type-scenes, motifs, and formulae, which, not only in their common elements, but in their ordering, can help to make a case for the literary relationship between texts.

Apart from content, genre, or cultural influence, another avenue for reading Ecclesiastes as a text influenced by Greek thought examines Qohelet's attitude toward ancient Israelite mythical traditions. Does Qohelet engage in a critique of his mythology in a manner similar to the way Greek philosophers did with theirs?[63] Here is a reading of my own where I show that both Ecclesiastes and Greek philosophical texts engage in a similar process of critiquing the mythical traditions of their respective cultures. The basis of this critique for both Qohelet and Greek philosophers is their belief in the radical transcendence of the divine that sees as inadequate anthropomorphic portrayal of deities in their respective mythologies.[64]

Criticisms of the standard Greek myths found in Homer and Hesiod[65] are put forward even by the pre-Socratics. By far the most explicit critic at this time is Xenophanes of Colophon.[66] Xenophanes charges both Homer and Hesiod with nothing less than blasphemy:

> πάντα θεοῖσ' ἀνέθηκαν Ὅμηρός θ' Ἡσίοδός τε, ὅσσα παρ' ἀνθρώποισιν ὀνείδεα καὶ ψόγος ἐστίν, κλέπτειν μοιχεύειν τε καὶ ἀλλήλους ἀπατεύειν.
> (DK 21b11)

> Homer and Hesiod attribute to the gods everything that among humankind is dishonorable and blameworthy—theft, adultery and deceiving each other.

This is because humanity erroneously believes the gods to be like human beings. In a caustic observation, which Cicero repeats five centuries later,[67] Xenophanes notes:

> ἀλλ' εἰ χεῖρας ἔχον βόες ἵπποι τ' ἠὲ λέοντες ἢ γράψαι χείρεσσι καὶ ἔργα τελεῖν ἅπερ ἄνδρες, ἵπποι μέν θ' ἵπποισι, βόες δέ τε βουσὶν ὁμοίας καί κε θεῶν ἰδέας ἔγραφον καὶ σώματ' ἐποίουν τοιαῦθ', οἷόν περ καὐτοὶ δέμας εἶχον ἕκαστοι.
> (DK 21b15)

> If oxen, horses or lions had hands, and drew with their hands and made things like men do, then horses would make the images of their gods look like horses, and cows make theirs to look like cows. Each would make the bodies similar to what they have.

Because God is ultimately transcendent, any attribution of human qualities, let alone human foibles, cannot be understood as true statements about the divine. What drives this critique is the intertwining in pre-Socratic thought of what only would later come to be known as science and theology, for these thinkers were on a quest for the ground of all being, which, because it would be prior to all reality, was also the true nature of the divine. This helps to explain not only their critiques of the gods in the mythological tradition, but also the claims they made for the divine in place of the old myths. Here is Xenophanes again

> εἷς θεὸς ἔν τε θεοῖσι καὶ ἀνθρώποισι μέγιστος, οὔ τι δέμας θνητοῖσιν ὁμοίιος οὐδὲ νόημα, οὖλος ὁρᾷ, οὖλος δὲ νοεῖ, οὖλος δέ τ' ἀκούει. ἀλλ' ἀπάνευθε πόνοιο νόου φρενὶ πάντα κραδαίνει. αἰεὶ δ' ἐν ταὐτῷ μίμνει κινεύμενος οὐδέν, οὐδὲ μετέρχεσθαί μιν ἐπιπρέπει ἄλλοτε ἄλλῃ.
>
> (DK 21b23–26)

> There is but one god who is the greatest among gods and humanity, like mortals in neither body nor intellect. He sees completely, knows completely, hears completely, but far from toil he moves everything by means of thought. Forever he remains in place, never moving, nor is it fitting for him to move here and there.

Similarly, Heraclitus, in his characteristically paradoxical way, asserts that "there is one alone who is wise, both willing and unwilling to be called by the name 'Zeus'" (ἓν τὸ σοφὸν μοῦνον λέγεσθαι οὐκ ἐθέλει καὶ ἐθέλει Ζηνὸς ὄνομα [DK B32]). Heraclitus's remark illustrates the complex and ambiguous relationship that ancient Greek intellectuals had with their myths. Even Plato, for all his animus toward myth, acknowledged that they were useful teaching devices for the young and used them himself in several of his dialogues.[68] Mythological traditions were given a new lease on life both in drama and allegory. While the development of prose allowed for both historiographical and philosophical texts, the older traditions could also be adapted and retold. The upshot is that the same kinds of claims about human existence could be made in poetic, historiographical, and philosophical texts.[69]

Elsewhere I have argued that Ecclesiastes portrays an adversarial relationship between humanity and God understood in metaphysical terms insofar as it revolves around the connection between knowledge and immortality. It is most succinctly expressed by Qohelet's recurring refrain הכל הבל ורעות רוח ("All is vanity[70] and a chasing after the wind," [NRSV]) which I translate as "All is mortal but strives for immortality."[71] An antagonistic understanding of the divine-human relationship can be found in ancient mythologies across the ancient Near East and Greece. Among them are mythic narratives offering etiologies for human mortality understood as something ordained by the gods to act as a limit on humankind's godlike cognitive abilities.[72] In each of these myths, a protagonist either acquires wisdom at the cost of immortality or in the realization that death is the irrevocable human lot, gains wisdom. At this juncture, it is worth pointing out that this is also a recurring theme in Greek tragedy, most poignantly expressed in Sophocles's retelling of the Oedipus cycle. As has been pointed out numerous times, the audience watching *Oedipus Tyrannos* would already have known that Oedipus is a patricide who has also committed incest with his mother. This is mentioned already in Homer (*Od.*

11.271–74). The play is not about what Oedipus has done. At the outset both heinous deeds have long since been committed. The play is about human knowledge: what human beings know about themselves and how one particular human being comes to know about who and what he truly is. And this knowledge is the source of pain. The chorus expresses this succinctly on seeing the self-mutilated king: δείλαιε τοῦ νοῦ τῆς τε συμφορᾶς ἴσον ("You are as wretched for knowing about what you have done as for having done it" *Oed. Tyr.* 1346).

Like these earlier narratives, Ecclesiastes views the human condition as one in which human knowledge—the trait that makes us like God—is the cause of human suffering because of death—the trait that distinguishes us from God. What is significant is how Qohelet chooses to express this situation. Rather than recount an etiological tale with a primeval human being symbolizing all of us who then engages in a struggle with an anthropomorphically portrayed deity, Qohelet's metaphysical conclusions are expressed in assertions based on his own life experiences and observations. Indeed, he takes a term that has already been personified in an etiological tale about the first human death (הבל is also the Hebrew name, "Abel"), restores it to its abstract sense, and uses it repeatedly to describe human existence. I think there are three places in Ecclesiastes where one can read Qohelet offering a critique of earlier Israelite myths. He is motivated to do so by an understanding of his god as transcendent and impossible to be validly described anthropomorphically in myths.

In Eccl 3:11, Qohelet critiques the creation myth of Genesis 2–3[73] in such a way as to reassert the transcendence and sovereignty of God.

> גם את העלם נתן בלבם מבלי אשר לא ימצא האדם את המעשה אשר עשה האלהים מראש ועד סוף
>
> [God] has put eternity into [humanity's] mind, but has made it so that humans cannot grasp the things which God has done from beginning to end.

This anthropology echoes the Eden Story in Genesis 2–3, where at the end the man and woman "have become like gods" (Gen 3:5, 22) in their acquisition of wisdom, but are still a part of the created world in their mortality.[74] This situation is due to the initiative of the man and woman in transgressing the prohibition set by God against eating from the tree of knowledge. Notice that for Qohelet, however, the human struggle between its godlike knowledge ("eternity into its mind") and its mortality is not due to an act of disobedience or rebellion on its own part, as in the myth of Genesis 2–3. It is the doing of God and seems to be a part of how things have been created to be. For Qohelet, there can be no question of human beings taking anything from God that the deity would not allow them to have. This is in marked contrast to the highly anthropomorphic portrayal of God in the Eden narrative, who creates with his hands (2:7), walks in the garden in the evenings (3:8), does not know where the man and woman are when they have hidden themselves (3:9), and feels threatened by the human couple's newfound power (3:22). Qohelet turns away from this Israelite myth about the struggles of the first couple with the limits put on them by God and in its place asserts that human knowledge has been *given* to human beings by God with limits already set and unable to be transgressed.

A second sustained mythological critique occurs in Qohelet's descriptions of human effort. He believes all human activity to be ultimately worthless and refers most often to it with terms derived from the root עמל ("toil").[75] What makes Qohelet's remarks about the futility of human effort is his equally insistent claim that toil has been given to human beings by God as their lot in life (Eccl 2:13, 2:24, 3:13, 5:18, 9:9). When Qohelet speaks of humanity's burden as a toil assigned to them by God, he is drawing on an ancient Near Eastern mythological tradition that stretches back to the Bronze Age. This tradition understands the rationale behind the creation of human beings as the gods' need for service. In *Enuma Elish*, Marduk creates the first people in order to cement his authority over the remainder of the divine assembly by having freed them from any need to work for themselves. Similarly, in the earliest complete version of the Mesopotamian flood narrative, *Atrahasis*, the high gods are faced with a revolt by the lower deities, who have become fed up with the onerous task of serving the elites of the divine world. To defuse the situation, Ea, the god of wisdom, in concert with the high god Enlil and the creator goddess Mami, create seven primordial human couples who will then procreate a world full of people for the specific purpose of serving the gods. This is also the case in a biblical creation myth. After planting a garden, Yahweh creates the first man "to work it and guard it" (לעבדה ולשמרה, Gen 2:15). A partial rationale for the view in these myths that human labor is ordained by the gods is that it supports the practice of offerings made to deities.[76] This belief that the gods need our service is subjected to critique by ancient philosophers, notably Plato in *Euthyphro*. There, after Euthyphro agrees that the making of offerings to the gods in exchange for blessings is a kind of trade between human beings and the gods, Socrates challenges Euthyphro

> φράσον δέ μοι, τίς ἡ ὠφελία τοῖς θεοῖς τυγχάνει οὖσα ἀπὸ τῶν δώρων ὧν παρ' ἡμῶν λαμβάνουσιν; ἃ μὲν γὰρ διδόασι παντὶ δῆλον· οὐδὲν γὰρ ἡμῖν ἐστιν ἀγαθὸν ὅτι ἂν μὴ ἐκεῖνοι δῶσιν. ἃ δὲ παρ' ἡμῶν λαμβάνουσιν, τί ὠφελοῦνται; ἢ τοσοῦτον αὐτῶν πλεονεκτοῦμεν κατὰ τὴν ἐμπορίαν, ὥστε πάντα τὰ ἀγαθὰ παρ' αὐτῶν λαμβάνομεν, ἐκεῖνοι δὲ παρ' ἡμῶν οὐδέν.
>
> (*Euthyphr*. 14e–15a)

> I wish that you would show me what benefit the gods gain from accepting our gifts. One thing that is clear is that there is no blessing for us that the gods do not give. But how do the things the gods receive from us help them? We must cheat them in this exchange, since we receive all blessings from them, while they receive nothing from us.

It is no coincidence that this is the same dialogue where Plato has Socrates question the validity of the Greek mythological tradition to speak truly about the divine. In response to Euthyphro's use of Hesiod as a prooftext to justify the prosecution of his own father, Socrates asks, "Do you really believe these things happened this way?" (Σύ ὡς ἀληθῶς ἡγῇ ταῦτα οὕτως γεγονέναι; [*Euthyphr*. 6b]). Similarly for Qohelet, a truly transcendent God cannot be in need of anything that human beings can provide. This helps to explain Qohelet's claim in Eccl 4:17 that it is better to listen during temple worship than to offer sacrifice.

Because it looks more at its method than its content, this aspect of the Greek philosophical tradition offers a point of contact with Ecclesiastes. For Qohelet, as for these Greek thinkers, the transcendence and power of God demands critique of the mythological tradition. Old stories must be reinterpreted or replaced by anthropological and theological statements that take into account what these thinkers believed to be the correct nature of the deity. The God described in Ecclesiastes is distant, seemingly capricious and without need of human beings. This corresponds to the understanding of the divine that comes out of early Greek philosophical tradition, where one often finds use of the term τὸ θεῖον ("the divine") in the pre-Socratics in order to avoid any connection between their understanding of God with the gods of the old stories.[77]

Ecclesiastes as Philosophy

There are other readings of Qohelet as a philosopher that do not rely on historical claims about Greek (or other) influences. For these readings, Ecclesiastes as a text and Qohelet as a thinker are placed alongside philosophies and philosophers from across time and cultures. This brings an element of timelessness to the book that lends it a cultural authority akin to the book's cache as inspired scripture for some readers. Part of the longstanding dichotomy between religion and philosophy that has marked much of the history of Jewish and Christian thought, readers for whom Qohelet is a theological iconoclast often describe him positively as a philosopher. Morris Jastrow's description of Qohelet as "a gentle cynic" comes to mind, Jastrow's use of "cynic" having little to do with the ancient philosophical school.

One of the most substantive readings of Ecclesiastes in this interpretive node is Michael Fox's use of the "absurd" in the thought of Albert Camus to understand Qohelet's concept of הבל.[78] Fox understands the absurd as

> a disjunction between two phenomena that are thought to be linked by a bond of harmony or causality, or that *should* be so linked . . . Absurdity arises from a contradiction between two undeniable realities.[79]

Camus advises revolt against an absurd world that will never make sense and to which the only rational response is suicide. To revolt against absurdity is, therefore, to live in a world where there is no meaning. Fox sees Qohelet's repeated cry that "all is absurd" (הכל הבל) as "ultimately a protest against God" and his call to a life of enjoyment an articulation of revolt.[80]

Mark Sneed classifies Qohelet as a pessimist which, while not a distinct philosophical school, is a philosophical stance based on how one views the world and the demands that view places on a person's choices. Like Fox, Sneed sees the problem not with Qohelet's thinking but with the world.[81] The particular dangers of Qohelet's historical context made pessimism an appropriate response to the world. It was the smart thing to do. Sneed goes further and points out that modern

American culture's fetishizing of optimism can and has been harmful. Qohelet's promotion of pessimism might also be good advice for us.

In a way similar to the readings discussed in the previous chapter that see Qohelet as working within the normative theological tradition, readings that see Ecclesiastes as a book of philosophy do not negatively evaluate Qohelet's thought. Rather they soften the blow of his words by pointing out how many of his observations about the world accurately describe the case. Building on this foundation, Qohelet's advice can be seen as helpful for modern readers, if not exactly affirming.

Discussion of this last interpret node allows me to move into a brief conclusion to this final chapter. Nobody, as far as I know, has read the words of Qohelet and said, "He's a nihilist. This book is evil."[82] That may be partly because Qohelet's is an intriguing personality: multifaceted and defiant of easy description. Few, if any, readers would agree equally with everything Qohelet says, but almost every reader has encountered at least one thing in Ecclesiastes that has evoked recognition and assent. That will keep us reading.

Notes

1. Much of this chapter draws upon papers I gave in Jerusalem (2009) and Madison, Wisconsin (2016). I am grateful for the feedback from the listeners at both gatherings.
2. American Bible Society, *The Good News Translation* (New York: American Bible Society, 1976).
3. Readers more knowledgeable than I about intellectual history will doubtless find fault with this statement. To them I can only say that I am aware that I am flattening a great deal of nuance here, but I think it warranted because the more generalized view was long prevalent in biblical studies.
4. Marc Van De Mieroop, *Philosophy before the Greeks: The Pursuit of Truth in Ancient Babylonia* (Princeton, NJ: Princeton University Press, 2016) 219.
5. One watershed moment being James Barr's dismantling of Thorleif Boman's argument (James Barr, *The Semantics of Biblical Language* [Oxford: Clarendon, 1961] in response to Thorleif Boman, *Das hebräische Denken im Vergleich mit dem Grieschichen* [Göttingen: Vandenhoeck & Ruprecht, 1954]).
6. Yoram Hazony, *The Philosophy of Hebrew Scripture* (Cambridge: Cambridge University Press, 2012).
7. Hazony, *The Philosophy of Hebrew Scripture*, 1–27.
8. Philip R. Davies, "Teaching the Bible as Philosophy," *Postscripts* 7 (2011): 213–24.
9. Hazony mentions Ecclesiastes in passing and in regard to the book's focus on observation as a source of knowledge. Dru Johnson is also an early contributor to this research, see his *Scripture's Knowing: A Companion to Biblical Epistemology* (Eugene, OR: Cascade, 2015). The Society of Biblical Literature now has annual meeting sections devoted to the Hebrew Bible and philosophy.
10. Thomas Street Millington, *The Testimony of the Heathen to the Truths of Holy Writ* (London: Seeley, Jackson, and Halliday,1863).
11. Millington, *Testimony of the Heathen*, vi.
12. "It has often been said that in our public schools too much time is bestowed upon the study of Greek and Latin classics. If the object of such study were merely the acquisition of languages, or if it were to be regarded only as a means of strengthening the mental powers and improving the taste, there might be some show of reason in the objection" (Millington, *Testimony of the Heathen*, x).
13. Millington, *Testimony of the Heathen*, xi.

14. John Van Seters, *In Search of History: Historiography in the Ancient World and the Origins of Biblical History* (New Haven: Yale University Press, 1983); Flemming Nielsen, *The Tragedy in History: Herodotus and the Deuteronomistic History*, LHBOTS (Sheffield: Sheffield Academic Press, 1997); Thomas M. Bolin, "History, Historiography, and the Use of the Past in the Hebrew Bible," in *The Limits of Historiography: Genre and Narrative in Ancient Historical Texts*, ed. Christina Kraus (Leiden: E. J. Brill, 1999) 113–40; Jan-Wim Wesselius, *The Origin of the History of Israel: Herodotus'* Histories *as Blueprint for the First Books of the Bible*, LHBOTS (Sheffield: Sheffield Academic Press, 2002); Katherine Stott, *Why Did They Write This Way? Reflections on References to Written Documents in the Hebrew Bible and Ancient Literature* (London/New York: T & T Clark, 2008). For a more thoroughgoing attempt to see points of contact between Greek thought and the Bible, see John Pairman. Brown, *Israel and Hellas*, 3 vols. (Berlin: De Gruyter, 1995–2001); abridged as *Ancient Israel and Ancient Greece: Religion, Politics, and Culture* (Minneapolis, MN: Fortress, 2003).
15. Philippe Wajdenbaum, *Argonauts of the Desert: Structural Analysis of the Hebrew Bible* (London: Routledge, 2014); Thomas L. Thompson and Philippe Wajdenbaum, eds., *The Bible and Hellenism: Greek Influence on Jewish and Early Christian Literature* (London: Routledge, 2014); Russell E. Gmirkin, *Plato and the Creation of the Hebrew Bible* (London: Routledge, 2016).
16. "And a final commentary: The present orientation towards the Hellenistic period as the time of origins of everything found in the Old Testament may at the end have counter-productive consequences similar to those that came as a result of the *Babel-Bibel Streit* some hundred years ago. After having argued for the Mesopotamian origins of practically every single element of Old Testament narrative and literature, nobody for several generations wanted to include anything except the occasional reference to Babylonian literature and culture thus blinding biblical scholars from seeing the perspective in arguing for more extensive Mesopotamian traits found in the Old Testament. A *Hellas-Bibel Streit* instead of a *Babel-Bibel Streit* could easily have the same unwanted consequences. The Old Testament may be a Jewish collection of literature dating to the Hellenistic and Roman Period, but it is definitely not a Greek or Roman book" (Niels Peter Lemche, "Does the Idea of the Old Testament as a Hellenistic Book Prevent Source Criticism of the Pentateuch?" *SJOT* 25 [2011]: 92, in explicit dialogue with his earlier article, "The Old Testament—A Hellenistic Book?" *SJOT* 7 [1993]: 163–93).
17. This in itself is a fascinating case that deserves more space than I can give it here. The Hebrew of Sirach 32:1 in Ms. B contains a parallelism: ראש סמוך אל תותר שבראש עשירים אל תסתורה, while the the LXX has only one phrase: Ἡγούμενόν σε κατέστησαν; μὴ ἐπαίρου. Hebrew text in Pancratius C. Beentjes, *The Book of Ben Sira in Hebrew*, VTSup 68 (Leiden: Brill, 2003) 109.
18. Hebrew text from Ms. B of Sirach, in Beentjes, *The Book of Ben Sira*, 58.
19. The Greek of Sirach 31:31 translates משתה היין literally: ἐν συμποσίῳ οἴνου.
20. A more sympathetic analysis of Ecclesiastes's Greek translator is in Françoise Vinel, *L'Ecclésiaste*, L'Bible d'Alexandrie 18 (Paris: Editions du Cerf, 2002) 49–62.
21. Not only in Ecclesiastes, but also in Isa 17:14. Dominic Rudman maintains that the meaning of חלק in Ecclesiastes is different from its other occurrences in the Hebrew Bible (*Determinism in the Book of Ecclesiastes*, JSOTSup 316 [Sheffield: Sheffield Academic Press, 2001] 55–60).
22. Martin Hengel, *Judaism and Hellenism: Studies in Their Encounter in Palestine during the Early Hellenistic Period*, trans. John Bowden, 2 vols. (Philadelphia, PA: Fortress Press, 1974) trans. of *Judentum und Hellenismus: Studien zu ihrer Begegnung unter besonderer Berücksichtigung Palästinas bis zur Mitte des 2 Jh.s v. Chr*, 2d. rev. ed., WUNT 10 (Tübingen: Mohr/Siebeck, 1973) 1.119–25.
23. Data in John Jarick, *A Comprehensive Bilingual Concordance of the Hebrew and Greek Texts of Ecclesiastes* (Atlanta: Scholars Press, 1993). Discussion of other terms in

Qohelet believed to be translations from Greek in Robert C. Harrison, Jr., "Qoheleth in Social-Historical Perspective," (PhD diss., Duke University, 1991) 71.

24. Ludger Schwienhorst-Schönberger, *Kohelet*, HThKAT (Freiburg: Herder, 2004).
25. Rudman, *Determinism*, 191.
26. Alain Buhlman, "The Difficulty of Thinking in Greek and Speaking in Hebrew (Qoheleth 3.18; 4.13–16; 5.8)," *JSOT* 90 (2000): 101–8.
27. *Prologue to the Commentary on the Song of Songs*, in Rowan A. Greer, *Origen: An Exhortation to Martyrdom, Prayer, and Selected Works*, CWS (New York: Paulist, 1979) 231–2.
28. Sara Klein-Braslavy, "The Alexandrian Prologue Paradigm in Gersonides' Writings, *JQR* 95 (2005): 260–1.
29. Detailed summaries of 19th-century readings in Christian Ginsburg, *Coheleth, Commonly Called the Book of Ecclesiastes* (London: Longman, Green, Longman and Roberts, 1861) and George A. Barton, *A Critical and Exegetical Commentary on the Book of Ecclesiastes*, ICC (Edinburgh: T & T Clark, 1908).
30. Compare the criticisms in Harrison, "Qoheleth in Social-Historical Perspective," 80–102.
31. Barton, *Ecclesiastes*, 43. For Barton's citation of the *Gilgamesh* parallel, see 39; for a detailed overview of 19th-century scholarship dealing with the question of Greek influence on Qohelet, see 32–43.
32. Oswald Loretz, *Qohelet und der alte Orient: Untersuchungen zu Stil und theologischer Thematik des Buches Qohelet* (Freiburg: Herder, 1964).
33. "Das Fehlen konkreter Bezüge zum griechischen Geistesleben . . . hat die Autoren nun dazu gerführt, sich mit allgemeinen Urteilen über einem angeblichen grieschischen Einfluß auf das Buch Qohelet zu begnügen. Die Schwäche dieser Theorie eines allgemeinen Einflusses des hellenistischen Zeitalters auf Qohelet liegt in der Tatsache, daß sie sich nur auf allgemeine Ähnlichkeiten zwischen dem Buch Qohelet und schriftlichen Zeugnissen aus der hellenistischen Epoche berufen kann." ("The lack of concrete connections to Greek intellectual life . . . means that scholars must be content with a general claim about alleged Greek influence on the Book of Qohelet. The weakness of the claim for an overall Hellenistic influence on Qohelet lies in the fact that only a general similarity can be found between the Book of Qohelet and written texts from the Hellenistic era." [Loretz, *Qohelet und der alte Orient*, 53).
34. "altlevantinischen Literaturgeschichte . . . die mesopotamische, ägyptische und levantinische Weisheitsliteratur der persischen und hellenistischen Zeit in ihrer ganzen Breite" (Christoph Uehlinger, "Qohelet im Horizont mesopotamischer, levantinischer und ägyptischer Weisheitsliteratur der persischen und hellenistischen Zeit," in *Das Buch Kohelet: Studien zur Struktur, Geschichte, Rezeption, und Theologie*, ed. Ludger Schweinhorst-Schönberger, BZAW 254 [Berlin: De Gruyter, 1997] 156).
35. Uehlinger, "Qohelet im Horizont," 229.
36. Those of you who bothered to come to this note are rewarded with my apologies for such wooden terminology.
37. Harry Ranston, *Ecclesiastes and the Early Greek Wisdom Literature* (London: Epworth, 1925). Robert Lowth had already made a connection between Eccl 11:1 and Theognis (*Lectures on the Sacred Poetry of the Hebrews Translated from the Latin by G. Gregory to Which Are Added the Principal Notes of Professor Michaelis and Notes By the Translator and Others*, 4th ed. [London: Thomas Tegg, 1849] 108).
38. Ranston, *Ecclesiastes*, 31–8, 66–71 see also his "Ecclesiastes and Theognis," *AJSL* 34 (1918): 99–122.
39. Ranston, *Ecclesiastes*, 150.
40. Walter Burkert, *The Orientalizing Revolution: Near Eastern Influence on Greek Culture in the Early Archaic Age* (Cambridge, MA: Harvard University Press, 1992), Martin West, *The East Face of Helicon: West Asiatic Elements in Greek Poetry and Myth* (New York: Oxford University Press, 1999).

41. Rainer Braun, *Kohelet und die frühhellenistische Popularphilosophie*, BZAW 130 (Berlin: De Gruyter, 1973). "Die Analysen der Motivverwendung, des Stils und der Komposition Kohelets beim Aufbau seiner Einzelsentenzen haben gezeigt, daß die frühhellenistische Bildung, insbesondere die griechischen und pessimistischen Stoffe und deren Traditionen, bestimmend auf Kohelet eingewirkt haben müssen." ("The analysis of the use of motifs, the style and the composition of Qohelet has shown that, when constructing his sentences, he must have utilized early Hellenistic learning, particularly Greek and pessimistic material and their traditions" [149]).
42. Braun, *Kohelet*, 168–9.
43. "Zusammenstellung der besprochenen griechischen Parallelen zu Kohelet und ihres Vorkommens im griechischen Denken" (*Kohelet*, 146–9). See also the critique in Harrison, "Qoheleth in Social-Historical Perspective," 74–6) Harrison characterizes Braun's use of Greek texts as "willy-nilly" (*ibid.*, 77).
44. John C. Gammie, "Stoicism and Anti-Stoicism in Qoheleth," *HAR* 9 (1985): 171. Also: "We may take it as probable, however, that the educated son of David in Jerusalem was not unfamiliar with the main tenets of Stoicism as taught by Zeno, Cleanthes, Chrysippus and Sphaerus—either mediated to him directly through writings or translations thereof, or through Hebrew and Aramaic renditions of excerpts carried to him in correspondence from compatriots—most likely from friends in the sizeable Jewish community in Alexandria" (184).
45. Ludger Schwienhorst-Schönberger, *'Nicht im Menschen gründet das Glück' (Koh 2,24): Kohelet im Spannungsfeld jüdischer Weisheit und hellenistischer Philosophie*, Herders Biblische Studien 2 (Freiburg: Herder, 1994); *idem*, *Kohelet*. For Schwienhorst-Schönberger, any investigation into the genre of Qohelet "muß sagen, mit welcher antiken literarischen Form das Buch Kohelet *als ganzes* die meisten Ähnlichkeiten besitzt" ("must determine which literary form *as a whole* the book of Ecclesiastes most resembles") in order to understand "wie das Buch Kohelet *als ganzes* im Horzont hellenistischer Philosophie verstanden werden kann"("how the book of Ecclesiastes can be understood *as a whole* in the context of Hellenistic philosophy." *'Nicht im Menschen gründet das Glück'*, 246).
46. Schwienhorst-Schönberger, *'Nicht im Menschen gründet das Glück'*, 274–8. "Wenn wir allerdings bedenken, daß die Frage nach dem Inhalt und den Bedingungen der Möglichkeit menschlichen Glücks im Zentrum der hellenistischen Philosophien einschließlich der Bewegung des Kynismus stand und dabei gleichzeitig berücksichtigen, daß sich etwa *eine* Generation nach Kohelet griechische Einflüsse in der jüdischen Literatur (Sir) mit einem hohen Grad an Wahrscheinlichkeit nachweisen lassen, dann ist es durchaus wahrscheinlich, daß Kohelet in seinem Denken von der hellenistischen Philosophie angeregt worden ist" ("However, if we consider that the question of the substance and the conditions for the possibility of human happiness stood in the center of Hellenistic philosophies, including the Cynic movement, and take into account at the same time that about a generation after Ecclesiastes, there is the high probability of Greek influence on Jewish literature (Sirach) then it is quite likely that Hellenistic philosophy influenced the thought of Ecclesiastes" [278]). For another example of seeing Greek influence in Qohelet, see Rudman, *Determinism in the Book of Ecclesiastes*.
47. Schwienhorst-Schönberger, *'Nicht im Menschen gründet das Glück'*, 247–8.
48. I have discussed this in Thomas M. Bolin, *Freedom beyond Forgiveness: The Book of Jonah Re-Examined*, JSOTSup 236 (Sheffield: Sheffield Academic Press, 1997) 46–53.
49. Loretz, *Qohelet und der alte Orient*, 54.
50. Harrison, "Qoheleth in Social-Historical Perspective," 76.
51. Hengel, *Judaism and Hellenism*, 1.115–30. Significantly, Hengel's larger project in his book (i.e., to argue for the thorough Hellenization of Palestine), is at odds with the Judaism versus Hellenism dichotomy that Loretz uses in claiming the absence of Greek influence on Qohelet (*Qohelet und der alte Orient*, 57).

52. Hengel, *Judaism and Hellenism*, 1.116, 119.
53. Hengel, *Judaism and Hellenism*, 1.124–7.
54. Morton Smith has argued there is sufficient literary and archaeological evidence to support Greek cultural, economic, and military presence in Palestine in the two centuries between the end of the Babylonian Exile and the conquest of Alexander (*Palestinian Parties and Politics that Shaped the Old Testament*, 2nd corrected ed. [London: SCM, 1987] 43–61). See also Ephraim Stern, *Archaeology of the Land of the Bible Volume II: The Assyrian, Babylonian, and Persian Periods (732–332 B.C.E.)*, AYBRL (New York: Random House, 2001) 217–27. Note especially Stern's conclusion: "From this combined evidence of both written documents and archaeological remains, it appears that, even before the arrival of the Assyrians, but mainly during and after their period of domination, there was Greek penetration into Palestine by traders and mercenaries. No discussion of the archaeology of Palestine of this period can ignore them" (227). This observation would seem to meet the criterion established by Harrison: "To establish Greek influence in Qoheleth convincingly, it is absolutely necessary to show that circumstances existed in Qoheleth's time which provide a plausible context for the transmission of Hellenistic forms and ideas from the Greek world to the biblical writer" ("Qoheleth in Social-Historical Perspective,"116).
55. Norbert Lohfink, *Qoheleth*, trans. Sean McEvenue, CC (Minneapolis, MN: Fortress Press, 2003) 44 trans. of *Kohelet*, NEchtB (Würzburg: Echter Verlag, 1980).
56. Lohfink, *Qoheleth*, 5. For a more nuanced articulation of this, see David Carr, *Writing on the Tablet of the Heart: Origins of Scripture and Literature* (New York: Oxford University Press, 2005).
57. Lohfink, *Qoheleth*, 6. See the list of connections in James Crenshaw, "Qoheleth in Current Research," *HAR* 7 (1984): 55–6, repr. as pages 520–34 in *Urgent Advice and Probing Questions: Collected Writings on Old Testament Wisdom* (Macon, GA: Mercer University Press, 1995) 527–8.
58. Lester Grabbe, *Judaism from Cyrus to Hadrian*, 2 vols. (Minneapolis, MN: Fortress Press, 1992) 1.175.
59. "Qoheleth's encounter with Hellenism was largely on a socio-economic plane. The idea that Greek intellectual and material culture was pervasive—or even generally present—in third century Judea was found to be insupportable in terms of archaeological evidence and documentation from first-hand historical sources." (Harrison, "Qoheleth in Social-Historical Perspective," 343).
60. Harrison, "Qoheleth in Social-Historical Perspective," 321–33.
61. So Reinhold Bohlen, "Kohelet Im Kontext Hellenistischer Kultur," in *Das Buch Kohelet: Studien zur Struktur, Geschichte, Rezeption und Theologie*, ed. L. Schwienhorst-Schönberger, BZAW 254 (Berlin/New York: De Gruyter, 1997) 249.
62. Miriam Lichtheim (*Late Egyptian Wisdom Literature in the International Context: A Study of Demotic Instructions*, OBO [Freiburg: Vandenhoeck & Ruprecht, 1983] 28–31) discusses what she refers to as "seven international proverbs," most of which have contacts with Qohelet.
63. Discussed in Hengel, *Judaism and Hellenism*, 1.125–7 and Hans-Peter Müller, "Plausibilitätsverlust Herkömmlicher Religion Bei Kohelet Und Den Vorsokratikern," in *Gemeinde ohne Tempel. Zur Substituierung und Transformation des Jerusalemer Tempels und seines Kults im Alten Testament, antiken Judentum und frühen Christentum*, eds. Beate Ego, Armin Lange, and Peter Pilhofer, WUNT 118 (Tübingen: Mohr Siebeck, 1999) 99–114.
64. I am not concerned with Plato's particular criticism of the idea of "myth" as a type of discourse, but rather with the criticism of traditional stories about the gods, which I refer to as "myths." I acknowledge that I am side-stepping a significant issue, but point the reader for detailed discussion of Plato's understanding of μῦθος to Bruce Lincoln, *Theorizing Myth: Narrative, Ideology, and Scholarship* (Chicago: University of Chicago Press, 1999) 3–43 and Luc Brisson, *How Philosophers Saved Myths: Allegorical*

Interpretation and Classical Mythology, trans. Catherine Tihanyi (Chicago: University of Chicago Press, 2004) 5–28; trans. of *Introduction à la philosophie du mythe: Sauver les mythes* (Paris: Librairie Philosophique J. Vrin, 1996).

65. By the end of the 6th century BCE, Homer and Hesiod represent a kind of canonical Greek mythological literature (Gregory Nagy, *Homeric Questions* [Austin, TX: University of Texas Press, 1996]).
66. For discussion see Georg Rechenauer, *Xenophanes von Kolophon. Ein Vorsokratiker zwischen Mythos und Philosophie* (Stuttgart: Teubner, 1996); Jonathan Barnes, *Early Greek Philosophy*, rev. ed. (New York: Penguin, 2001) 40–7.
67. An tu aquilam aut leonem aut delphinum ullam anteferre censes figuram suae? Quid igitur mirum, si hoc eodem modo homini natura praescripsit, ut nihil pulchrius quam hominem putaret? Eam esse causam, cur deos hominum similis putaremus ("Do you think that an eagle, a lion or a dolphin prefers any shape to its own? And if nature has given this characteristic to us too, so that a person should find nothing more beautiful than another person, then isn't this really why we imagine the gods to look like human beings? If animals were rational, don't you think that each species would make itself the crown of creation?" [*de nat. deor.* 1.77]).
68. E.g., *Gorgias* 320c-323a; *Symposium* 189c-193e; 201d-212c; *Republic* 614b-621d. On the complex role of myth in ancient Greek intellectual life, see Paul Veyne, *Did the Greeks Believe in Their Myths? An Essay on the Constitutive Imagination*, trans. Paula Wissing (Chicago: University of Chicago Press, 1988), trans. of *Les Grecs ont-ils cru à leurs mythes?* (Paris: Editions du Seuil, 1983).
69. E.g., compare *Oedipus Tyrannos* with Herodotus's story (1.30–32) of the exchange between Solon and Croesus on the true nature of human happiness discussed above in chapter two.
70. The use of "vanity" to translate הבל is due largely to the influence of Jerome, who followed the LXX and rendered ματαιότης as "vanitas." The immense amount of scholarship spent trying to define exactly what Qohelet means by הבל is beyond the scope of my discussion. A recent overview is Russell L. Meek, "Twentieth- and Twenty-first-century Readings of *Hebel* (הבל) in Ecclesiastes," *CurBR* 14 (2016): 279–97.
71. The phrase is in Eccl 1:14; 2:11, 17, 26; 4:4, 16; 6:9. See Thomas M. Bolin, "Rivalry and Resignation: Girard and Qoheleth on the Divine-Human Relationship," *Bib* 86 (2005): 245–58.
72. Shlomo Izre'el, *Adapa and the South Wind: Language Has the Power of Life and Death* (Winona Lake, IN: Eisenbrauns, 2001) 120–49; Tryggve N. D. Mettinger, *The Eden Narrative: A Literary and Religio-historical Study of Genesis 2–3* (Winona Lake, IN: Eisenbrauns, 2007). Jerome Segal argues that the idea of conflict between God and humankind is the overarching theme of the entire Pentateuch (*Joseph's Bones: Understanding the Struggle between God and Mankind in the Bible* (New York: Penguin, 2007).
73. For others who think that Qohelet knows the garden story, see R. Norman Whybray, "Qoheleth as a Theologian," in *Qohelet in the Context of Wisdom*, ed. Anton Schoors (Leuven: Peeters, 1998), 239–65; Horacio Simian-Yofre, "Conoscere la Sapienza: Qohelet e Genesi 2–3," in *Il Libro Del Qohelet: Tradizione, redazione, teologia*, eds. G. Bella and A Passaro, Cammini nello Spirito Biblica 44 (Milan: Paulist, 2001) 314–36. Katharine Dell argues that there is no intertextual connection between the two texts ("Exploring Intertextual Links between Ecclesiastes and Genesis 1–11," in *Reading Ecclesiastes Intertextually*, eds. Katharine Dell and Will Kynes, LHBOT 587 (London: Bloomsbury, 2014) 9–10, but does so on the basis that Ecclesiastes does not have a notion of a fall.
74. See also Mettinger, *The Eden Narrative*, 123–35.
75. Roots derived from עמל occur 35 times in Ecclesiastes; see Jarick, *A Comprehensive Bilingual Concordance*.
76. This is discussed in greater detail in Thomas M. Bolin, "The Role of Exchange in Ancient Mediterranean Religion and Its Implications for Reading Genesis 18–19," *JSOT* 39 (2004): 37–56.

77. Anton Schoors has argued for a similar understanding of Qohelet's exclusive use of the term אלהים. ("God in Qoheleth," in *Schöpfungsplan und Heilsgeschichte: Frestschrift für Ernst Haag zum 70. Geburtstag*, ed. R. Broshdscheidt [Trier: Paulinus, 2002] 251–70).
78. Michael V. Fox, *A Time to Tear Down and a Time to Build Up: A Rereading of Ecclesiastes* (Grand Rapids, MI: Eerdmans, 1999) 8–14, 27–49. See Diethelm Michel, *Untersuchungen zur Eigenart des Buches Qohelet*, BZAW 183 (Berlin: Walter De Gruyter, 1989), 40–51; and Benjamin Berger, "Qoheleth and the Exigencies of the Absurd," *BibInt* 9 (2001): 141–79.
79. Fox, *A Time to Tear Down*, 31.
80. Fox, *A Time to Tear Down*, 49.
81. Mark Sneed, *The Politics of Pessmism in Ecclesiastes: A Social-Science Perspective*, AIL 12 (Atlanta, GA: SBL Press, 2012) 231–53. Similarly, Stuart Weeks sees the problem with Qohelet's world instead of his thinking: "It is not scepticism or even pessimism that characterizes Qohelet's ideas, then, so much as a sense that humans are missing the point . . . If his analysis is largely negative, that is because, in a world of illusion, there is value in disillusion" (*Ecclesiastes and Scepticism*, LHBOTS [London: T & T Clark, 2012] 169).
82. The key words being, "as far as I know." I await correction and education from readers and reviewers.

Conclusion

An Anticipatory *Apologia*

As I bring this book to a close, I am acutely aware of its shortcomings. Reception history is a deep engagement with what we usually call "secondary" literature. It was impossible to discuss all of the interpretations of Ecclesiastes, but I have tried my best to be representative. I read much more than I have included, and there is yet much more left to read. This book is a first foray into this kind of reception history, an exploratory trench in the large tell constituted of readings of Ecclesiastes. I ignored a good part of the early modern period because many readings of Ecclesiastes from that era are themselves literary works and I wanted to focus on theological and academic readings of the book. Thankfully Eric Christianson has treated a number of these readings in his excellent reception history of Ecclesiastes.[1] I engaged some readings more than others—the Midrash, Gregory of Nyssa, Jerome—because in all honesty they were richer than other readings; their multivalence matched that of Ecclesiastes itself. It is sometimes the case in reception history that some readers are more sensitive than others to a range of potential interpretations in a text and are able to dwell with the kind of polysemy such texts produce. I need not have separated chapters 1 and 2, which both discuss readings of Qohelet as a king, but I chose to do so because of the importance of Solomonic readings for so much of the reception history of Ecclesiastes. In contrast, I grouped older and newer readings together in the chapters on contradiction and on Qohelet as saint and sinner. These were judgment calls on my part and can rightfully be second guessed. Some readers may think the book too short, given the topic. To them I can only say that this was never conceived as an exhaustive reception history. I think such a thing impossible to be honest; instead I intend this book to be a first attempt and a roadmap for future scholars to take up. In particular, the individual interpretive nodes I have described can be further broken down into smaller groups of readings. I hope there are readers who are willing to do this work.

Reception History and Historical Criticism

This book is not an indictment of historical criticism. I am trained as a historical critic, and most of my research and publications are in that wheelhouse. Nor am I trying to prove that historical-critical readings of Ecclesiastes are the same as earlier ones in every respect. But I have demonstrated that modern scholarly readings of Ecclesiastes are part of an interpretive tradition that extends back to antiquity and that they are in part shaped by the potential meanings in the text. For example, when the non-Solomonic authorship of Ecclesiastes became widely accepted, it did not resolve the tension between the authorial voices in the book. Instead it opened up new interpretive possibilities now that readers were free to construct profiles of the biblical authors beyond the limits imposed by the traditional descriptions of Solomon, creative as those traditions are. But the theological problem of Qohelet's orthodoxy remained, and so some of the interpretive problems at work in pre-modern Jewish and Christian readings of the book persist in modern biblical scholarship. Academic treatments of Ecclesiastes problematize differences between Qohelet's theological views and those in the rest of the Hebrew Bible, as did the rabbis. Qohelet's expressions of despair or exhortations to pleasure are as much moral problems in need of solutions for historical critics, such as Norbert Lohfink or Eunny Lee, as they are for Gregory of Nyssa or Martin Luther. This is not how other ancient literature is read by modern scholars. The wrath of Achilles in the *Iliad* raises questions about the Homeric narrative, characterization, heroic values, and a host of literary and historical issues. It is not a problem about wrath itself that the scholar must tackle. What biblical scholars have failed to notice, and what reception history can help to reveal, is the existence of a blind spot in historical critical exegesis that gives its practitioners the illusion of an entirely objective point of view. An example of this blind spot at work, but with a contemporary non-scholarly reading rather than one from the past, is Harold Bloom's book on the Yahwist. Bloom, a literary critic and not an exegete, engaged in a thought experiment, imagining a woman at King Solomon's court as the author of a theologically daring narrative of Israel's origins.[2] *The Book of J* was vigorously criticized by biblical scholars for problems with its translation of the Hebrew, and Bloom's alleged interpretive liberties with the biblical text. What was passed over with little critique is the fact that Bloom offers a reading of a text that does not exist, but that was created by biblical scholars. Bloom's Solomonic Yahwist is based on the historical work of Gerhard von Rad. His reading of later redactors as theologically constricting J's enigmatic, surprising, and capricious Yahweh could have been taken right from Wellhausen's work on the Pentateuch. This irony was lost on those biblical scholars who shook their heads at Bloom's perceived flights of fancy without noticing their similarities with respected academic readings of the Pentateuch.[3] All this is to say that biblical scholarship is itself a part of reception history. Indeed, so is the practice of reception history. We do not watch the stream flow by from the riverbank. We are in the stream.

I want to continue this discussion of reception history and historical-critical exegesis with the help of three more readings of Ecclesiastes.

> In hoc capitulo, diversa omnium explanatio fuit, et tot pene sententiae, quot homines (The interpretations of this chapter are so diverse that there are as many opinions are there are people.)
>
> (Jerome, *Commentary on Ecclesiastes*, 12:1)[4]

> This book is one of the more difficult books in all of Scripture, one which no one has ever completely mastered. Indeed, it has been so distorted by the miserable commentaries of many writers that it is almost a bigger job to purify and defend the author from the notions which they have smuggled into him than it is to show his real meaning.
>
> (Martin Luther, *Notes on Ecclesiastes* 15:7)[5]

> To Fox he is a seeker of truth eager to communicate his experiences. To Frye he is a realist embarked on a critique of the way of wisdom. To Patterson he is a journal-keeping humanist. To Whybray he is a distinctly Jewish philosopher. To Zimmerman he is a melancholy storyteller. To each of them Qoheleth is a character who (according to Ecclesiastes) interacted with the world and left it with his consequent thoughts and judgments. In each instance the tendency is to assume the presence of a cohesive narrative character at the heart of Ecclesiastes."
>
> (Eric S. Christianson)[6]

Jerome's comment might be cause for despair, but he is reading a text that for him contains meaning on multiple levels and that can tolerate a limited amount of ambiguity so long as it is framed by theological orthodoxy. A historical critic would see Jerome's wry comment as a challenge to cull later interpretations from any potential original meanings of the words with the aim of recovering the author's thoughts.[7] The aim of this process is to eliminate readings and narrow the range of interpretations. Less is better. This is the bread and butter of biblical criticism. Luther writes with one foot in Jerome's world and the other in the nascent era of historical criticism. He seeks a meaning that is both original in a literary sense—gone for him are the multiple senses of Scripture—but also consonant with the intent of the divine author of scripture. The scholars listed in the quote by Christianson all seek a single, unified voice in Ecclesiastes that can be placed in recognizable descriptive labels, part of a larger intellectual taxonomy with multiple examples for each category.

In contrast reception history places no normative value on whether there are few or many interpretations of a text. In this regard it is descriptive, but not merely descriptive. This is because, as Brennan Breed makes clear, readings are not simply things brought to the text by readers but determined by the text's own interpretive potential. The descriptive power of reception history is focused on the text, isolating some of the strands of its polyvalence. In Breed's words, reception history allows us to envision "the text as the protagonist."[8] This text-centered focus is what places reception history in the realm of biblical criticism, which John Barton points out is an essentially literary, and not historical, task.[9]

Here the difference between reception history and historical criticism appears. Ambiguity is a problem for historical critics. Multiple potential readings must be weighed and ranked. This is part of the reason why Breed's discussion of reception history begins with textual criticism. It is the premier exegetical method aimed at eliminating ambiguity. But historical criticism has met its match in Ecclesiastes, a book where, in one instance, the Hebrew word for "foolishness" (סכלות) is written as the word for "intelligence" (שכלות).[10] In a book-length study on ambiguities in Ecclesiastes, Doug Ingram argues that they are intentional.[11] If this is the case, then the ways readers make sense of those ambiguities are important for the historical-critical project of trying to get at a text's ancient meaning. Reception history can help that project, because it does not see ambiguity as a problem to be solved but rather an interpretive opportunity to be mined for all it's worth. All this being said, reception history does not need to justify its validity on the grounds of its utility for historical criticism.

Reception history of the author in Ecclesiastes shows that one of the book's most prominent textual features (i.e., its multiple authorial voices) has continuously exercised the creativity of readers. Some reconciled the voices of the book with an externally created figure called "Solomon." Others parsed different theological positions from among the voices and ranked them according to externally imposed theological criteria. In almost every case the result was that the readers had in some way inscribed themselves and their theological biases into the text. How else could Jerome have taken a book that repeatedly urges its readers to take pleasure in food and drink and read it as a treatise on the merit of self-mortification? How else could Jastrow and Longman be in agreement concerning major compositional aspects of Ecclesiastes, yet diverge so completely in their respective evaluations of these literary phenomena?[12]

To group and examine these readings by their semantic nodes instead of by religious tradition or chronology allows Breed's interpretive marbles not to fall where they may, but to fall in a certain way that tells us much about the interpretive richness of the text alongside the biases and creativity of the interpreters. This makes reception history more than a curio shop displaying odd or interesting readings. Reception history does not erase all genre distinctions between readings and the different aims readers bring to texts. It shows how the finite number of potential readings in a text limits the kinds of meanings readers construe, even when these readers occupy different historical times, carry different confessional commitments, and write in different genres. Nor does reception history make historical criticism irrelevant. Historical criticism remains necessary to biblical studies, but it ought no longer be privileged in relation to other forms of biblical interpretation. Reception history is an engagement with the Bible that is nothing less than a reconception of biblical scholarship.[13]

Notes

1. Eric S. Christianson, *Ecclesiastes through the Centuries*, Blackwell Bible Commentaries (Malden, MA: Wiley-Blackwell, 2007) 40–65.
2. Harold Bloom and David Rosenberg, *The Book of J: Translated by David Rosenberg and Interpreted by Harold Bloom* (New York: Grove Weidenfeld, 1990).
3. An exception is Edwin M. Good's review of *The Book of J*: "that Bloom gives us here a superbly crafted, subtle, shrewd reading of a document that is itself a fiction, that never existed and exists only in fictive imagination—Bloom's and also those of other folks, some scholars and some not. Bloom's reading of J is magnificent, but if J and its author

are the products of scholarly or literary speculation, constructed by modern readers to answer some questions that had to be raised about the Torah, then the reading is of a text that came to be in the modern imagination, not in any ancient one" (Edwin M. Good, review of *The Book of J*, by Harold Bloom and David Rosenberg, *USQR* 45 [1991]: 139). In contrast, Walter Brueggemann's major critique is that "There is more than a little danger that this sort of commentary becomes a clever, safe aesthetic program. It seems clear that literary criticism and commentary (of which Bloom is a skillful practitioner) need to be done alongside or in the presence of sociological criticism. In this case, readers might refer to *The Bible's First History* by Robert B. Coote and David Robert Ord, which is a hard-nosed sociological analysis of J" (Walter Brueggemann, review of *The Book of J*, by Harold Bloom and David Rosenberg, *ThTo* 48 [1991]: 240). To praise a book as "a hard-nosed sociological analysis" of a text that does not exist is as telling an example of biblical scholarship's blind spot as I can imagine.

4. PL 23:1105a.
5. Jaroslav Pelikan and Hilton C. Oswald, *Notes on Ecclesiastes, Lectures on the Song of Solomon, Treatise on the Last Words of David*, Luther's Works 15 (St. Louis: Concordia Press, 1972) 7.
6. *A Time to Tell: Narrative Strategies in Ecclesiastes*, JSOTSup 280 (Sheffield: Sheffield Academic Press, 1998) 21, quoted in Kyle Greenwood, "Debating Wisdom: The Role of Voice in Ecclesiastes," *CBQ* 74 (2012): 477–8. Compare also my discussion in this conclusion with Christianson's section, "How Might This Reception History Inform the Discipline?" in *Ecclesiastes through the Centuries*, 261–3.
7. This is itself no mean feat. The scholarly bibliography on Ecclesiastes 12 is massive.
8. Brennan Breed, *The Nomadic Text: A Theory of Biblical Reception History*, ISBL (Bloomington: Indiana University Press, 2014) 205.
9. John Barton, *The Nature of Biblical Criticism* (Louisville, KY: Westminster John Knox Press, 2007) 9–30.
10. Eccl 1:17. This is addressed at least as far back as Rashbam (Sara Japhet and Robert B Salters, *The Commentary of R. Samuel Ben Meir Rashbam on Qoheleth* [Jerusalem: Magnes Press, 1985] 98); Mark Sneed, "(Dis)closure in Qohelet: Qohelet Deconstructed," *JSOT* 27 (2002): 124–5; and Anton Schoors, *The Preacher Sought to Find Pleasing Words: A Study of the Language of Qoheleth. Part II: Vocabulary*, OLA 143 (Leuven: Peeters, 2004) 19. *DCH* lists סכל as a by-form of שכל.
11. Doug Ingram, *Ambiguity in Ecclesiastes*, LHBOTS 431 (London: T & T Clark, 2006).
12. An illustration of Jacques Berlinerblau's observation that "the strange way in which the Hebrew Bible was assembled in antiquity impacts how it is read in modernity" (*The Secular Bible: Why Nonbelievers Must Take Religion Seriously* [New York: Cambridge University Press, 2005] 89).
13. Breed, *Nomadic Text*, 206.

Bibliography

(Formatted according to *The SBL Handbook of Style* [2nd edition] and *The Chicago Manual of Style* [16th edition].)

Anderson, Bernhard W. *Understanding the Old Testament*. 3rd ed. Englewood Cliffs, NJ: Prentice Hall, 1975.

Anderson, William H. U. "Philosophical Considerations in a Genre Analysis of Qoheleth." *VT* 48 (1998): 289–300.

Aurifaber, Joannes. *Tischreden; oder, Colloquia Doct. Mart. Luthers mit einem Nachwort von Johannes Adler*. Eisleben: Gaubisch, 1566.

Bachmann, E. Theodore. *Word and Sacrament I*. Luther's Works 35. Philadelphia: Fortress Press, 1960.

Baden, Joel and Candida Moss. "Can Hobby Lobby Buy the Bible?" *Atlantic Monthly* 317 (January–February 2016): 70–77. http://www.theatlantic.com/magazine/archive/2016/01/can-hobby-lobby-buy-the-bible/419088/.

Barbour, Jennie. *The Story of Israel in the Book of Qohelet: Ecclesiastes as Cultural Memory*. Oxford Theological Monographs. Oxford: Oxford University Press, 2012.

Barnes, Jonathan. *Early Greek Philosophy*. Rev. ed. New York: Penguin, 2001.

Barr, James. *The Semantics of Biblical Language*. Oxford: Clarendon, 1961.

———. *The Concept of Biblical Theology*. Minneapolis, MN: Fortress Press, 1999.

Bart, William Hamilton. *Discussions on Philosophy and Literature: Education and University Reform*. New York: Harper and Brothers, 1861.

Bartholomew, Craig. *Reading Ecclesiastes: Old Testament Exegesis and Hermeneutical Theory*. AnBib 139. Rome: Pontifical Biblical Institute, 1993.

———. *Ecclesiastes*. Grand Rapids, MI: BCOTWP, 2009.

Barton, George. *A Critical and Exegetical Commentary on the Book of Ecclesiastes*. ICC. Edinburgh: T & T Clark, 1908.

Barton, John. *The Nature of Biblical Criticism*. Louisville, KY: Westminster John Knox Press, 2007.

Beckett, Samuel. *Krapp's Last Tape and Other Dramatic Pieces*. New York: Grove Press, 1960.

Beentjes, Pancratius C. *The Book of Ben Sira in Hebrew*. VTSup 68. Leiden: Brill, 2003.

Berger, Benjamin. "Qoheleth and the Exigencies of the Absurd." *BibInt* 9 (2001): 141–79.

Berlinerblau, Jacques. *The Secular Bible: Why Nonbelievers Must Take Religion Seriously*. New York: Cambridge University Press, 2005.

Bickerman, Elias. *Four Strange Books of the Bible: Jonah, Daniel, Koheleth, Esther*. New York: Schocken, 1985.

Binder, Gerhard and Leo Liesenborghs. *Didymos der Blinde: Kommentar zum Ecclesiastes (Tura-Papyrus) Teil I.1.* Bonn: Rudolf Habelt Verlag, 1979.

Bloom, Harold and David Rosenberg. *The Book of J: Translated by David Rosenberg and Interpreted by Harold Bloom.* New York: Grove Weidenfeld, 1990.

Boda, Mark J., Tremper Longman III, and Cristian G. Rata, eds. *The Words of the Wise Are like Goads: Engaging Qohelet in the 21st Century.* Winona Lake, IN: Eisenbrauns, 2013.

Bolin, Thomas M. "'Should I Not also Pity Nineveh?'—Divine Freedom in the Book of Jonah." *JSOT* 67 (1995): 109–20.

———. *Freedom beyond Forgiveness: The Book of Jonah Re-Examined.* JSOTSup 236. Sheffield: Sheffield Academic Press, 1997.

———. "History, Historiography, and the Use of the Past in the Hebrew Bible." Pages 113–40 in *The Limits of Historiography: Genre and Narrative in Ancient Historical Texts.* Edited by Christina Shuttleworth Kraus. Leiden: Brill, 1999.

———. "The Role of Exchange in Ancient Mediterranean Religion and Its Implications for Reading Genesis 18–19." *JSOT* 39 (2004): 37–56.

———. "Rivalry and Resignation: Girard on Qoheleth and the Divine-Human Relationship." *Bib* 86 (2005): 245–59.

———. "The Biblical Commission's Instruction, *On the Historical Truth of the Gospels* (*Sancta Mater Ecclesia*) and Present Magisterial Attitudes toward Biblical Exegesis." *Gregorianum* 93 (2012): 765–85.

———. "Qohelet and the Covenant: Some Preliminary Observations." Pages 357–67 in *Covenant in the Persian Period: From Genesis to Chronicles.* Edited by Richard J. Bautch and Gary N. Knoppers. Winona Lake, IN: Eisenbrauns, 2015.

Bolt, Robert. *A Man for All Seasons.* New York: Vintage, 1990.

Boman, Thorleif. *Das hebräische Denken im Vergleich mit dem Grieschichen.* Göttingen: Vandenhoeck & Ruprecht, 1954.

Bottèro, Jean. *Mesopotamia: Writing, Reasoning, and the Gods.* Translated by Zainab Bahrani and Marc Van De Mieroop. Chicago: University of Chicago Press, 1992. Translation of *Mésopotamie. L'écriture, la raison et les dieux.* Paris: Gallimard, 1987.

Braun, Rainer. *Kohelet und die frühhellenistische Popularphilosophie.* BZAW 130. Berlin: De Gruyter, 1973.

Breed, Brennan. *The Nomadic Text: A Theory of Biblical Reception History.* ISBL. Bloomington: Indiana University Press, 2014.

Briant, Pierre. *From Cyrus to Alexander: A History of the Persian Empire.* Translated by Peter T. Daniels. Winona Lake, IN: Eisenbrauns, 2002. Translation of *Histoire de l'Empire perse: de Cyrus à Alexandre.* Paris: Fayard, 1996.

Brisson, Luc. *How Philosophers Saved Myths: Allegorical Interpretation and Classical Mythology.* Translated by Catherine Tihanyi. Chicago: University of Chicago Press, 2004. Translation of *Introduction à la philosophie du mythe: Sauver les mythes.* Paris: Librairie Philosophique J. Vrin, 1996.

Brown, John Pairman. *Israel and Hellas.* 3 vols. Berlin: De Gruyter, 1995–2001.

———. *Ancient Israel and Ancient Greece: Religion, Politics, and Culture.* Minneapolis, MN: Fortress, 2003.

Brown, William P. *Ecclesiastes.* IBC. Louisville, KY: John Knox Press, 2000.

Broyde, Michael J. "Defilement of the Hands, Canonizationo of the Bible, and the Special Status of Esther, Ecclesiastes, and Song of Songs." *Judaism* 44 (1995): 65–79.

Brueggemann, Walter. "Review of *The Book of J*, by Harold Bloom and David Rosenberg." *ThTo* 48 (1991): 234–40.

———. *Theology of the Old Testament: Testimony, Dispute, Advocacy.* Minneapolis: Fortress Press, 1997.

Buhlman, Alain. "The Difficulty of Thinking in Greek and Speaking in Hebrew (Qoheleth 3.18; 4.13–16; 5.8)." *JSOT* 90 (2000): 101–8.

Bundvad, Mette. *Time in the Book of Ecclesiastes*. Oxford Theological Monographs. Oxford: Oxford University Press, 2015.

Burkert, Walter. *The Orientalizing Revolution: Near Eastern Influence on Greek Culture in the Early Archaic Age*. Cambridge, MA: Harvard University Press, 1992.

Burkes, Shannon. *Death in Qoheleth and Egyptian Biographies of the Late Period*. SBLDS 170. Atlanta, GA: Society of Biblical Literature, 1999.

Camporeale, Salvatore I. "Lorenzo Valla's 'Oratio' on the Pseudo-Donation of Constantine: Dissent and Innovation in Early Renaissance Humanism." *Journal of the History of Ideas* 57 (1996): 9–26.

Carr, David. *Writing on the Tablet of the Heart: Origins of Scripture and Literature*. New York: Oxford University Press, 2005.

———. *The Formation of the Bible: A New Reconstruction*. New York: Oxford University Press, 2011.

Casey, Maurice. "Porphyry and the Origin of the Book of Daniel." *JTS* 27 (1976): 15–33.

Christianson, Eric. *A Time to Tell: Narrative Strategies in Ecclesiastes*. JSOTSup 280. Sheffield: Sheffield Academic Press, 1998.

———. "Voltaire's *Precis* of Ecclesiastes: A Case Study in the Bible's Afterlife." *JSOT* 29 (2005): 455–84.

———. *Ecclesiastes through the Centuries*. Blackwell Bible Commentaries. Malden, MA: Wiley-Blackwell, 2007.

———. "Ecclesiastes in Premodern Reading: Before 1500 C.E." Pages 3–36 in *The Words of the Wise Are like Goads: Engaging Qohelet in the 21st Century*. Edited by Mark J. Boda, Tremper Longman III, and Cristian G. Rata. Winona Lake, IN: Eisenbrauns, 2013.

Collins, John. *The Bible after Babel: Historical Criticism in a Postmodern Age*. Grand Rapids: Eerdmans, 2005.

Crenshaw, James L. "Impossible Questions, Sayings, and Tasks." *Semeia* 17 (1980): 19–34.

———. "Qoheleth in Current Research." *HAR* 7 (1984): 41–56. Reprinted as pages 520–34 in *Urgent Advice and Probing Questions: Collected Writings on Old Testament Wisdom*. Macon, GA: Mercer University Press, 1995.

———. *Ecclesiastes*. OTL. Philadelphia: Westminster Press, 1987.

———. "Ecclesiastes: Odd Book In." *BRev* 31 (1990): 28–33.

Curkpatrick, Stephen. "A Disciple for Our Time: A Conversation." *Int* 55 (2001): 285–91.

Davies, Philip R. *In Search of "Ancient Israel": A Study in Biblical Origins*. JSOTSup 148. Sheffield: Sheffield Academic Press, 1992.

———. "Method and Madness: Some Remarks on Doing History with the Bible." *JBL* 114 (1995): 699–705.

———. "Teaching the Bible as Philosophy." *Postscripts* 7 (2011): 213–24.

Dawood, Nessim Joseph. *Tales from the Thousand and One Nights*. Rev. ed. London: Penguin, 1973.

Delitzsch, Franz. *Biblischer Commentar Über Die Poetischen Bücher des Alten Testaments Vierter Band: Hoheslied und Koheleth*. Leipzig: Dörffling and Franke, 1875.

Dell, Katharine. "Ecclesiastes as Wisdom: Consulting Early Interpreters." *VT* 44 (1994): 301–29.

———. *Interpreting Ecclesiastes: Readers Old and New*. Critical Studies in the Hebrew Bible 3. Winona Lake, IN: Eisenbrauns, 2013.

———. "Exploring Intertextual Links between Eccleisastes and Genesis 1–11." Pages 3–14 in *Reading Ecclesiastes Intertextually*. Edited by Katharine Dell and Will Kynes. LHBOT 587. London: Bloomsbury, 2014.

Dell, Katharine and Will Kynes, eds. *Reading Ecclesiastes Intertextually*. LHBOTS. London: Bloomsbury, 2014.

Dever, William G. *What Did the Biblical Writers Know and When Did They Know It?: What Archeology Can Tell Us about the Reality of Ancient Israel*. Grand Rapids, MI: Eerdmans, 2001.

Dobbs-Allsopp, F.W. *On Biblical Poetry*. New York: Oxford University Press, 2015.

Drummond, Andrew L. "Alexander Geddes 1737–1802: Roman Catholic Priest and Higher Critic in the Age of Reason." *Historical Magazine of the Protestant Episcopal Church* 35 (1966): 73–85.

Eco, Umberto. *The Name of the Rose*. Translated by William Weaver. New York: Harvest, 1983. Translation of *Il nome della rosa*. Milan: Fabbri-Bompiani, 1980.

Eissfeldt, Otto. *The Old Testament: An Introduction*. Translated by Peter Ackroyd. New York: Harper and Row, 1965. Translation of *Einleitung in das Alte Testament*. 3 Auflage. Tübingen: Mohr Siebeck, 1964.

England, Emma and William John Lyons, eds. *Reception History and Biblical Studies: Theory and Practice*. LHBOTS. London: Bloomsbury, 2015.

Evans, Robert. *Reception History, Tradition, and Biblical Interpretation: Gadamer and Jauss in Current Practice*. LBHOTS. London: Bloomsbury, 2014.

Fagles, Robert. *Sophocles: Three Theban Plays*. Rev. ed. New York: Penguin, 1984.

———. *Homer: The Odyssey*. New York: Penguin, 1996.

Förstemann, K. E. and H. E. Bindseil. *D. Martin Luthers Tischreden oder Colloquia nach Aurifaber's erster Ausgabe*. 4 vols. Berlin: Gebauer'sche Buchhandlung,1844–1848.

Foster, Benjamin. "On Authorship in Akkadian Literature." *Annali di Istituto Universitario Orientali di Napoli* 51 (1991): 17–32.

Foster, Donald. *Elegy by W.S.: A Study of Attribution*. Newark, DE: University of Delaware Press, 1989.

Foucault, Michel. "What Is An Author?" Translated by Donald Bouchard and Sherry Simon. Pages 178–93 in *Professing the New Rhetorics: A Sourcebook*. Edited by Theresa Enos and Stuart C. Brown. Englewood Cliffs, NJ: Prentice Hall, 1994. Translation of "Qu'est ce qu'un auteur?" *Bulletin de la société française de philosophie* 63 (1969): 73–104.

Fox, Michael V. "Frame-Narrative and Composition in the Book of Qohelet." *HUCA* 48 (1977): 83–106.

———. *Qohelet and His Contradictions*. JSOTSup 71. Sheffield: Almond Press, 1989.

———. *A Time to Tear Down and a Time to Build Up: A Rereading of Ecclesiastes*. Grand Rapids, MI: Eerdmans, 1999.

Frahm, Eckart. "Keeping Company with Men of Learning: The King as Scholar." Pages 508–32 in *The Oxford Handbook of Cuneiform Culture*. Edited by Karen Radner and Eleanor Robinson. New York: Oxford University Press, 2011.

Fry, Gérard. *Jérôme Lit l'Ecclésiaste*. Les Pères dans la Foi 79–80. Paris: Migne, 2001.

Gadamer, Hans-Georg. *Truth and Method*. Translated by Joel Weinsheimer and Donald G. Marshall. 2nd rev. ed. New York: Crossroad, 1989. Translation of *Gesammelte Werke* 1. Rev. and expanded ed. Tübingen: Mohr Siebeck, 1986.

Galling, Kurt. "Koheleth-Studien." *ZAW* 50 (1932): 276–99.

Gammie, John. "Stoicism and Anti-Stoicism in Qoheleth." *HAR* 9 (1985): 169–87.

George, Andrew R. *The Babylonian Gilgamesh Epic: Introduction, Critical Edition, and Cuneiform Texts*. 2 vols. Oxford: Oxford University Press, 2003.

Gese, Hartmut. "The Crisis of Wisdom in Koheleth." Translated by Lester Grabbe. Pages 141–53 in *Theodicy in the Old Testament*. Edited by James Crenshaw. IRT 4.

Philadelphia, PA: Fortress, 1983. Translation of "Die Krisis der Wiesheit bei Koheleth." Pages 139–51 in *Le sagesses du Proche-Orient ancien*. Paris: Presses Universitaires de France, 1963.

Ginsburg, Christian D. *Coheleth, Commonly Called the Book of Ecclesiastes*. London: Longman, Green, Longman and Roberts, 1861.

Ginzberg, Louis. *Legends of the Bible*. Philadelphia, PA: Jewish Publication Society, 1956.

Gmirkin, Russell E. *Plato and the Creation of the Hebrew Bible*. London: Routledge, 2016.

Goldman, Yohanan A. P. "Qoheleth." in *Megilloth*. BHQ 18. Stuttgart: Deutsche Bibelgesellschaft, 2004.

Gómez-Aranda, Mariano. "Ibn Ezra and Rashbam on Qohelet: Two Perspectives in Contrast." *HS* 46 (2005): 236–58.

———. "The Influence of Isaac Ibn Ghayyat on Abraham Ibn Ezra's Commentary on Ecclesiastes." *JJS* 63 (2012): 84–104.

Good, Edwin M. "Review of *The Book of J*, by Harold Bloom and David Rosenberg." *USQR* 45 (1991): 138–42.

Goodrich, Richard J. and David J. D. Miller. *Jerome: Commentary on Ecclesiastes*. ACW. Mahwah, NJ: Paulist Press, 2012.

Grabbe, Lester. *Judaism from Cyrus to Hadrian*. 2 vols. Minneapolis, MN: Fortress Press, 1992.

———. "Intertextual Connections between the Wisdom of Solomon and Qoheleth." Pages 201–13 in *Reading Ecclesiastes Intertextually*. Edited by Katherine Dell and Will Kynes. LHBOTS. London: Bloomsbury, 2014.

Gramberg, Carl Peter Wilhelm. *Kritische Geschichte der Religionsideen des alten Testaments*. 2 vols. Berlin: n.p., 1830.

Greenfield, Sayre N. *The Ends of Allegory*. Newark, DE: University of Delaware Press, 1998.

Greenspan, Ezra. *Walt Whitman's "Song of Myself" A Sourcebook and Critical Edition*. New York: Routledge, 2005.

Greenwood, Kyle. "Debating Wisdom: The Role of Voice in Ecclesiastes." *CBQ* 73 (2012): 476–91.

Greer, Rowan A. *Origen: An Exhortation to Martyrdom, Prayer, and Selected Works*. CWS. New York: Paulist, 1979.

Greidanus, Sidney. *Preaching Christ from Ecclesiastes*. Grand Rapids, MI: Eerdmans, 2010.

Grotius, Hugo. *Annotationes in Vetus Testamentum in Hugonis Grotii Opera omnia theologica, in tres tomos divisa, ante quidem per partes, nunc autem conjunctim et accuratius edita, curis Petri Grotii*. 4 vols. London: Moses Pitt, 1679.

Hall, Stuart George, ed. *Gregory of Nyssa: Homilies on Ecclesiastes*. Berlin: de Gruyter, 1993.

Halperin, David J. "The 'Book of Remedies', the Canonization of the Solomonic Writings, and the Riddle of Pseudo-Eusebius." *JQR* 2/72 (1982): 269–92.

Halton, Charles. "Allusions to the Stream of Tradition of Neo-Assyrian Oracles." *ANES* 46 (2009): 50–61.

Harding, James. "What Is Reception History and What Happens to You If You Do It?" Pages 31–44 in *Reception History and Biblical Studies: Theory and Practice*. Edited by Emma England and William John Lyons. LHBOTS. London: Bloomsbury, 2015.

Harrison, Robert C. "Qoheleth in Social-Historical Perspective." PhD diss., Duke University, 1991.

Hatch, Robert. "Laughter at Your Own Risk." *Horizon: A Magazine of the Arts* 3 (January 1960): 112–16.

Hattaway, Michael. "Paradoxes of Solomon: Learning in the English Renaissance." *Journal of the History of Ideas* 29 (1968): 499–530.

Haubold, Johaness. *Greece and Mesopotamia: Dialogues in Literature*. Cambridge: Cambridge University Press, 2013.

Haupt, Paul. "Ecclesiastes." *The American Journal of Philology* 26 (1905): 125–71.

Hayes, John H. and Frederick Prussner. *Old Testament Theology: Its History and Development*. Atlanta, GA: John Knox Press, 1985.

Hazony, Yoram. *The Philosophy of Hebrew Scripture*. Cambridge: Cambridge University Press, 2012.

Hendel, Ronald. "Mind the Gap: Modern and Postmodern in Biblical Studies." *JBL* 133 (2014): 422–43.

Hengel, Martin. *Judaism and Hellenism: Studies in Their Encounter in Palestine during the Early Hellenistic Period*. Translated by John Bowden. 2 vols. Philadelphia, PA: Fortress Press, 1974. Translation of *Judentum und Hellenismus: Studien zu ihrer Begegnung unter besonderer Berücksichtigung Palästinas bis zur Mitte des 2 Jh.s v. Chr*. 2d. Rev. ed. WUNT 10. Tübingen: Mohr/Siebeck, 1973.

Hirshman, Marc. "The Greek Fathers and the Aggada on Ecclesiastes: Formats of Exegesis in Late Antiquity." *HUCA* 59 (1988): 143–7.

Holm-Nielsen, Svend. "On the Interpretation of Qoheleth in Early Christianity." *VT* 24 (1974): 168–77.

———. "The Book of Ecclesiastes and the Interpretation of It in Jewish and Christian Theology." *ASTI* 10 (1975): 38–96.

Hossfeld, Frank-Lothar. "Die Theologische Relevanz des Buches Kohelet." Pages 377–89 in *Das Buch Kohelet: Studien zur Struktur, Geschichte, Rezeption, und Theologie*. Edited by Ludger Schweinhorst-Schönberger. BZAW 254. Berlin: De Gruyter, 1997.

Hyde, Lewis. *Trickster Makes This World: Mischief, Myth, and Art*. New York: Farrar, Strauss, and Giroux, 1998.

Ingram, Doug. *Ambiguity in Ecclesiastes*. LHBOTS 431. London: T. & T. Clark, 2006.

Isaksson, Bo. *Studies in the Language of Qoheleth, with Special Emphasis on the Verbal System*. Studia Semitica Upsaliensia. Uppsala: University of Uppsala Press, 1987.

Izre'el, Shlomo. *Adapa and the South Wind: Language Has the Power of Life and Death*. Winona Lake, IN: Eisenbrauns, 2001.

Japhet, Sara and Robert B. Salters. *The Commentary of R. Samuel Ben Meir Rashbam on Qoheleth*. Jerusalem/Leiden: Magnes/Brill, 1985.

Jarick, John. *A Comprehensive Bilingual Concordance of the Hebrew and Greek Texts of Ecclesiastes*. Atlanta: Scholars Press, 1993.

———. "The Hebrew Book of Changes: Reflections on *Hakkol Hebel* and *Lakkol Zeman* in Ecclesiastes." *JSOT* 90 (2000): 79–99.

Jastrow, Morris. *A Gentle Cynic: Being a Translation of the Book of Koheleth Commonly Known as Ecclesiastes, Its Origin, Growth and Interpretation*. Philadelphia, PA: Lippincott, 1919. Reprinted in New York: Oriole, 1972.

———. *Zionism and the Future of Palestine*. New York: Macmillan, 1919.

Johnson, Dru. *Scripture's Knowing: A Companion to Biblical Epistemology*. Eugene, OR: Cascade, 2015.

Jong, Stephan de. "God in the Book of Qohelet: A Reappraisal of Qohelet's Place in Old Testament Theology." *VT* 47 (1997): 154–67.

Kelly, J.N.D. *Jerome: His Life, Writings, and Controversies*. New York: Harper and Row, 1975.

Kelly, Joseph Ryan. "Sources of Contention and the Emerging Reality Concerning Qohelet's *Carpe Diem* Advice." *Antiguo Oriente* 8 (2010): 117–34.

Kidner, Derek. *The Wisdom of Proverbs, Job and Ecclesiastes: An Introduction to Wisdom Literature*. Downers Grove, IL: InterVarsity, 1985.

Klein-Braslavy, Sara. "The Alexandrian Prologue Paradigm in Gersonides' Writings." *JQR* 95 (2005): 257–89.

Knobel, Peter. *The Targum of Job, the Targum of Proverbs, the Targum of Qohelet*. ArBib. Collegeville, MN: Liturgical Press, 1991.

Koh, Y. V. *Royal Autobiography in the Book of Qoheleth*. BZAW 369. Berlin: De Gruyter, 2006.

Konkel, August and Tremper Longman, III. *Job, Ecclesiastes, Song of Songs*. Cornerstone Biblical Commentary 6. Carol Stream, IL: Tyndale House, 2006.

Kraus, Matthew. "Christians, Jews, and Pagans in Dialogue: Jerome on Ecclesiastes 12:1–7." *HUCA* 70–71 (1999–2000): 183–231.

Krüger, Thomas. *Qoheleth*. Hermeneia. Minneapolis: Fortress, 2004.

Kuhrt, Amélie. *The Persian Empire: A Corpus of Sources from the Achaemenid Period*. New York: Routledge, 2007.

Laird, Martin. "Under Solomon's Tutelage: The Education of Desire in the Homilies on the Song of Songs." *Modern Theology* 18 (2002): 507–25.

Lambert, David A. *How Repentance Became Biblical: Judaism, Christianity, and the Interpretation of Scripture*. New York: Oxford University Press, 2016.

Lee, Eunny P. *The Vitality of Enjoyment in Qohelet's Theological Rhetoric*. BZAW 353. Berlin: De Gruyter, 2005.

Legaspi, Michael. *The Death of Scripture and the Rise of Biblical Studies*. OSHT. New York: Oxford University Press, 2010.

Lemche, Niels Peter. "The Old Testament—A Hellenistic Book?" *SJOT* 7 (1993): 163–93.

———. *The Israelites in History and Tradition*. LAI. Louisville, KY: Westminster John Knox, 1998.

———. "Does the Idea of the Old Testament as a Hellenistic Book Prevent Source Criticism of the Pentateuch?" *SJOT* 25 (2011): 75–92.

Levine, Amy-Jill. *Short Stories By Jesus*. New York: HarperOne, 2014.

Lewis, Charlton T. and Charles Short. *A Latin Dictionary*. Oxford: Clarendon, 1879.

Lichtheim, Miriam. *Late Egyptian Wisdom Literature in the International Context: A Study of Demotic Instructions*. OBO. Freiburg: Vandenhoeck & Ruprecht, 1983.

Limburg, James. *Encountering Ecclesiastes: A Book for Our Time*. Grand Rapids, MI: Eerdmans, 2006.

Lincoln, Bruce. *Theorizing Myth: Narrative, Ideology, and Scholarship*. Chicago: University of Chicago Press, 1999.

Loader, James A. *Polar Structures in the Book of Qohelet*. BZAW 152. Berlin: De Gruyter, 1979.

———. *Ecclesiastes: A Practical Commentary*. Translated by John Vriend. Text and Interpretation. Grand Rapids, MI: Eerdmans, 1986. Translation of *Prediker: Een praktische bijbelverklaring*. Tekst en Toelichting. Kampen: Kok, 1984.

Lohfink, Norbert. *Qoheleth*. Translated by Sean McEvenue. CC. Minneapolis, MN: Fortress Press, 2003. Translation of *Kohelet*. NEchtB. Würzburg: Echter Verlag, 1980.

———. "Qoheleth 5:17–19: Revelation by Joy." *CBQ* 52 (1990): 625–35.

Longman, Tremper. *Ecclesiastes*. NICOT. Grand Rapids: Eerdmans, 1998.

Loretz, Oswald. *Qohelet und der Alte Orient: Untersuchungen zu Stil und theologischer Thematik des Buches Qohelet*. Freiburg: Herder, 1964.

Lowth, Robert. *De sacra poesi hebraeorum*. Oxford: Clarendon, 1753.

———. *Lectures on the Sacred Poetry of the Hebrews Translated from the Latin by G. Gregory to Which Are Added the Principal Notes of Professor Michaelis and Notes By the Translator and Others*. 4th ed. London: Thomas Tegg, 1849.

Luther, Martin. *Dr. Martin Luthers Werke: Kritische Gesamtausgabe, Tischreden*. 6 vols. Weimar: Hermann Bohlaus, 1912–1921.

Macnaghten, William H. *The Alif Laila, or Book of the Thousand Nights and One Night*. 4 vols. London: W.H. Allen, 1839–42.

McKenna, John. "The Concept of *Hebel* in the Book of Ecclesiastes." *SJT* 45 (1992): 19–28.

Meek, Russell L. "Twentieth- and Twenty-first-century Readings of *Hebel* (הבל) in Ecclesiastes." *CurBR* 14 (2016): 279–97.

Mettinger, Tryggve N. D. *The Eden Narrative: A Literary and Religio-historical Study of Genesis 2–3*. Winona Lake, IN: Eisenbrauns, 2007.

Michel, Diethelm. *Untersuchungen zur Eigenart des Buches Qohelet*. BZAW 183. Berlin: De Gruyter, 1989.

Miller, Douglas L. "What the Preacher Forgot: The Rhetoric of Ecclesiastes." *CBQ* 62 (2000): 215–35.

Millington, Thomas Street. *The Testimony of the Heathen to the Truths of Holy Writ*. London: Seeley, Jackson, and Halliday,1863.

Mills, Mary E. *Reading Ecclesiastes: A Literary and Cultural Exegesis*. Heythrop Studies in Contemporary Philosophy, Religion, and Theology. Aldershot: Ashgate, 2003.

Moore, Stephen D. and Yvonne Sherwood. *The Invention of the Biblical Scholar: A Critical Manifesto*. Minneapolis, MN: Fortress Press, 2011.

Morgan, Jonathan. "Visitors, Gatekeepers, and Receptionists: Reflections on the Shape of Biblical Studies and the Role of Reception History." Pages 61–76 in *Reception History and Biblical Studies: Theory and Practice*. Edited by Emma England and William John Lyons. LHBOTS. London: Bloomsbury, 2015.

Mroczek, Eva. "'Aramaisms' in Qohelet: Methodological Problems in Identification and Interpretation." Pages 343–63 in *The Words of the Wise Are like Goads: Engaging Qohelet in the 21st Century*. Edited by Mark J. Boda, Tremper Longman III, and Cristian G. Rata. Winona Lake, IN: Eisenbrauns, 2013.

———. *The Literary Imagination in Jewish Antiquity*. New York: Oxford University Press, 2016.

Müller, Hans-Peter. "Wie Sprach Qohälät von Gott?" *VT* 18 (1968): 507–21.

———. "Der Begriff 'Rätsel' Im Alten Testament." *VT* 20 (1970): 465–89.

———. "Plausibilitätsverlust Herkömmlicher Religion Bei Kohelet Und Den Vorsokratikern." Pages 99–114 in *Gemeinde ohne Tempel. Zur Substituierung und Transformation des Jerusalemer Tempels und seines Kults im Alten Testament, antiken Judentum und frühen Christentum*. Edited by Beate Ego, Armin Lange, and Peter Pilhofer. WUNT 118. Tübingen: Mohr Siebeck, 1999.

Murphy, Roland E. "Qohelet Interpreted: The Bearing of the Past on the Present." *VT* 32 (1982): 331–7.

Nagy, Gregory. *Homeric Questions*. Austin, TX: University of Texas Press, 1996.

Niditch, Susan. *Oral World and Written Word: Ancient Israelite Literature*. LAI. Louisville: Westminster John Knox, 1996.

Nielsen, Flemming. *The Tragedy in History: Herodotus and the Deuteronomistic History*. LHBOTS. Sheffield: Sheffield Academic Press, 1997.

Nongbri, Brent. *Before Religion: A History of a Modern Concept*. New Haven, CT: Yale University Press, 2013.

Norris, Richard A., Jr. *Gregory of Nyssa Homilies on the Song of Songs*. Atlanta, GA: Society of Biblical Literature, 2012.

Ogden, Graham S. "Qoheleth xi 7–xii 8: Qoheleth's Summons to Enjoyment and Reflection." *VT* 34 (1984): 27–38.

Ong, Walter. *Orality and Literacy: The Technologizing of the Word*. New York: Methuen, 1982.

Pahk, Johan Y.-S. "Qohelet e le Tradizioni Sapienziali del Vicino Oriente Antico." Pages 117–43 in *Il Libro Del Qohelet: Tradizione, Redazione, Teologia*. Edited by Giuseppe Bellia and Angelo Passaro. Cammini nello Spirito Biblica 44. Milan: Paulist, 2001.

Payne, Michael. "The Voices of Ecclesiastes." *College Literature* 15 (1988): 262–8.

Pelikan, Jaroslav and Hilton C. Oswald. *Notes on Ecclesiastes, Lectures on the Song of Solomon, Treatise on the Last Words of David*. Luther's Works 15. St. Louis: Concordia Press, 1972.

Perry, Theodore. *Dialogues with Kohelet: The Book of Ecclesiastes*. College Park, PA: Penn State University Press, 1993.

———. *The Book of Ecclesiastes (Qohelet) and the Path to Joyous Living*. New York: Cambridge University Press, 2015.

Person, Raymond F., Jr. "The Problem of 'Literary Unity' from the Perspective of Oral Traditions." Pages 217–36 in *Empirical Models Challenging Biblical Criticism*. Edited by Raymond F. Person, Jr. and Robert Rezetko. Atlanta: Society of Biblical Literature, 2016.

Plumptre, Edward H. *Ecclesiastes, or the Preacher*. Cambridge Bible for Schools and Colleges. Cambridge: Cambridge University Press, 1888.

Provan, Iain. "Ideologies, Literary and Critical: Reflections on Recent Writing on the History of Israel." *JBL* 114 (1995): 585–606.

Radner, Karen and Eleanor Robson, eds. *The Oxford Handbook of Cuneiform Culture*. New York: Oxford University Press, 2011.

Ranston, Harry. "Ecclesiastes and Theognis." *AJSL* 34 (1918): 99–122.

———. *Ecclesiastes and the Early Greek Wisdom Literature*. London: Epworth, 1925.

Rechenauer, Georg. *Xenophanes von Kolophon. Ein Vorsokratiker zwischen Mythos und Philosophie*. Stuttgart: Teubner, 1996.

Rogerson, John. *Old Testament Criticism in the Nineteenth Century: England and Germany*. London: SCM, 1984.

Roth, Wolfgang M. W. *Numerical Sayings in the Old Testament: A Form-Critical Study*. Vetus Testamentum Supplements. Leiden: Brill, 1965.

Rudman, Dominic. *Determinism in the Book of Ecclesiastes*. JSOTSup 316. Sheffield: Sheffield Academic Press, 2001.

Samet, Nili. "'The Tallest Man Cannot Reach Heaven; The Broadest Cannot Cover Earth'—Reconsidering the Proverb and Its Biblical Parallels." *JHebS* 10 (2010). doi:10.5508/jhs.2010.v10.a18.

———. "The Gilgamesh Epic and the Book of Qohelet: A New Look. *Biblica* 96 (2015): 375–90.

———. "Religious Redaction in Qohelet in Light of Mesopotamian Vanity Literature." *VT* 65 (2015): 1–16.

Sandberg, Ruth. *Rabbinic Views of Qohelet*. Lewiston, NY: Mellen, 1999.

Sanders, Jack T. "When Sacred Canopies Collide: The Reception of the Torah of Moses in the Wisdom Literature of the Second-Temple Period." *JSJ* 32 (2001): 121–36.

Schniedewind, William M. *A Social History of Hebrew: Its Origins through the Rabbinic Period*. ABRL. New Haven, CT: Yale University Press, 2013.

Schoors, Anton, ed. *Qohelet in the Context of Wisdom*. Leuven: Leuven University Press, 1998.

———. "The Verb *hāyâ* in Qoheleth." Pages 229–38 in *Shall Not the Judge of All the Earth Do What Is Right? Studies on the Nature of God in Tribute to James L. Crenshaw*. Edited by David Penchansky and Paul L. Redditt. Winona Lake, IN: Eisenbrauns, 2000.

———. "God in Qoheleth." Pages 251–70 in *Schöpfungsplan und Heilsgeschichte: Festschrift für Ernst Haag zum 70*. Geburtstag. Edited by Renate Brandscheidt. Trier: Paulinus, 2002.

———. *The Preacher Sought to Find Pleasing Words: A Study of the Language of Qoheleth. Part II: Vocabulary*. OLA 143. Leuven: Peeters, 2004.

———. *Ecclesiastes*. HCOT. Leuven: Peeters, 2013.

Schultz, Richard L. "Unity or Diversity in Wisdom Theology? A Canonical and Covenantal Perspective." *TynBul* 48 (1997): 271–305.

Schwienhorst-Schönberger, Ludger. *'Nicht im Menschen gründet das Glück' (Koh 2,24): Kohelet im Spannungsfeld jüdischer Weisheit und hellenistischer Philosophie*. Herders Biblische Studien 2. Freiburg: Herder, 1994.

———, ed. *Das Buch Kohelet: Studien zur Struktur, Geschichte, Rezeption, und Theologie*. BZAW 254. Berlin: De Gruyter, 1997.

———. *Kohelet*. HThKAT. Freiburg: Herder, 2004.

Segal, Jerome. *Joseph's Bones: Understanding the Struggle between God and Mankind in the Bible*. New York: Penguin, 2007.

Seow, Choon Leong. *Ecclesiastes*. AB 18C. New York: Doubleday, 1997.

Sharp, Carolyn. "Ironic Representation, Authorial Voice, and Meaning in Qohelet." *BibInt* 12 (2004): 37–68.

Sheppard, Gerald. "The Epilogue to Qohelet as Theological Commentary." *CBQ* 39 (1977): 182–9.

Shields, Martin A. "Ecclesiastes and the End of Wisdom." *TynBul* 50 (1999): 117–39.

———. "Re-Examining the Warning of Eccl XII 12." *VT* 50 (2000): 123–7.

———. *The End of Wisdom: A Reappraisal of the Historical and Canonical Function of Ecclesiastes*. Winona Lake, IN: Eisenbrauns, 2006.

———. "Qohelet and Royal Autobiography." Pages 117–36 in *The Words of the Wise Are Like Goads: Engaging Qohelet in the 21st Century*. Edited by Mark J. Boda, Tremper Longman III, and Cristian G. Rata. Winona Lake, IN: Eisenbrauns, 2013.

Simian-Yofre, Horacio. "Conoscere la Sapienza: Qohelet e Genesi 2–3." Pages 314–36 in *Il Libro Del Qohelet: Tradizione, redazione, teologia*. Edited by Giuseppe Bellia and Angelo Passaro. Cammini nello Spirito Biblica 44. Milan: Paulist, 2001.

Ska, Jean-Louis. *Introduction to Reading the Pentateuch*. Translated by P. Dominique. Winona Lake, IN: Eisenbrauns, 2006. Translation of *Introduzione alla lettura del Pentateuco. Chiavi per l'interpretazione dei primi cinque libri della Bibbia*. Edizioni Dehoniane: Rome, 1996.

Smith, Morton. *Palestinian Parties and Politics that Shaped the Old Testament*. 2nd corrected ed. London: SCM, 1987.

Sneed, Mark. "(Dis)closure in Qohelet: Qohelet Deconstructed." *JSOT* 27 (2002): 115–26.

———. *The Politics of Pessmism in Ecclesiastes: A Social-Science Perspective*. AIL 12. Atlanta, GA: SBL Press, 2012.

———, ed. *Was There a Wisdom Tradition? New Prospects in Israelite Wisdom Studies*. AIL 23. Atlanta, GA: SBL Press, 2015.

Spangenberg, Izak. "Irony in the Book of Qohelet." *JSOT* 72 (1996): 57–69.

Stern, Ephraim. *Archaeology of the Land of the Bible Volume II: The Assyrian, Babylonian, and Persian Periods (732–332 B.C.E.)*. AYBRL. New York: Random House, 2001.

Stott, Katherine. *Why Did They Write This Way? Reflections on References to Written Documents in the Hebrew Bible and Ancient Literature*. London/New York: T & T Clark, 2008.

Tamez, Elsa. *When the Horizons Close: Rereading Ecclesiastes*. Maryknoll, NY: Orbis, 2000.

———. "Ecclesiastes: Reading from the Periphery." *Int* 55 (2001): 250–9.

Tapett, Theodore. *Table Talk*. Luther's Works 54. Philadelphia: Fortress Press, 1967.

Thompson, Thomas L. *The Early History of the Israelite People: From the Written and Archeological Sources*. SHANE 4. Leiden: Brill, 1992.

———. "A Neo-Albrightean School in History and Biblical Scholarship." *JBL* 114 (1995): 683–98.

Thompson, Thomas L. and Philippe Wajdenbaum, eds. *The Bible and Hellenism: Greek Influence on Jewish and Early Christian Literature*. London: Routledge, 2014.

Tolkien, John Ronald Reuel. *The Hobbit, or, There and Back again*. Boston: Houghton Mifflin, 1966.

Torczyner, Harry. "The Riddle in the Bible." *HUCA* 1 (1924): 125–49.

Turner, James. *Philology: The Forgotten Origins of the Modern Humanities*. Princeton, NJ: Princeton University Press, 2014.

Uehlinger, Christoph. "Qohelet im Horizont mesopotamischer, levantinischer und ägyptischer Weisheitsliteratur der persischen und hellenistischen Zeit." Pages 155–247 in *Das Buch Kohelet: Studien zur Struktur, Geschichte, Rezeption, und Theologie*. Edited by Ludger Schweinhorst-Schönberger. BZAW 254. Berlin: De Gruyter, 1997.

Van De Mieroop, Marc. *Philosophy before the Greeks: The Pursuit of Truth in Ancient Babylonia*. Princeton, NJ: Princeton University Press, 2016.

Van Seters, John. *In Search of History: Historiography in the Ancient World and the Origins of Biblical History*. New Haven: Yale University Press, 1983.

Vayntrub, Jacqueline. "Proverbs and the Limits of Poetry." PhD diss., University of Chicago, 2015.

Veyne, Paul. *Did the Greeks Believe in Their Myths? An Essay on the Constitutive Imagination*. Translated by Paula Wissing. Chicago: University of Chicago Press, 1988. Translation of *Les Grecs ont-ils cru à leurs mythes?* Paris: Editions du Seuil, 1983.

Vinel, Françoise. *Grégoire de Nysse: Homélies sur l'Ecclésiaste*. SC 416. Paris: Éditions du Cerf, 1996.

———. *L'Ecclésiaste*. L'Bible d'Alexandrie 18. Paris: Editions du Cerf, 2002.

Von Rad, Gerhard. *Wisdom in Israel*. Translated by James Martin. London: SCM Press, 1972. Translation of *Weisheit in Israel*. Neukirchen-Vluyn: Neukirchener Verlag, 1970.

Wachler, Gottfried. "The Inspiration and Inerrancy of Scripture: An Examination of Hermann Sasse's Sacra Scriptura Based on the History of Doctrinal Theology and Dogmatics." *Wisconsin Lutheran Quarterly* 81 (1984): no pages.

Wajdenbaum, Philippe. *Argonauts of the Desert: Structural Analysis of the Hebrew Bible*. London: Routledge, 2014.

Walch, Johannes Georg. *Dr. Martin Luther's Sämmtliche Schriften* 22. St. Louis: Concordia Publishing House, 1890.

Wechsler, Harold S. "Pulpit or Professoriate: The Case of Morris Jastrow." *American Jewish History* 74 (1985): 338–55.

Weeks, Stuart. *Ecclesiastes and Scepticism*. LHBOTS. London: T & T Clark, 2012.

———. "The Inner-Textuality of Qoheleth's Monologue." Pages 142–53 in *Reading Ecclesiastes Intertextually*. Edited by Katharine Dell and Will Kynes. LHBOT 587. London: Bloomsbury, 2014.

———. *The Making of Many Books: Printed Works on Ecclesiastes 1523–1875*. Winona Lake, IN: Eisenbrauns, 2014.

Wesselius, Jan-Wim. *The Origin of the History of Israel: Herodotus'* Histories *as Blueprint for the First Books of the Bible*. LHBOTS. Sheffield: Sheffield Academic Press, 2002.

West, Martin. *The East Face of Helicon: West Asiatic Elements in Greek Poetry and Myth*. New York: Oxford University Press, 1999.

———. "The Invention of Homer." *Classical Quarterly* 49 (1999): 364–82.

White, Graham. "Luther on Ecclesiastes and the Limits of Human Ability." *Neue Zeitschrift für systematische Theologie und Religionsphilosophie* 29 (1987): 180–94.

Whybray, R. Norman. "The Identification and Use of Quotations in Ecclesiastes." Pages 435–51 in *Congress Volume Vienna 1980*. Edited by John Adney Emerton. Vetus Testamentum Supplements 32. Leiden: Brill, 1981.

———. *Ecclesiastes*. NCB. Grand Rapids, MI: Eerdmans, 1989.

———. "Qohelet as a Theologian." Pages 238–65 in *Qohelet in the Context of Wisdom*. Edited by Anton Schoors. Leuven: Leuven University Press, 1998.

Wimsatt, William K. and Monroe C. Beardsley. "The Intentional Fallacy." Pages 2–18 in *The Verbal Icon: Studies in the Meaning of Poetry*. Lexington: University of Kentucky Press, 1954.

Wright, J. Robert, ed. *Proverbs, Ecclesiastes, Song of Solomon*. ACCS. Old Testament IX. Downers Grove, IL: Inter Varsity, 2005.

Wright, J. Stafford. "Interpretation of Ecclesiastes." *EvQ* 18 (1946): 18–34.

Yesudian-Storfjell, Suseela C. "The Reception of Qoheleth in a Selection of Rabbinic, Patristic and Nonconformist Texts." PhD diss., University of Sheffield, 2003.

Zimmerli, Walther. "The Place and Limit of the [sic] Wisdom in the Framework of the [sic] Old Testament Theology." *SJT* 17 (1964): 146–58. Translation of "Ort und Grenze der Weisheit im Rahmen der alttestamentlichen Theologie." Pages 300–15 in *Gottes Offenbarung: Gesammelte Aufsätze zum Alten Testament*. München: Kaiser, 1963.

———. "Das Buch Kohelet—Traktat Oder Sentenzensammlung?" *VT* 24 (1974): 221–30. Reprinted in IOSOT (2013): 77–86.

Index